P9-DFM-728

An Eighteenth-Century
Musical Chronicle

AN EIGHTEENTH-CENTURY MUSICAL CHRONICLE

Events 1750-1799

Compiled by
CHARLES J. HALL

Music Reference Collection, Number 25

GREENWOOD PRESS
New York • Westport, Connecticut • London

Ref
ML
195
H28
1990

Library of Congress Cataloging-in-Publication Data

Hall, Charles J.
  An eighteenth-century musical chronicle : events 1750-1799 /
compiled by Charles J. Hall.
    p. cm. — (Music reference collection, ISSN 0736-7740 ; no.
25)
  ISBN 0-313-26576-3 (lib. bdg. : alk. paper)
  1. Music—18th century—Chronology. I. Title. II. Series.
ML195.H28 1990
780'.9'033—dc20   89-71527

British Library Cataloguing in Publication Data is available.

Library of Congress Catalog Card Number: 89-71527
ISBN: 0-313-26576-3
ISSN: 0736-7740

First published in 1990

Greenwood Press, 88 Post Road West, Westport, CT 06881
An imprint of Greenwood Publishing Group, Inc.

Printed in the United States of America

The paper used in this book complies with the
Permanent Paper Standard issued by the National
Information Standards Organization (Z39.48-1984).

10 9 8 7 6 5 4 3 2 1

Contents

Preface

An Eighteenth-Century Musical Chronicle is the last of three volumes chronicling musical history since 1750. This project originated as program notes for a radio show broadcast in Michigan in the mid-70s in which musical selections of a given year were accompanied by commentary on contemporaneous events. The resulting books present musical events year-by-year in the context of political, social, and cultural history. Emphasis is on "art" music, but some highlights in popular genres are included. Information has been gathered from myriad sources--recognized authorities, magazines, newspapers and, when possible, directly from the original sources. Where different sources yield conflicting information about musical events, the author has chosen for the most part to accept the authority of the *New Grove Dictionary of Music and Musicians*.

Each year begins with selected World Events and Cultural Highlights. Musical Events follow, divided into nine sections:

A. Births
B. Deaths
C. Debuts
D. New Positions
E. Prizes and Honors
F. Biographical Highlights
G. Institutional Openings
H. Musical Literature
I. Musical Compositions

Category C covers three types of debuts: the original debut (with location); a U.S. debut (also with location) when it is separate from the preceding, and the Metropolitan Opera debut for singers and conductors. Other debuts, such as those in Paris, Vienna or Covent Garden, may be found under F. Biographical Highlights. The dates given for compositions under Category I are actual completion dates rather than premieres; however, it is not always possible to make the distinction. A detailed index provides access from the name or term to the year and category letter.

A word of acknowledgment should be given to those who helped and gave encouragement, to the many students who pored over the tomes in search of obscure items and pounded the typewriter keys, and to my wife who patiently put up with me in the hectic days of getting all the resources together; and a special word of thanks is due Allyn Craig, without whose computer expertise I could not have survived.

Charles J. Hall
B.M., M.M., Ph.D.

Abbreviations

COUNTRIES

Am	United States	Fin	Finland	Pan	Panama
Arm	Armenia	Fr	France	Peru	Peru
Arg	Argentina	Ger	Germany	Phil	Philippines
Aus	Austria	Gr	Greece	Pol	Poland
Aust	Australia	Hol	Holland	Por	Portugal
Azer	Azerbaijan	Hun	Hungary	P.R.	Puerto Rico
Bel	Belgium	Ind	India	Rom	Romania
Boh	Bohemia	Ir	Ireland	Rus	Russia
Bol	Bolivia	Iran	Iran	Scot	Scotland
Br	Great Britain	Is	Israel	Serb	Serbia
Bra	Brazil	It	Italy	S.Af.	South Africa
Bul	Bulgaria	Jp	Japan	Sp	Spain
Can	Canada	Kor	Korea	Swe	Sweden
Chi	China	Lat	Latvia	Swi	Switzerland
Chil	Chile	Leb	Lebanon	Tai	Taiwan
Cub	Cuba	Lith	Lithuania	Tur	Turkey
Cz	Czechoslovakia	Man	Manchuria	Urg	Uruguay
Den	Denmark	Mex	Mexico	Ven	Venezuela
Egypt	Egypt	Nor	Norway	Yug	Yugoslavia
Est	Estonia	N.Z.	New Zealand		

PROFESSIONS

acous	acoustics	fl.m	flute maker	org	organist
act	actor, actress	folk	folk music	org.m	organ maker
alto	contralto	gui	guitarist	pat	patron of arts
arr	arranger	harm	harmonica	ped	pedagogue
au	author	hn	horn virtuoso	perc	percussion
bal	ballet	hp	harpist	pop	popular artist
band	band	hp.m	harp maker	pn	pianist
bar	baritone	hps	harpsichord	pt	poet
bn	bassoonist	hum	humorist	pub	publisher
bs	bass	hymn	hymn writer	rec	recorder
cas	castrato	imp	impresario	rel	religion
cb	contrabass	ind	industrialist	sax	saxophonist
cd	conductor	inst.m	instrument maker	sing	singer
cel	cellist			sop	soprano
clar	clarinetist	inv	inventor	ten	tenor
cm	composer	lib	librettist	the	theory
cri	music critic	mez	mezzosoprano	tpt	trumpeter
c.ten	countertenor	m.ed	music educator	vn	violinist
ed	educator	mus	musicology or music history	vla	violist
film	film music			voc	vocalist
fl	flutist	ob	oboist	ww.m	woodwind maker

The above abbreviations are found primarily in the Births and Deaths of each year. The country given in each case is the country of birth, except in rare cases where the parents are residing temporarily in another country.

THE CHRONICLE, 1750-1799

1750

World Events:

In the New World, the British Parliament passes the Iron Act which seeks to restrict iron manufacture in the colonies and benefit the mother country; the Ohio Company begins the exploration of its western territories; Barbourville, Kentucky, becomes the first settlement to be founded west of the Alleghenies; the Conestoga Wagon, the original "prairie schooner" makes its appearance as does the River Flatboat in Pennsylvania; the University of Pennsylvania is founded; the first coal mine in the New World opens in Virginia. Internationally, this is the general beginning of the Industrial Revolution, which takes place mainly in Great Britain but which continues to spread and grow into the new century; Spain and Portugal settle their claims in South America by a treaty drawn up by the Pope which gives Brazil to Portugal and all the rest of the southern continent to Spain; John V of Portugal dies.

Cultural Highlights:

Samuel Johnson begins printing his periodical, *The Rambler*; Giovanni Battista Piazzetta becomes director of the newly formed Venetian Academy of Fine Arts; Laurent Delvaux becomes court sculptor at Lorraine; Frederick the Great calls Voltaire to the Prussian court; Jonathan Edwards is dismissed from his pastorate after disputes over his theological views. Births in the literary field include American poet John Trumbull, author Lemuel Hopkins, German poets Johann Martin Miller and Count Friedrich Leopold Stolberg, British dramatist Elizabeth Anspach and novelist Sophia Lee, Scotch poet Robert Fergusson and Spanish poet Tomás de Iriarte y Oropesa; deaths include American author John Tufts and Italian poet and scholar Apostolo Zeno. Births in the art world include German artist Johann Friedrich Tischbein and British artist John Downman; deaths include American artist Robert Feke, Dutch artists Rachel Ruysch and Cornelis Troost, Italian architect Juste Meissonier and German sculptor Equid Quirin Asam. Other highlights include:

Art: Edme Bouchardon, *Cupid Making a Bow from Hercules' Club*; John Cornish, *William Hayes*; Robert Feke, *Self-Portrait*; Pietro Longhi, *Man Selling Doughnuts*: Jean-Marc Nattier, *Comtesse de Tillieres*; Thomas Gainsborough, *View of Dedham*; Giovanni Battista Tiepolo, *Antony and Cleopatra* and *Martyrdom of St. Agatha*; Paul Troger, *Frescoes, Bressanone Cathedral*

Literature: Joseph Bellamy, *True Religion Delineated*; Carlo Goldoni, *The Café*; Françoise Grafigny, *Cénie*; Friedrich von Hagedorn, *Moralische Gedichte*; Friedrich Gottlieb Klopstock, *To Lake Zurich*; Jean François Marmontel, *Cléopâtre*; Samuel Richardson, *Clarissa*; Jean-Jacques Rosseau, *Discours sur les Sciences et sur les Arts*; William Whitehead, *The Roman Father*

MUSICAL EVENTS

A. Births:

Jan 25	Johann G. Vierling (Ger-org)	Nov 16	Giuseppe Serassi, Jr. (It-org.m)
Jan 31	Franz C. Hartig (Ger-ten)	Nov 27	Anton Stamitz (Ger-cm-cd)
Mar	John S. Smith (Br-org)	Dec 3	Johann F. Sterkel (Ger-org)
Mar 21	Franz C. Neubaur (Cz-vn-cm)	Dec 25	John C. Beckwith (Br-org)
Apr 18	Jean B. Mercadier (Fr-the)		Antonio Abreu (Por-gui)
Jun 17	Michel Woldemar (Fr-vn)		Antonio Bianchi (ii) (It-cm)
Jun 23	J. J. Kriegk (Ger-vn-cel)		Giacomo Davide (It-ten)
Jul 19	Alessio Prati (It-cm)		Charles G. Foignet (Fr-cm)
Aug 10	Daniel Türk (Ger-cm-the)		Franz Kotzwara (Boh-cm)
Aug 18	Antonio Salieri (It-cm)		Wenzel Krumpholtz (Boh-vn)
Sep 2	Pehr Frigel (Swe-cm)		Peter A. Van Hagen (Hol-cm)
Sep 22	Christoph Breitkopf (Ger-pub)		Giulio Visconti (It-cm)

B. Deaths:

Jan	Louis G. Bourgeois (Fr-ten)	Sep 15	Karl T. Pachelbel (Ger-cm)
Feb 2	Johann Graf (Ger-vn-cm)	Sep 28	Sperontes (J. Scholze) (Ger-cm)
Mar 7	Domenico Montagnana (It-vn.m)	Oct 3	Mathias G. Monn (Aus-cm)
May	Jean B. Ballard (Fr-pub)	Oct 15	Sylvius Weiss (Ger-lute)
May 29	Giuseppe Porsile (It-cm)	Oct 31	Francesco Veracini (It-vn)
Jun 2	Johann Rathgeber (Ger-cm)	Nov	Giuseppe Sammartini (It-cm)
Jun 14	Franz Maichelbeck (Ger-cm)	Nov 15	Pantaleon Hebenstreit (Ger-vn)
Jun 24	Robert Woffington (Ir-org)	Nov 25	Francesco Feroci (It-org)
Jul 28	Johann S. Bach (Ger-org-cm)	Dec 7	Johann G. Lösel (Ger-cm)
Aug 27	Joseph Timmer (Aus-ten)		Henry Holcombe (Br-voc-cm)

C. Debuts:
Other - Michael Arne (London), Marie Jeanne Larrivée (Paris)

D. New Positions:
Conductors: Georg Anton Benda (kapellmeister, Saxe-Gotha), Angelo Antonio Caroli (maestro di cappella, Church of the Filippini, Bologna), Georg Gebel (kapellmeister, Rudolstadt), Gottlob Harrer (kantor, Leipzig Thomaskirche), Johann Adolph Hasse (kapellmeister, Dresden), Guillaume Kennis (kapellmeister, St. Pierre, Louvain), Ignaz F. Kurtzinger (kapellmeister, Württemberg), Padre Antonio Soler (maestro de capilla, Lérida)

Educational: Corrado Giaquinto (President, Academy of St. Luke, Rome)

Others: Anton Cajetan Adlgasser (organ, Salzburg Cathedral), John Alcock, Sr. (vicar-choral and organ, Lichfield Cathedral), Laurent Desmazures (organ, Cathedral of St. Lazare d'Autun), Joaquin de Oxinaga (organ, Toledo Cathedral), Anton Ignaz Werndle (organ, Vienna Court)

E. Prizes and Honors:
Honors: François Colin de Blamont (Letters of Nobility by Louis XV of France), Farinelli (Carlo Broschi) (Cross of Calatrava by Ferdinand VI of Spain)

F. Biographical Highlights:
Johann Friedrich Agricola experiences his first success as a composer in Potsdam; Johann Christian Bach, following his father's death, goes to Berlin to live with and to study with his brother Carl Philipp Emanuel Bach; Christian Cannabich is sent by the Elector of Mannheim to study music with Niccolò Jommelli in Rome; Giovanni Carestini joins the court of Frederick the Great; Francesca Cuzzoni is arrested for debts while in London but is rescued by the Prince of Wales; the Tommaso Giordani family moves to Frankfurt am Main; Christoph Willibald Gluck settles for a while in Vienna and marries Marianna Pergin, daughter of a well-to-do merchant; Christoph Graupner becomes totally blind; André Ernest Grétry, age nine, enters the St. Denis church in Liège as a chorister; George Frederic Handel donates an organ to the Foundling Hospital in London and makes a last visit to Germany; Franz Joseph Haydn, age 18, visits Rome and begins serious music study; Gaetano Pugnani returns to Turin after a year of study in Rome; Antonio Soler takes on Holy Orders at El Escorial.

G. Institutional Openings:
Other: W. E. Hill and Sons, Violin Makers (London); King Street Theatre (Birmingham); Movable Type for Music Printing (by Johann Breitkopf of Leipzig); St. Petersburg Court Theater; Stuttgart Music Theater; George Winter, Music Printer and Publisher (Berlin)

H. Musical Literature:

Arne, Thomas A., *Vocal Melody II*
Batteux, Charles, *Cours de belles-lettres V*
Marpurg, Friedrich W., *Die Kunst das Clavier zu spielen I*
    Der critische Musicus an der Spree
Rameau, Jean-Philippe, *Demonstration du principe de l'harmonie*
Ruetz, Caspar, *Widerlegte Vorurtheile von Ursprung der Kirchenmusik I*
Tessarini, Carlo, *Nouvelle Methode pour apprendre par theorie*

I. Musical Compositions:

Abos, Girolamo, *Adriano in Siria* (opera)
Adolfati, Andrea, *Adrianna* (opera)
Agricola, Johann F., *Il filosofo convinto in amore* (opera)
Araia, Francesco, *Bellerofonte* (opera)
Arne, Thomas, *Cymon and Iphigenia* (cantata)
    Don Saverio (opera)
    The Sacrifice of Iphigenia (opera)
    Romeo and Juliet (incidental music)
Boyce, William, *8 Symphonies in 8 Parts, Opus 2*
    The Roman Father (opera)
Burney, Charles, *Queen Mab* (incidental music)
Durante, Francesco, *Litany in F Minor*
Galuppi, Baldassare, *Archifanfano* (opera)
    Il mondo della luna (opera)
    Il mondo alla roversa (opera)
    La vittoria d'Imeneo (cantata)
    Aqua e rupe Horeb (oratorio)
Gluck, Christoph W., *Ezio* (opera)
Graun, Carl H., *Il Mitridate* (opera)
    Fetonte (opera)
Handel, George F., *The Choice of Hercules* (oratorio)
    Theodora (oratorio)
Hasse, Johann A., *Attilio Regolo* (opera)
Haydn, Franz J., *Missa Brevis in F Major*
    Lauda Sion
Jommelli, Niccolo, *Andromeda* (incidental music)
    Euridice (pastorale)
    Le sposa di Elcana (sacred drama)
    Il sacrificio di Abramo (oratorio)
Leclair, Jean Marie (l'aine), *Apollon et Climene* (opera)
Perez, David, *Semiramide* (opera)
Pescetti, Giovanni, *Arianna e Teseo* (opera)
    Adriano in Siria (opera)
Reutter, Georg, *La rispettosa tenerezza* (opera)
Royer, Joseph N., *Myrtil* (opera)
Sammartini, Giovanni, *Paride riconosciuto* (cantata)
Scarlatti, Giuseppe, *Antigona* (opera)
Tartini, Giuseppe, *12 Trio Sonatas*
Telemann, Georg P., *Passion According to Matthew III*
Terradellas, Domingo, *Didone abbandonata* (opera)
Tessarini, Carlo, *6 Violin Duets, Opus 15*
Wagenseil, Georg C., *Antigono* (opera)
    Andromeda (opera)
    Euridice (opera)

1751

World Events:

In the U.S., Parliament passes the Currency Act forbidding the issuance of paper money by any of the New England colonies; the Ohio Company begins the colonization of the Ohio Valley with English settlers thereby causing rivalry with France to increase; Georgia is formed as a Royal Colony; the Academy and College of Philadelphia is established; the Pennsylvania Hospital becomes the first hospital to be opened in the colonies; Manchester, New Hampshire, is incorporated; future President James Madison is born; Benjamin Franklin publishes his *Experiments and Observations on Electricity* and his *Observations Concerning the Increase of Mankind*. Internationally, the British Parliament finally changes the English calendar to the Gregorian, the change going into effect in 1752; the element Nickel is isolated by A. Cronstadt; King William IV of the Netherlands dies and is succeeded by King William V; King Frederick II of Sweden dies and is succeeded by King Adolphus Frederick; Chinese forces invade Tibet; French philosopher Voltaire publishes his book, *Le Siècle de Louis XV*.

Cultural Highlights:

Charles Natoire is appointed director of the French Academy in Rome; Jonathan Edwards accepts the appointment as missionary to the Indians of Massachusetts. Births in the world of art include American portrait painter Ralph Earl, British portrait painter James Sharples, German artists Heinrich Friedrich Füger and Johann Friedrich August Tischbein, and Italian sculptor Giuseppe Ceracchi; deaths in the art world include Scottish-born artist John Smibert, French artist Charles Antoine Coypel and Italian sculptor Nicola Salvi. Births in the literary field include German poets Jakob Michael Reinhold Lenz and Johann Heinrich Voss, Swedish poet and critic Johan Henrik Kellgren, Russian poet Nikolai L'vov, French satirical poet Nicolas Joseph Laurent Gilbert as well as Irish dramatist and parliamentarian Richard Brinsley Sheridan. Other highlights include:

Art: François Boucher, *The Toilet of Venus* and *The Reclining Girl*; Jean-Baptiste Chardin, *The Bird Organ*; Étienne Falconet, *Allegory of Music* (marble); Robert Feke, *Isaac Winslow*; Thomas Gainsborough, *Artist, Wife and Child*; William Hogarth, *Cheap Gin and Beer Street*; Maurice de La Tour, *Self-Portrait*; Pietro Longhi, *The Painter in His Studio*; Giovanni Tiepolo, *Ceiling of the Kaisersaal* (Würzburg)

Literature: Richard Cambridge, *Scribleriad*; Nathaniel Cotton, *Visions in Verse*; Denis Diderot, *Encyclopédie I*; Henry Fielding, *Amelia*; Thomas Gray, *Elegy Written in a Country Church Yard*; James Harris, *Hermes, or a Philosophical Inquiry*; Henry Home, *Essays on the Principles of Morality and Natural Religion*; Friedrich Gottlieb Klopstock, *Messias I*; Gotthold Lessing, *Kleinigkeiten*; Tobias Smollett, *The Adventures of Peregrine Pickle*

MUSICAL EVENTS

A. Births:

Jan 14	Corona Schröter (Ger-sop)	Aug 23	Nikolaus Simrock (Ger-pub)
Jan 18	Ferdinand Kauer (Aus-cm-cd)	Sep 1	Emanuel Schikaneder (Aus-lib)
Jan 21	Josephus Fodor (Hol-vn-cm)	Sep 10	Bartolomeo Campagnoli (It-vn)
Feb 4	Blas de Laserna (Sp-cm)	Oct 27	David M. Michael (Ger-vn)
Feb 18	Karl Haack (Ger-vn-cm)		Benjamin Blake (Br-vn)
Mar 5	Jan Kucharcz (Boh-org)		Dmitri Bortniansky (Rus-cm-cd)
Apr 3	Jean Baptiste Lemoyne (Fr-cm)		Mary Ann Pownall (Br-sop)
Apr 9	Supply Belcher (Am-cm)		Carl D. Stegmann (Ger-ten)
Jul 30	Anna Mozart (Aus-pn-ped)		

B. Deaths:

Jan 17	Tomaso Albinoni (It-cm)	Oct 2	Pierre Dumage (Fr-org)
Feb	Giuseppe Alberti (It-vn-cm)	Oct 9	Jacobus Moreau (Hol-org.m)
Feb 25	Georg K. Schürmann (Ger-cm)	Oct 26	Philip Doddridge (Br-hymn)
May	Christopher Schrider (Br-org.m)	Nov 22	Anton Englert (Ger-org)
May 14	Henry Reinhold (Ger-bs)	Dec 7	Heinrich Bokemeyer (Ger-the)
May 20	Domingo Terradellas (Sp-cm)	Dec 7	Nicolò Girolamo (It-vn)
Jul 25	John F. Lampe (Ger-cm-the)		Giuseppe M. Alberti (It-vn)

C. Debuts:

Other - Carlo F. Chiabrand (London), Joseph Vernon (London), Isabella Young (London)

D. New Positions:

Conductors: Ignazio Fiorillo (kapellmeister, Brunswick), Manuel Gaytán y Arteaga (maestro de capilla, Córdoba Cathedral), Ignaz Jakob Holzbauer (kapellmeister, Stuttgart), Antonio Mazzoni (maestro di cappella, S. Giovanni, Monte), José Nebra (music director, Royal Chapel, Madrid)

Others: Charles Burney (organ, St. Margaret's, King's Lynn), François Francoeur and François Rebel (co-directors, Paris Opera), Johann Christian Kittel (organ, Langensalza), John Worgen (organ, Vauxhall Gardens)

E. Prizes and Honors:

Honors: Johann Friedrich Agricola (court composer to Frederick the Great), Francois Colin de Blamont (Order of St. Michel), Quirino Gasparini (Accademia Filarmonica, Bologna), Johann Philipp Kirnberger (violinist to Frederick the Great)

F. Biographical Highlights:

Johann Friedrich Agricola marries soprano Benedetta Molteni; Giuseppe Aprile begins voice study at a private school in Naples; François Bainville marries organist Marie-Claude Renault; Faustina Bordoni retires from the stage but continues singing in the court; Charles Burney moves his family to King's Lynn for a nine-year stay; Marie Camargo retires from the ballet; Carl Ditters von Dittersdorf enters the service of the Prince of Sachsen-Hilburghausen; Elizabeth Duparc returns to the concert stage; Felice de' Giardini begins his London career as a violin virtuoso; Johann Gottlieb Goldberg joins the musical court of Count von Brühl; Francois Joseph Gossec arrives in Paris with a letter of introduction to Rameau; François Granier moves to Lyons as teacher and composer; George Frederic Handel is stricken with blindness; Pieter Hellendaal leaves Leiden to settle permanently in London as organist and teacher; Johann Adam Hiller enters the law school of the University of Leipzig; Johann Philipp Kirnberger returns to Dresden after a ten-year stay in Poland; Jean Pantaléon LeClerc retires and gives his publishing business to his daughter.

G. Institutional Openings:

Performing Groups: Maresch Hunting Horn Ensemble (St. Petersburg)

Educational: James Logan Library (bequeathed to the City of Philadelphia)

Other: Johann A. Stein, Organ Builder (Augsburg); Teatro Nuovo (Padua); Peter Thompson Music Publishing House (London)

H. Musical Literature:

Arne, Thomas, *Vocal Melody III*
Blainville, Charles-Henri, *Essai sur un troisième mode*
Estève, Pierre, *Nouvelle découverte du principe de l'harmonie*
Geminiani, Francesco, *Art of Playing the Violin* (Third Edition)

Hahn, Georg J., *Wohl unterwiesene General-Bass Schüller*
Hayes, William, *The Art of Composing Music by a Method Entirely New*
Nauss, Johann X., *Gründlicher Unterricht der General-Bass recht zu erlernen*
Wagenseil, Georg C., *Geig-Fundamenta, oder Rudimenta panduristae*

I. Musical Compositions:

Abos, Girolamo, *Tito Manlio* (opera)
Adolfati, Andrea, *Adriano in Siria* (opera)
    La gloria e il piacere (opera)
Agricola, Johann F., *La ricamatrice divenuta dama* (opera)
Araia, Francesco, *La clemenza de Tito* (opera--may be by Hasse)
Arne, Thomas, *The Country Lasses* (incidental music)
    8 Overtures
Avison, Charles, *6 Concertos in 7 Parts, Opus 3*
Bertoni, Ferdinando, *Le Pescatrici* (opera)
Blainville, Charles, *6 Symphonies, Opus 2*
Bonno, Giuseppe, *Il re pastore* (opera)
Boyce, William, *The Shepherd's Lottery* (opera)
Duni, Egidio, *La semplice curiosa* (opera)
Galuppi, Baldassare, *Dario* (opera)
    Antigona (opera)
    Lucio Papirio (opera)
    Artaserse (opera)
Giardini, Felice de', *6 Violin Sonatas, Opus 1*
Graun, Carl H., *Britannico* (opera)
    L'Armida (opera)
Handel, George F., *Jephtha* (oratorio)
Hasse, Johann A., *Ciro riconosciuto* (opera)
    Mass in D Minor
    Te Deum in D Major
Jommelli, Niccolò, *Talestri* (opera)
    Ifigenia in Aulide (opera)
    Cesare in Egitto (opera)
    Ipermestra (opera)
    L'uccellatrice (intermezzo)
Logroscino, Nicola, *Amore figlio del piacere* (opera)
Pasquali, Nicolo, *12 Overtures*
Pescetti, Giovanni, *Artaserse* (opera)
Rameau, Jean-Philippe, *Linus* (opera)
    La guirlande (ballet)
    Acante et Céphise (pastorale)
Reutter, Georg, *La virtuosa emulazione* (opera)
Rinaldo di Capua, *Gli impostori* (opera)
    Il ripiego in amore di Flaminia (opera)
Terradellas, Domingo, *Sesostri* (opera)
Traetta, Tommaso, *Il Farnace* (opera)

1752

World Events:
In the U.S., the "Liberty Bell" is installed in Philadelphia but cracks on its first trial and has to be recast; the Treaty of Logstown with the Indians settles the Allegheny Mountain problems and opens the territory for colonial expansion; Benjamin Franklin performs his electricity experiments with the kite in a thunderstorm thereby proving that lightning is electricity and also invents the lightning rod. Internationally, the Treaty of Aranjuez is signed between Spain and the Holy Roman Empire; Madame Pompadour is made a Duchess by the French monarch; the Great Moscow Fire destroys over 18,000 houses; the British break the French siege of Trichinopoly in India; David Hume publishes his *Political Discourses* and Henry Bolingbroke his *Letters on the Study of History.*

Cultural Highlights:
The Madrid Academy of Fine Arts opens its doors; Jean Honoré Fragonard receives the Prix de Rome in Art; Corrado Giaquinto becomes court painter in Madrid; Johann Heinrich Wilhelm Tischbein, Sr., becomes court painter at Hesse-Kassel; Pierre Antoine Verschaffelt becomes court painter in Mannheim; Jean Baptiste Pigalle becomes professor at the Royal Academy in Paris; Anna Williams becomes a part of the Johnson household; Jean Baptiste Oudry publishes his *Discours sur la Pratique de la Peinture;* In the art world, British artist John Robert Cozens is born; dead are French artists Charles Antoine Coypel and Jean François de Troy. Births in the literary field include American poets Timothy Dwight and Philip Morin Freneau, Italian poet Giuseppe Carpani, German novelist Friedrich Maximilian von Klinger, British novelist Fanny Burney, poet Thomas Chatterton and French poet Antoine de Bertin; deaths include British philosopher and theologian Joseph Butler and French dramatist Louis Fuzelier. Other highlights include:

Art: François Boucher, *Sunrise and Sunset;* Jean-Honoré Fragonard, *Jeroboam Sacrificing to Idols;* Corrado Giaquinto, *Birth of the Virgin;* Pietro Longhi, *The Family Concert;* Anton Mengs, *Domenico Annibali;* Joshua Reynolds, *Lady Chambers;* Giovanni Battista Tiepolo, *Beatrix Arrival to the Emperor* and *The Investiture of Bishop Harold;* Paul Troger, *Dome of the Church of Dreieichen*

Literature: William Dodd, *The Beauties of Shakespeare;* Jonathan Edwards, *Misrepresentations Corrected and Truth Vindicated;* Friedrich von Hagedorn, *Oden und Lieder III;* Soame Jenyns, *Poems;* Charlotte Lennox, *The Female Quixote;* Jean F. Marmontel, *Les Héraclides;* William Mason, *Elfrieda;* Michel Jean Sedaine, *Poésies Fugitives;* Christopher Smart, *Poems on Several Occasions*

MUSICAL EVENTS

A. Births:

Jan 23	Muzio Clementi (It-pn-cm)	Sep 4	Friedrich Benda (Ger-cm)
Feb 20	Charles Broche (Fr-org)	Sep 25	Carl Stenborg (Swe-cm)
Feb 22	Charles Knyvett, Sr. (Br-c.ten)	Sep 30	Justin H. Knecht (Ger-org)
Mar 7	Carl F. Cramer (Ger-pub)	Oct 2	Ambrogio Minoja (It-cm)
Mar 13	Josef Reicha (Cz-cel)	Nov 2	Andreas Rasumovsky (Rus-pat)
Mar 19	José Mauricio (Por-the)	Nov 25	Johann F. Reichardt (Ger-cm)
Mar 22	Johann Spangler (Aus-ten)	Dec	André de Silva Gomes (Bra-cm)
Apr 2	Edward Jones (Br-hp)	Dec 9	Georg F. Fuchs (Fr-cl-cm)
Apr 4	Niccolo Zingarelli (It-cm)	Dec 30	Leopold Kozeluch (Boh-cm)
Apr 5	Sébastien Érard (Fr-pn.m)		Anton Kraft (Aus-cel)
Apr 6	Johann F. Kranz (Ger-vn)		Isidore Bertheaume (Fr-vn)
May 2	Ludwig A. Lebrun (Ger-ob)		Francesco Bianchi (It-cm-cd)
May 17	Johann Dalberg (Ger-cm)		John Dodd (Br-bow.m)

B. Deaths:

Feb 29   Pietro Castrucci (It-vn)
Jul 20   John C. Pepusch (Ger-cm)
Jul 24   Michael C. Festing (Br-vn)
Aug 16   Nicolas Vibert (Fr-vn-cm)
Sep 19   Louis Fuzelier (Fr-lib)
Nov 20   John Shore (Br-tpt)

Nov 23   Conrad Schneider (Ger-org)
Dec 3   Henri G. Hamal (Bel-cd-cm)
Johann Benda (Boh-vn-cm)
Agostino Coletti (It-cm)
Girolamo Donnini (It-cm)

C. Debuts:
Other - Jean-Louis Laruette (Paris)

D. New Positions:
Conductors: Antonio Brunetti (maestro di cappella, Pisa Cathedral), Benjamin Cooke (Academy of Ancient Music, London), Christoph Willibald Gluck (conductor to Prince Sachsen-Hildburghausen), Adolph Carl Kunzen (kapellmeister, Mecklenburg-Schwerin), David Pérez (maestro di capella, Royal Chapel, Lisbon), Giuseppe Sarti (Faenza Theater), Joseph Umstatt (kapellmeister, Bamburg)

Others: Ferdinando Bertoni (organ, St. Mark's, Venice), Capel Bond (organ, Holy Trinity, Coventry)

F. Biographical Highlights:
Anton Cajetan Adlgasser marries Maria Josepha Eberlin, the daughter of the Salzburg kapellmeister; composer Maria Teresa Agnesi marries Pier Antonio Pinottini; Pasquale Anfossi leaves the Loreto Conservatory in Naples to play the violin in local theater orchestras; Raniero Cazabigi is given royal publishing privileges for printing music in Paris and France; the family of Tommaso Giordani, comprising a traveling opera group of their own, makes their Amsterdam debut; François Joseph Giraud travels to Paris where he begins playing violin in the Opera orchestra; Christoph Willibald Gluck goes to Naples to oversee the performance of his commissioned opera, *La clemenza di Tito*; Nicola Antonio Porpora is pensioned from the Dresden Court and moves to Vienna where he begins private teaching, Franz Joseph Haydn becoming one of his students; Gaetano Pugnani becomes concertmaster of the Turin Court orchestra; Antonio Soler takes the Holy Orders at El Escorial and remains there for the rest of his life; Francesco Antonio Uttini joins the traveling Mingotti Opera Troupe for a short time as a singer.

G. Institutional Openings:
Educational: Académie de Musique de Reims

Other: *Covent Garden Journal*; *Gray's Inn Journal*; Samuel Lee, Music Store and Publisher (Dublin); Rococo Theater (Schwetzingen)

H. Musical Literature:
Alembert, Jean d', *Treatise on Rameau's Theories*
    The Elements of Music
Arne, Thomas, *Vocal Melody IV*
Avison, Charles, *Essay on Musical Expression*
Krause, Christian G., *Von der musikalischen Poesie*
Provedi, Francesco, *Paragone della musica antica e della moderna*
Quantz, Johann J., *Versuch einer Anweisung, die Flöte traversiere zu spielen*
Rameau, Jean-Philippe, *Nouvelle reflexions...sur la manière de former la voix*
Riepel, Joseph, *Anfangsgründe zur musikalischen Setzkunst*
Ruetz, Caspar, *Widerlegte vorurtheile von der Beshaffenheit der heutigen Kirchenmusik...*

I. Musical Compositions:
Abos, Girolamo, *Erifile* (opera)

    Lucio Vero (opera)
Adolfati, Andrea, *Vologeso* (opera)
    Ipermestra (opera)
Almeida, Francisco de, *L'Ippolito* (serenade)
Arne, Thomas, *Harlequin Sorcerer* (opera)
    The Oracle (incidental music)
Bertoni, Ferdinando, *Antigono* (opera)
Bonno, Giuseppe, *L'eroe cinese* (opera)
Dauvergne, Antoine, *Les amours de Tempé* (ballet)
Galuppi, Baldassare, *Didone abbandonato* (opera)
    Le virtuose ridicole (opera)
    La calamità de' cuori (opera)
    Gerusalemme convertita (oratorio)
Gluck, Christoph W., *La clemenza di Tito* (opera)
    Issipile (opera)
    Concerto in G Major for Flute and Orchestra
Graun, Carl H., *L'Orfeo* (opera)
    Il giudicio di Paride (pastorale)
Hasse, Johann A., *Adriano in Siria* (opera)
Haydn, Franz J., *Der krumme teufel* (singspiel)
Jommelli, Nicolò, *I rivali delusi* (opera)
    La natività della beatissima Vergine (oratorio)
Logroscino, Nicola, *La Griselda* (opera)
    Lo finto Perziano (opera)
Mondonville, Jean de, *Vénus et Adonis* (opera)
    Concerto for Violin, Voice, Chorus and Orchestra
Pérez, David, *Demofoönte* (opera)
Piccinni, Niccolò, *Gioas, re di Giuda* (oratorio)
Rinaldo di Capua, *La donna superba* (intermezzo)
    La forza della pace (opera)
Rousseau, Jean-Jacques, *Le devin du village* (intermezzo)
Royer, Joseph N., *Pandore* (opera)
Sarti, Giuseppe, *Pompeo in Armenia* (opera)
Scarlatti, Domenico, *30 Keyboard Sonatas, Volume I* (publication)
    30 Keyboard Sonatas, Volume II (publication)
Scarlatti, Giuseppe, *Adriano in Siria* (opera)
    Demetrio (opera)
    L'impostore (opera)
    I portentosi effetti della Madre Natura (opera)
    L'amor della Patia (serenade)
Telemann, Georg P., *7 Duets for Flutes*

1753

World Events:
In the U.S., Fort Presque Isle (present-day Erie, Pennsylvania) and other forts are built by the French in the Ohio Territory--George Washington is sent by the Virginia governor to demand French withdrawal from the Territory; Benjamin Franklin receives the Copley Medal for his work with electricity and receives many international honors as well as three honorary degrees; the first known steam engine is brought to the colonies by J. Schuyler in New Jersey. Internationally, the British Parliament finally ends an era of prejudice in the British Empire and provides for the naturalization of all Jews; the British Marriage Act prevents marriages by unlicensed ministers; Austria, Russia and France unite against Frederick II of Prussia; the last Burmese dynasty is formed and Rangoon is rebuilt.

Cultural Highlights:
The British Museum Library is built upon the base of the donation of the Hans Sloane Collection; German actor Konrad Ekhof opens his Dramatic Academy in Schwerin; Voltaire, quarreling with Frederick the Great, leaves the Prussian court and returns to France; Giuseppe Baretti (pen-name of Aristarco Scannabue) publishes his *Dissertation on Italian Poetry*; William Hogarth brings out his *Analysis of Beauty*; Jean Baptiste Perroneau is inducted into the Royal Academy in Paris. Births in the art field include British artist William Beechey, artist and engraver Thomas Bewick, collector and artist George Howland Beaumont; deaths in the field include German artist and architect Georg Wenzeslaus Knobelsdorff and architect Balthasar Neumann. Births in the literary field include British actress and author Elizabeth Inchbald, African-born poet Phillis Wheatley, French author Joseph Marie de Maistre and German author August Gottlieb Meissner; Irish philosopher George Berkeley dies. Other highlights include:

Art: François Boucher, *Setting of the Sun*; Jean-Baptiste Chardin, *The Blind Man*; John Singleton Copley, *Reverend William Welsteed*; François de Cuvilliés, *The Residenz Theater, Munich*; Maurice de La Tour, *Le Rond d'Alembert*; Jean-Baptiste Oudry, *A Dog Guarding Dead Game*; Jean-Baptiste Perroneau, *Jean-Baptiste Oudry*; Joshua Reynolds, *Commodore Keppel*; Giovanni Domenico Tiepolo, *Frescoes, Kaisersaal, Würzburg*

Literature: Philippe Destouches, *Le Dissipateur*; Samuel Foote, *The Englishman in Paris*; Richard Glover, *Boadicea*; Carlo Goldoni, *Mistress of the Inn*; Thomas Gray, *Hymn to Adversity*; Carolus Linnaeus, *Species Plantarum*; Robert Lowth, *De Sacra Poesi Hebraeorum*; Jean Francois Marmontel, *Funérailles de Sésostris*; Edward Moore, *The Gamester*; Samuel Richardson, *History of Sir Charles Grandison*; Christopher Smart, *Hilliad*; Tobias George Smollett, *Ferdinand, Count Fathom*

MUSICAL EVENTS

A. Births:

Jan 9	Luiza Rosa Todi (Por-sop)	Oct 14	Anton Dimler (Ger-hn)
Jan 22	Peter Fuchs (Aus-vn)	Nov 3	Friedrich Gestenitz (Ger-cm)
Feb 24	Carl Türrschmidt (Ger-hn)	Nov 3	Antoine M. Lemoine (Fr-pub)
Mar 9	Jean J. Imbault (Fr-vn-pub)	Nov 6	Jean B. Bréval (Fr-cel)
Jun 8	Nicolas Dalayrac (Fr-cm)	Nov 19	Stanislas Champein (Fr-cm)
Jun 28	Anton Stadler (Aus-cl)	Nov 25	Otto Kospoth (Ger-cm)
Aug 22	Christian Ruppe (Hol-the)	Nov 30	Johann Schenk (Aus-cm-cd)
Aug 29	Johann Braun (Ger-vn-cm)		Angelo Baldan (It-rel-cm)
Sep 12	Friedrich Baumbach (Ger-cm)		Giuseppe Giordani (It-cm)
Sep 29	Johann G. Schicht (Ger-cm)		Giovanni Rubinelli (It-cas)

B. Deaths:

Jan 1	Louis de la Pierre (Fr-cm)		Aug 2	Joseph C. Deichel (Ger-vn-cm)
Feb 6	Barnabas Gunn (Br-org)		Aug 4	Gottfried Silbermann
Feb 7	Giovanni Ristori (It-cm)			(Ger-org.m)
Feb 16	Giacomo Facco (It-vn-cm)		Nov	Carl Einwald (Aus-org)
Feb 25	François Grenet (Fr-cm)		Nov 4	Johann N. Bach (Ger-org)
Mar 6	Gerhardus Havingha (Hol-org)		Nov 16	Nicolas de Grandval (Fr-cm)
Apr	James Worgen (Br-org)			Domenico Auleta (It-org)
May 17	Jacques Aubert (Fr-vn)			Giovanni Bononcini (It-vn)

C. Debuts:
Other - Giuseppe Aprile (Naples)

D. New Positions:
Conductors: Andrea Bernasconi (kapellmeister, Munich), Gioacchino Cocchi (maestro di cappella, Conservatorio degli Incurabili, Venice), Ignaz Holzbauer (kapellmeister, Mannheim), Niccolò Jommelli (kapellmeister, Stuttgart), Giuseppe Sarti (Italian Opera, Copenhagen)

Others: Christlieb Siegmund Binder (organ, Dresden Court), Richard Langdon (organ, Exeter Cathedral), Johann Gottfried Müthel (organ, Lutheran Church, Riga)

F. Biographical Highlights:
Francesco Algarotti, suffering from ill health, leaves Berlin and returns to Italy; Joseph Marie Dall'Abaco leaves the Vienna Court and goes to Verona with his wife; the operatic family of Tommaso Giordani moves on to England and makes their debut at Covent Garden; Gioacchino Conti (Gizziello) retires from the operatic stage; André Rosa Curioni maker her London debut; Ernest Grétry, age twelve, is dismissed from the choir of the St. Denis church and begins taking violin and singing lessons; music historian John Hawkins marries into a wealthy family leaving him free to devote his time to music and literature study; Franz Joseph Haydn meets and receives encouragement from Carl Ditters von Dittersdorf; William Tuckey arrives in the U.S. and sets himself up as a teacher of voice in New York.

G. Institutional Openings:
Other: Hummel Music Publishing Co. (Amsterdam); Residenztheater (Cuvilliéstheater, Munich)

H. Musical Literature:
Arne, Thomas, *Agreeable Musical Choice I*
Avison, Charles, *A Reply to the Author of Remarks on the Essay on Musical Expression*
Bach, C. P. E., *The Proper Method of Playing Keyboard Instruments I*
Corrette, Michel, *Le maître de clavecin*
Estève, Pierre, *L'esprit des beaux-arts*
Grimm, Friedrich, *Le petit prophète de Boemischbroda*
Hayes, William, *Remarks on Avison's Essay on Musical Expression*
Marpurg, Friedrich, *Abhandlung von der Fuge I*
Riedt, Friedrich, *Versuch über die musikalischen Intervalle*
Rousseau, Jean-Jacques, *Lettre sur la musique française*
Travenol, Louis, *Histoire du théâtre de l'Opéra en France*

I. Musical Compositions:
Adolfati, Andrea, *La clemenza di Tito* (opera)
Agnesi, Maria Teresa, *Ciro in Armenia* (opera)
Arne, Thomas, *Lethe* (incidental music)
Bertoni, Ferdinando, *Ginevra* (opera)

I bagni d'Abano (opera)
Blavet, Michel, *La fête de Cythère* (opera)
   Le jeux olympiques (ballet)
Dauvergne, Antoine, *Les troqueurs* (intermezzo)
   La coquette trompée (opera)
   La sibylle (ballet)
Durante, Francesco, *Mass in A Major*
Ferrandini, Giovanni, *Catone in Utica* (opera)
Galuppi, Baldassare, *I bagni d'Abano* (opera, with Bertoni)
   Sofonisba (opera)
   L'eroe cinese (opera)
Giraud, Francois, *Les hommes* (ballet)
Graun, Carl H., *Silla* (opera)
   Il trionfo della fedeltà (opera)
Hasse, Johann A., *Solimano* (opera)
   L'eroe cinese (opera)
Holzbauer, Ignaz, *Il figlio delle selve* (opera)
Jommelli, Niccolò, *Demetrio* (opera)
   La clemenza di Tito (opera)
   Fetonte (opera)
   Bajazette (opera)
   Demofoonte II (opera)
Lampugnani, Giovanni, *Vologeso* (opera)
Leclair, Jean Marie (l'aîné), *3 Ouvertures et sonates en trio, Opus 13*
Logroscino, Nicola, *Olimpiade* (opera)
   Elmira generosa (opera)
   La Pastorella scaltra (intermezzo)
Mondonville, Jean de, *Titon et l'Aurore* (opera)
Rameau, Jean-Philippe, *Daphnis et Églé* (pastorale)
   Les Sybarites (ballet)
Reutter, Georg, *Primo omaggio di canto*
Rinaldo di Capua, *La Zingara* (intermezzo)
   L'amante deluso (opera)
   La serva sposa (intermezzo)
Rutini, Giovanni M., *Sémiramide* (opera)
. Sammartini, Giovanni, *La reggia de' fati* (cantata)
   La pastorale offerta (cantata)
Sarti, Giuseppe, *Il re pastore* (opera)
Scarlati, Domenico, *30 Keyboard Sonatas, Volume III*
   30 Keyboard Sonatas, Volume IV
Scarlatti, Giuseppe, *Alessandro nell'Indie* (opera)
   De gustibus non est disputandum (opera)
Talon, Pierre, *6 Symphonies, Opus 1*
Tessarini, Carlo, *6 Trio Sonatas, Opus 16*
Traetta, Tommaso, *I pastori felici* (opera)

1754

World Events:
In the U.S., the first skirmish of the French and Indian War takes place at the Battle of Great Meadows and George Washington, in charge of the Virginia militia, is forced to surrender Fort Necessity; the Albany Plan seeks united action of the English and colonial forces against the French and their Indian allies; Fort Duquesne (modern day Pittsburgh) is founded by the French; King's College (Columbia University) is founded in New York City. Internationally, England and France begin their prolonged battles in the New World (French and Indian War) and the Old (Seven Years War); the French withdraw their colonial governor from India, bringing to an end their dream of a French empire there; Mahmum I of Turkey dies and is succeeded by Othman III; China's population reaches 185 million; Charles Talleyrand, famous French statesman is born.

Cultural Highlights:
The Society of the Encouragement of Arts and Manufactures is founded in England; the magazine *L'Année Littéraire* begins publication in Paris with Élie Fréron as editor; Anton Raphael Mengs becomes the new director of the Academy of Fine Arts in Rome; Jean le Rond d'Alembert is taken into the French Academy; British furniture designer and maker, Thomas Chippendale, publishes his *Gentleman and Cabinet Maker's Director*; David Hume publishes the first volume of his *History of England*. Births in the art world include German artist Asmus Jakob Carstens and Italian artist Andrea Appiani; deaths in the field include French sculptor Nicholas Pineau, Italian artist Giovanni Battista Piazzetta and Scottish architect James Gibbs. Births in the literary field include American poet and diplomat Joel Barlow, Italian poet Vincenzo Monti, Spanish poet Juan Meléndez-Valdés, British poet George Crabbe, Irish poet William Drennan, Swedish poet Anna Maria Lenngren as well as French philosopher Antoine Destutt de Tracy; deaths in the literary world include Norwegian dramatist Ludvig Holberg, Scottish poet William Hamilton, French dramatist Philippe Destouches, British novelist Henry Fielding, German poet Friedrich von Hagedorn and Spanish author Ignacio de Suelves y Gurrea. Other highlights include:

Art: François Boucher, *The Captive Cupid*; John Singleton Copley, *Galatea*; Étienne Maurice Falconet, *Milo of Croton*; Jean-Honoré Fragonard, *Psyche with Cupid's Presents*; William Hogarth, *An Election I*; Jean-Baptiste Pigalle, *Louis XV* (statue); Francesco Rastrelli, Winter Palace, St. Petersburg; Claude-Joseph Vernet, *Ports of France I*; Richard Wilson, *Lake Albano and Castelgandolfo*

Literature: Isaac Hawkins Browne, *De Animi Immortalitate*; Étienne Bonnot de Condillac, *Treatise on Sensation*; Crébillon, *Triumvirat*; Denis Diderot, *Pensées sur l'interpretaion de la Natur*; Jonathan Edwards, *Freedom of the Will*; Salomon Gessner, *Daphnis*; Jean-Jacques Rousseau, *On the Inequality of Man:* Thomas Wharton, *Observations on the Fairy Queen of Spencer*; Thomas Whitehead, *Creusa*

MUSICAL EVENTS

A. Births:

Feb 19	Matteo Babbini (It-ten)	Sep 5	Elizabeth Ann Linley (Br-sop)
Feb 23	David von Apell (Ger-cm-cd)	Sep 8	Anton Teyber (Aus-cm)
Mar	Josefa Dusek (Cz-sop)	Sep 25	Luigi Caruso (It-cm)
Apr 9	Anton Becvarovsky (Boh-org)	Oct 1	François Callinet (Fr-org.m)
May 2	Vicente Martín y Soler (Sp-cm)	Oct 21	Camillus Camilli (It-vn-cm)
May 12	Franz Hoffmeister (Ger-pub)		Maddalena Allegranti (Br-sop)
Jun 3	Gaetano Marinelli (It-cm)		Franciscus Geissenhof
Aug 28	Peter Winter (Ger-cm)		(Aus-vn.m)

B. Deaths:

Feb 21	Johann J. Schnell (Ger-vn)	Oct	Johann C. Hertel (Ger-vn)
Apr 19	Ferdinando Lazzari (It-org)	Oct 21	Camillus Camilli (It-vn.m)
May 16	Giovanni C. Clari (It-cm)		Louis de la Coste (Fr-cm)
Aug 7	Friedrich Schwindl (Aus-vn)		Gaetano M. Schiassi (It-cm)

C. Debuts:
   Other - Anna Lucia de Amicis (Florence), Rosa Curioni (London),

D. New Positions:
   Conductors: Pierre-Montan Berton (Paris Opera), Giovan Brunetti (maestro di cappella, Pisa), Ignazio Fiorillo (kapellmeister, Braunschweig), Christoph Willibald Gluck (kapellmeister, Vienna), Francesco Antonio Uttini (kapellmeister, Stockholm)
   Educational: Johann Hiller (tutor to the nephew of Count Bruhl, Dresden)

   Others: John Christopher Smith (organ, Foundling Hospital Chapel, London)

E. Prizes and Honors:
   Honors: Gregorio Ballabene (Accademia Filarmonica, Bologna)

F. Biographical Highlights:
   Johann Christian Bach travels to Bologna where he begins music study with Padre Martini; Francois Bainville moves to Paris; Giovanni Carestini, disilllusioned by the Berlin Court, goes to St. Petersburg for a two-year stay; Franz Joseph Haydn becomes a valet-pupil of Porpora who gives him composition lessons in exchange for menial tasks; Francis Hopkinson's *Ode to Music* is the first known work by a native American; Regina Mingotti makes her London debut at the King's Theater; Pierre-Alexandre Monsigny, fired by a performance of Pergolesi's *La Serva padrona*, decides to engage in opera writing; Giovanni Paisiello, on the recommendation of his choir director, Guaducci, is sent to the Conservatorio de S. Onofrio in Naples; Niccolo Piccinni has his first opera buffa, *Le Donne dispettose*, performed at the Teatro dei Fiorentini in Naples; Gaetano Pugnani begins concertizing as a concert violinist throughout Europe; Jean-Jacques Rousseau returns to Geneva and re-enters the Calvinist faith; Domenico Scarlatti leaves Madrid and returns to Naples; Johann Anton Stamitz, on the invitation of Alexandre La Poupliniere, conducts the Orchestre de Passy in Paris as well as at the Concerts Spirituels.

G. Institutional Openings:
   Other: Robert Bremner, Music Publisher (Edinburgh); Drottningholm Palace Theater I (Stockholm); *Historisch-Kritische Beytrage zur Aufnahme der Musik*; Inventionshorn (by Anton Hampel); Teatro Filarmonico II (Verona)

H. Musical Literature:
   d'Alembert, Jean-le-Rond, *Reflexions sur la musique en general...*
   Arne, Thomas, *Agreeable Musical Choice II*
   Bethizy, Jean de, *Exposition de la theorie et de la pratique de la musique*
   Blainville, Charles-Henri, *L'Esprit de l'art musical*
   Blamont, Francois Colin de, *Essai sur les gouts...de la musique francaise*
   Geminiani, Francesco, *Guida Armonica*
   Hiller, Johann A., *Abhandlung uber die Nachahmung der Natur in der Musik*
   Marpurg, Friedrich, *Abhandlung von der Fuge II*
   Rameau, Jean-Philippe, *Observations sur notre instinct pour la musique*
   Scheibe, Johann A., *Abhandlung vom Ursprung und Alter der Musik*
   Schmidt, Johann M., *Musico-Theologia*
   Tartini, Giuseppe, *Trattata di musica secondo la vera sienza dell'armonia*

I. Musical Compositions:

Adlgasser, Anton, *Christ on the Mount of Olives* (oratorio)
Agricola, Johann, *Cleofide* (opera)
    La nobiltà delusa (opera)
Arne, Thomas, *Eliza* (opera)
Bernasconi, Andrea, *L'huomo* (opera)
Bertoni, Ferdinando, *Sesostri* (opera)
    La moda (opera)
Bonno, Giuseppe, *L'isola disabitata* (opera)
Durante, Francesca, *S. Antonio di Padua* (sacred drama)
Galuppi, Baldassare, *Siroe* (opera)
    Il filosofo di campagna (opera)
    Alessandro nelle Indie (opera)
García, Manuel, *Le finta schiava* (opera)
Gluck, Christoph W., *Le cinesi* (opera)
Granier, François, *6 Solos for Cello*
Graun, Carl H., *Semiramide* (opera)
Hasse, Johann A., *Artemisia* (opera)
Holzbauer, Ignaz, *L'isola disabitata* (opera)
    L'issipile (opera)
    La Passione de Gesú Christo (oratorio)
Hopkinson, Francis, *Ode to Music*
Jommelli, Nicolò, *Lucio Vero* (opera)
    Catone in Utica (opera)
    Don Falcone (intermezzo)
    La reconciliazione della Virtù e della Gloria (oratorio)
Mondonville, Jean de., *Daphnis et Alcimadure* (opera)
Pescetti, Giovanni, *Tamerlano* (opera)
Piccinni, Niccolò, *Le donne dispettose* (opera)
Porpora, Nicola, *12 Violin Sonatas* (publication)
Rameau, Jean-Philippe, *Anacréon I* (ballet)
    La naissance d'Osiris (ballet)
Reutter, Georg, *Il tributo di Rispetto e d'Amore* (opera)
    La Corona (opera)
Richter, Franz X., *6 Concertos for Horn and Orchestra*
Rinaldo di Capua, *Attalo* (opera)
    La Chiavarina (intermezzo)
Sarti, Giuseppe, *Antigono* (opera)
    Vologeso (opera)
    Ciro riconosciuto (opera)
Scarlatti, Domenico, *30 Keyboard Sonatas, Volume VII*
    30 Keyboard Sonatas, Volume VIII
    30 Keyboard Sonatas, Volume IX
Scarlatti, Giuseppe, *Caio Mario* (opera)
    Antigono (opera)
    La madamigella (opera)
Smith, John C., *The Fairies* (opera)
Traetta, Tommaso, *Le nozze contrastate* (opera)

1755

World Events:
In the U.S., General Braddock is mortally wounded at the Battle of the Wilderness and George Washington takes over command of the retreat; the Arcadian French from Nova Scotia are deported to Maryland by the British; Bethlehem, Pennsylvania, introduces the first municipal water system; Jonathan Roberts becomes the first known prescription druggist in the colonies; the first maps of the middle colonies are published. Internationally, the Great Lisbon Earthquake kills more than 60,000 people and causes extensive damage; the British sign a Treaty of Alliance with Russia; Moscow University is founded; the Island of Corsica becomes a free republic; Austrian princess Marie Antoinette is born.

Cultural Highlights:
Giovanni Battista Tiepolo becomes President of the newly formed Venetian Academy of Art; Olof von Dalin becomes the historiographer for the Swedish Court; Johann Joachim Winckelmann publishes his *Gedanken über die Nachahmung der Griechischen Werke in der Malerei und Bilderkunst*; Samuel Johnson's *Dictionary of the English Language* is published. Births in the art world include American artist Gilbert Charles Stuart, British artist Thomas Stothard and sculptor John Flaxman and French artist Marie Anne Elisabeth Vigée-Lebrun; deaths include Swedish portrait painter Gustavus Hesselius, French artist Jean Baptiste Oudry and sculptor Jacques Caffiéri. Births in the field of literature include Scottish author Anne Grant and French dramatist Jean François Collin d'Harleville; deaths include French author Charles de Secondat Montesquieu and Italian dramatist Francesco Scipione de Maffei. Other highlights include:

Art: François Boucher, *Shepherd and Shepherdess*; Étienne Falconet, *The Punishment of Cupid*; Thomas Gainsborough, *Milkmaid and Woodcutter*; Jean-Baptiste Greuze, *Father Reading His Bible to the Children*; Maurice de La Tour, *Madame de Pompadour*; Pietro Longhi, *Excursion on Horseback*; Jean-Baptiste Oudry, *The White Duck*; Louis-François Roubillac, *Sir Isaac Newton*

Literature: Thomas Amory, *Memoirs*; Henry Fielding, *Journal of a Voyage to Lisbon*; Francis Hutcheson, *System of Moral Philosophy*; Immanuel Kant, *General History of Nature and Theory of the Heavens*; Gotthold Lessing, *Miss Sara Sampson*; Charles Palissot de Montenoy, *Le Cercle*; William Shenstone, *Pastoral Ballad*; Voltaire, *La Pucelle d'Orléans*

MUSICAL EVENTS

A. Births:

Jan 18	François Garnier (Fr-ob-cm)	Aug 1	Giuseppe Capuzzi (It-vn)
Feb 11	Albert Dies (Ger-art-mus)	Aug 8	Luigi Marchesi (It-cas)
Feb 17	Manuel Doyague (Sp-m.ed)	Sep 22	Christian Kalkbrenner (Ger-the)
Mar 2	Antoine Gresnick (Bel-cm)	Nov 10	Franz A. Ries (Ger-vn)
Mar 10	François Hérold (Fr-pn)	Nov 12	Sabina Hitzelberger (Ger-sop)
Mar 10	Philipp Kayser (Ger-pn)	Dec	Thomas Busby (Br-org-cri)
Mar 14	Pierre L. Couperin (Fr-org)	Dec 21	Caspar Reutz (Ger-cm)
Apr 4	Vincenz Mašek (Boh-cd-cm)		John E. Betts (Br-vn.m)
May 12	Giovanni B. Viotti (It-vn)		Thomas H. Butler (Br-ten)
May 22	Gaetano Andreozzi (It-cm)		Louis Chardiny (Fr-bar)
Jun 1	Federigo Fiorillo (It-vn)		Francesca Gabrielli (It-sop)
Jun 18	Louise Dugazon (Ger-sop)		M. Josephine Laguerre (Fr-sop)
Jul 29	Franz Götz (Boh-cm-vn)		Pierre Leduc (Fr-vn-pub)
Jul 12	Gaspard C. Prony (Fr-hp)		John C. Moller (Ger-org)

B. Deaths:

Jan 11	Joseph N. Royer (Fr-cm)	Aug 14	Jean Baptiste Anet (Fr-vn)
Jan 15	Azzolino Della Ciaia (It-org.m)	Sep 24	Georg Gebel, Jr. (Ger-org)
Mar 5	François Estienne (Fr-cm)	Sep 30	Francesco Durante (It-cm)
Mar 24	Theodor Reinhold (Ger-org)	Oct 28	Joseph de Boismortier (Fr-cm)
Apr	Anastasia Robinson (Br-alto)	Nov 25	Georg J. Pisendal (Ger-vn)
Jun 21	Giovanni Porta (It-cm)	Dec 1	Maurice Greene (Br-org)
Jun 23	Johann Bachofen (Swi-cm)	Dec 8	Jean Baptiste Stuck (It-cel-cm)
Jul 6	Pietro P. Bencini (It-cm)		Alexander Gordon (Scot-ten)
Jul 9	Gottlob Harrer (Ger-cm)		Francisco de Almeida (Por-cm)

C. Debuts:

Other - Charlotte Brent (Dublin), Henri Larrivée (Paris), Frederick C. Reinhold (London)

D. New Positions:

Conductors: Andrea Bernasconi (kapellmeister, Munich), Giovanni Battista Costanzi (maestro di cappella, St. Peter's, Rome), Antoine Dauvergne (Royal Orchestra, Paris), Johann Friedrich Doles (cantor, Leipzig Thomaskirche), José Durán (maestro de capilla, Palau, Barcelona), Francisco García (maestro di cappella, Terni Cathedral), Felice de' Giardini (Italian Opera, London), Johann Andreas Giulini (kapellmeister, Augsburg Cathedral), Gottfried August Homilius (cantor, Dresden Kreuzkirche), Jean Joseph de Mondonville (Concerts Spirituel, Paris), David Pérez (Lisbon Opera), Giuseppe Sarti (kapellmeister, Copenhagen)

Educational: Fedele Fenaroli (composition, Conservatorio della Pieta, Naples)

Others: Johann G. Albrechtsberger (organ, Raab), Edmund Ayrton (organ, Minster Cathedral), John Jones (organ, St. Paul's, London)

E. Prizes and Honors:

Honors: William Boyce (Master of the King's Music), Antoine Dauvergne (Composer to the King, Paris)

F. Biographical Highlights:

Paolo Tommaso Alberghi begins playing first violin in the Faenza Cathedral orchestra; John Alcock, Sr., earns his Bachelor of Music degree from Oxford; Francesco Araia writes the first known opera to be based on a Russian libretto, *Cephal i Prokris*; Thomas Arne and his wife separate over his affair with the soprano Charlotte Brent; Gioacchino Conti survives the great Lisbon earthquake but is impressed by his escape to enter a monastery; Caterina Gabrielli makes her Vienna debut to great acclaim; Bortolomeo Giacometti enters the choir school at the Verona Cathedral; Christoph Willibald Gluck, traveling in Italy, meets Franz Joseph Haydn; Michael Haydn is dropped from the St. Stephen's choir when his voice changes; Nicola Antonio Porpora leaves Vienna to return to Naples; Giovanni Battista Sammartini marries Rosalinda Acquanio; Francesco Antonio Uttini goes to Stockholm as conductor of an Italian opera group and stays there permanently.

G. Institutional Openings:

Other: Thomas Cahusec, Music Publisher (England); W. Hill and Son, Organ Builders (London); Municipal Theater on the Place Stanislas (Nancy); Teatro des Pacos de Ribeira (Lisbon)

H. Musical Literature:

Algarotti, Francesco, *Saggio sopra l'opera in musica*
Bérard, Jean-Antoine, *L'art du chant*
Caffiaux, Philippe, *Histoire de la musique*
Geminiani, Francesco, *The Art of Accompaniment*

Marpurg, Friedrich W., *Anleitung zum Clavierspielen...*
　　Handbuch bey dem General basse und der Composition
Nichelmann, Christoph, *Die melodie nach ihren Wesen*
Roussier, Pierre, *Observations sur différents points d'harmonie*
Tans'ur, William, *The Royal Melody Compleat*
Tonelli, Antonio, *Trattado di Musica*

I. Musical Compositions:

Adolfati, Andrea, *Sesostri, re d'Egitto* (opera)
Agricola, Johann F., *Il tempio d'amore* (opera)
Araia, Francesco, *Alessandro nell'Indie* (opera)
Arne, Thomas, *Britannia* (opera)
Avison, Charles, *8 Concertos in 7 Parts, Opus 4*
Bernasconi, Andrea, *Adriano in Siria* (opera)
Boyce, William, *Lyra britannica* (song cycle)
Duni, Egidio, *Olimpiade* (opera)
Ferrandini, Giovanni B., *Diana placata* (opera)
Galuppi, Baldassare, *Attalo* (opera)
　　Le nozze (opera)
　　La diavolessa (opera)
　　Il poverto superbo (opera)
García, Manuel, *La pupilla* (opera)
　　Pompeo Magno in Armenia (opera)
Giardini, Felice de', *6 Cembalo Sonatas, Opus 3 (with violin obbligato)*
Giordani, Tommaso, *La comediante fatta cantatrice* (opera)
Giraud, François, *Deucalion et Pyrrha* (ballet)
Gluck, Christoph W., *La danza* (pastorale)
　　L'innocenza giustificata (opera)
Graun, Carl H., *Ezio* (opera)
　　Montezuma (opera)
　　Der tod Jesu (cantata)
Hasse, Johann A., *Ezio II* (opera)
　　Il ré pastore (opera)
　　Il Calandrano (intermezzo)
Holzbauer, Ignaz, *Don Chisciotte* (opera)
Jommelli, Niccolò, *Pelope* (opera)
　　Enea nel Lazio (opera)
　　Il giardino incanto (serenade)
　　Gerusalemme convertita (oratorio)
Lampugnani, Giovanni, *Siroe* (opera)
Pérez, Davide, *Ezio* (opera)
　　Alessandro nell'Indie (opera)
Philidor, François, *6 Quartets for Oboe and Strings*
Piccinni, Niccolò, *Le Gelosie* (opera)
Reutter, George, *La Gara* (opera)
Scarlatti, Domenico, *30 Keyboard Sonatas, Volume X*
　　30 Keyboard Sonatas, Voume XI
Scarlatti, Giuseppe, *Caio Mario* (opera)
　　La Madamigella (opera)
Smith, John C., *The Fairies* (opera)
Tartini, Giuseppe, *6 Trio Sonatas II*
Traetta, Tommaso, *L'incredulo* (opera)
Uttini, Francesco, *Il re pastore* (opera)
Wagenseil, Georg, *3 Symphonies, Opus 1*
　　Le cacciatrici amanti (opera)
　　Gioas, re di Giuda (oratorio)
　　La redenzione (oratorio)

1756

World Events:
In the U.S., the French capture and destroy Fort Oswego in New York thereby taking over control of Lake Ontario but their forces return to Montreal without consolidating their victories; stagecoach service begins between New York City and Philadelphia; the *New Hampshire Gazette,* one of the country's longest running newspapers, is founded. Internationally, the Seven Years War, a part of the French and Indian War in the New World, begins with Great Britain against most of the rest of the European nations; the Treaty of Westminster is signed between England and Prussia; over one hundred British Soldiers die from suffocation in the infamous Black Hole of Calcutta; the first chocolate factory opens in Germany.

Cultural Highlights:
The magazine *Critical Review,* begins publication in London as does Samuel Johnson's *The Literary Magazine, or Universal Review;* Jacques Francois Blondel is inducted into the Royal Academy of Architecture in France; George Lyttelton receives a baronet; Edmund Burke publishes his *A Philosophical Enquiry into the Origin of Our Ideas of the Sublime and Beautiful* while Joseph Warton publishes his *Essays on the Genius and Writings of Pope.* Births in the art world include American artist John Trumbull, portrait painter Joseph Wright and sculptor William Rush, British artist Peter Francis Bourgeois, portrait painter and caricaturist Thomas Rowlandson, Scotch artist Henry Raeburn as well as German artist Johann Peter von Langer; deaths in the art field include British artist George Vertue and French sculptor Jean-Louis Lemoyne. Births in the literary field include British poet and critic William Gifford, as well as philosopher and novelist William Godwin and Dutch poet Willem Bilderdijk; British poet Thomas Cooke dies. Other highlights include:

Art: Francois Boucher, *The Nativity;* John Singleton Copley, *Ann Tyng;* Johann Baptiste Hagenauer, *Christ Tied to the Column;* Pietro Longhi, *The Fortune Teller;* Charles-Joseph Natoire, *San Sebastian and the Angel;* Giovanni Battista Piranesi, *Le Antichità Romane;* Joshua Reynolds, *Admiral Holbourne and His Son* and *Horace Walpole;* Luigi Vanvitelli, *Palazzo Calabritto* (Naples)

Literature: Thomas Amory, *The Life of John Buncle I;* Marie Anne Boccage, *La Colombiade;* Salomon Gessner, *Idyllen;* John Home, *Douglas;* William Mason, *Odes;* Edward Moore, *Poems, Fables and Plays;* Arthur Murphy, *The Apprentice;* Michel Jean Sedaine, *Le Diable a Quatre;* Emanuel Swedenborg, *The Heavenly Arcana;* Voltaire, *Essai sur les Moeurs*

MUSICAL EVENTS

A. Births:

Jan 22	Vincenzo Righini (It-cm)	Jun 20	Joseph M. Kraus (Ger-cm-cd)
Jan 27	Wolfgang A. Mozart (Ger-cm)	Aug 10	Daniel G. Turk (Ger-org)
Jan 30	Joseph Preindl (Aus-cm)	Aug 14	Olof Ahlstrom (Swe-org)
Mar 18	Johann C. Vogel (Ger-cm)	Oct 2	Jozef Jawurek (Pol-pn-cd)
Mar 21	Augustus Kollmann (Ger-the)	Oct 24	Charles P. Caraffe (Fr-vn)
Apr 8	Joseph Gehot (Bel-vn)	Nov 15	Franz Teyber (Aus-cm)
Apr 23	Alexander Reinagle (Br-cm)	Nov 30	Ernst Chladni (Ger-acous)
May 2	Carl A. Grenser (Ger-inst.m)	Dec 15	A. Saint-Huberty (Fr-sop)
May 5	Thomas Linley, Jr. (Br-vn)	Dec 26	Bernard Lacepede (Fr-the)
May 23	Nikolaus Hullmandel (Fr-hps)	Dec 30	Paul Wranitzky (Cz-vn-cm)
Jun 13	Henrik Klein (Ger-cm)		Cecilia Davies (Br-sop)
Jun 19	Laurent F. Boutmy (Br-org)		Antoine Lacroix (Fr-vn)

B. Deaths:

Mar 16	Antonio Bernacchi (It-cas)	Oct 24	Charles Caraffe (Fr-vn)
Mar 23	Georg G. Wagner (Ger-vn)	Oct 26	Johann Römhildt (Ger-org)
Apr 10	Jacopo A. Perti (It-cm)	Nov 7	Jean Demars (Fr-org)
Apr 13	Johann G. Goldberg (Ger-pn)		Riccardo Broschi (It-cm)
Sep	Johann C. Donati (Ger-org.m)		John Byfield, Sr. (Br-org.m)
Oct 3	William McGibbon (Scot-vn)		Catherine Tofts (Br-sop)

C. Debuts:

Other - Luigi Boccherini (Italy), Rosalia Guerrero (Madrid), Pierre Vachon (Paris), Elizabeth Young (Dublin)

D. New Positions:

Conductors: Antonio Aurisicchio (maestro di cappella, S. Giacomo degli Spagnuoli), Johann Ernst Bach (kapellmeister, Weimar), Giuseppe Maria Carretti (maestro di cappella, S. Petronio, Bologna), Francisco Javier García (maestro di cappella, Saragossa Cathedral), François Giroust (maître de musique, Orleans Cathedral), Johann Valentin Görner (kapellmeister, Hamburg Cathedral), Jakob Friedrich Kleinknecht (kapellmeister, Bayreuth), Luis Misón (Royal Opera, Madrid), Fabián García Pacheco (maestro de capilla, Soledad Church, Madrid), Giuseppe Paolucci (maestro di cappella, S. Maria Gloriosa, Venice), Hermann Friedrich Raupach (St. Petersburg Opera), Johann Michael Schmid (kapellmeister, Mainz)

Educational: Johann Friedrich Doles (cantor, St. Thomaskirche, Leipzig)

Others: Franz Xaver Brixi (organ, Prague Cathedral), Franz Vollrath Buttstett (organ, Weikersheim an der Tauber), John Camidge (organ, York Minster), Felice de' Giardini (impresario, Italian Opera, London), Johann Christian Kittel (organ, Barfüsskirche, Erfurt), Johann Ludwig Krebs (organ, Altenburg), James Nares (organ, Chapel Royal, London), Johann Philipp Sack (organ, Berlin Cathedral), Alexander Sumarokov (director, St. Petersburg Theater)

E. Prizes and Honors:

Honors: Giovan G. Brunetti (Accademia Filarmonica, Bologna), Pierre de La Garde (Chamber Composer to the King, Paris), Christoph Willibald Gluck (Order of the Golden Spur), Pietro Longhi (Venice Academy)

F. Biographical Highlights:

Anton Cajetan Adlgasser marries his second wife, Maria Barbara Schwab; Caffarelli retires from the opera stage and, with his considerable fortune, buys the dukedom of Santo-Durato in Naples; Giovanni Carestini retires and returns to Italy; Christoph Johann August Eberhard begins the study of theology at the University of Halle; Filippo Maria Gherardeschi begins composition studies with Padre Martini in Bologna; François Giroust is ordained a priest; Christoph Willibald Gluck goes to Rome to oversee the production of his *Antigono*, then returns to Vienna to oversee the production of his *Il re pastore*; Franz Joseph Haydn begins the limited teaching of music; Jean Jacques Rousseau is set up at the Hermitage by Mme. d'Epinay.

G. Institutional Openings:

Other: Breitkopf und Härtel, Music Publishers (Breitkopf since 1719, Leipzig); Thomas Haxby, Instrument Maker (York); Princes Street Rooms (Bristol); Russian Royal Court Theater (first known permanent Russian theater); *Samenspraaken over Musikaale Beginselen*

H. Musical Literature:

Baron, Ernst, *Abriss einer Abhandlung von der melodie*
Blanchet, Joseph, *L'art ou les principes philosophiques du chant*

Bremner, Robert, *The Rudiments of Music*
Caffiaux, Philippe, *Nouvelle méthode de solfier la musique*
Durazzo, Giacomo, *Lettre sur le Méchanisme de l'Opéra Italien*
Estève, Pierre, *Dialogue sur les Arts*
Fournier, Pierre, *Essai d'un nouveau caractères de fonte pour l'impression de la musique*
Fritz, Barthold, *Tuning of Keyboard Instruments*
Martini, Giovanni, *Regole agli organiste per accompagnare il canto fermo*
Mozart, Leopold, *Fundamentals of Violin Playing*

I. Musical Compositions:

Arne, Thomas, *The Pincushion* (opera)
    Injured Honor (incidental music)
Avison, Charles, *6 Sonatas, Opus 5, for 2 Violins, Cello and Harpsichord*
Bernasconi, Andrea, *Didone abbandonata* (opera)
Duni, Egidio, *La buona figliuola* (opera)
Ferrandini, Giovanni B., *Demetrio* (opera)
Galuppi, Baldassare, *Idomeneo* (opera)
    Le nozze di Paride (opera)
    La cantarina (opera)
    Le pescatrici (opera)
García, Francisco, *Lo Scultore deluso* (opera)
Gasparini, Quirino, *Artaserse* (opera)
Giardini, Felice de', *Olimpiade* (opera)
Giordani, Tommaso, *La Comediante fatta cantatrice* (opera)
Giraud, François, *La gageure de village* (opera)
Gluck, Christoph W., *Antigono* (opera)
    Il rè pastore (opera)
Gossec, François, *6 Symphonies, Opus 3*
Graun, Carl H., *La Merope* (opera)
    I fratelli nemici (opera)
    Te Deum
Hasse, Johann A., *L'Olimpiade* (opera)
Haydn, Franz J., *Organ Concerto No. 1 in C Major*
    Salve Regina in E Major
Holzbauer, Ignaz, *Le nozze d'Arianna* (opera)
    Il filosofo di campagna (opera)
Insanguine, Giacomo, *Lo funnaco revotato* (opera)
Jommelli, Niccolò, *Missa pro defunctis in E-flat Major*
    Artaserse II (opera)
Logroscino, Nicola, *I disturbi* (opera)
    Le finte magie (opera)
Philidor, François, *Le diable à quatre* (opera)
    Le retour du printemps (opera)
Piccinni, Niccolò, *Zenobia* (opera)
    L'astrologa (opera)
    Il curioso del proprio Danno (opera)
Rinaldo di Capua, *Il capitano napolitano* (opera)
Sacchini, Antonio, *Fra Donato* (intermezzo)
Sarti, Giuseppe, *Arianna e Teseo* (opera)
Scarlatti, Domenico, *30 Keyboard Sonatas, Volume XII*
    Salve Regina for Soprano and Strings
Smith, John C., *The Tempest* (opera)
Tartini, Giuseppe, *12 Trio Sonatas, Opus "3"*
Telemann, Georg P., *Der Tod Jesu* (oratorio)
Traetta, Tommaso, *La fante furba* (opera)
    Buovo d'Antona (opera)
Wagenseil, Georg C., *Il roveto di Mose* (oratorio)
    6 Symphonies, Opus 2

1757

World Events:
In the U.S., the French forces under General Montcalm capture Fort William Henry in upper New York--on the march, many of the English captives are massacred by the Indian allies of the French; Benjamin Franklin is sent to London as a special agent representing the colonies; Franklin's publication, *Poor Richard's Almanac*, reaches its final publication; Philadelphia introduces the first street lights, oil lamps designed by Benjamin Franklin; George Washington acquires his famous estate at Mount Vernon. Internationally, in the Seven Years War, Prussia suffers a defeat at the hands of the Austrians at Koln but gains victories against the French at Rossbach and Leuthen; Robert Clive defeats the French in India and consolidates the British influence in that country; the Chinese emperor curtails all foreign trade and limits it to the city of Canton; Othman III of Turkey is succeeded by Mustapha III; the London *Chronicle* begins publication.

Cultural Highlights:
The magazine *American Magazine and Monthly Chronicle* with William Smith as editor begins publication in Philadelphia; also making its appearance is the *Bibliothek der Schönen Wissenschaften und Freien Kunste* in Germany; the St. Petersburg Academy of Fine Arts is founded in Russia; Jonathan Edwards becomes President of the College of New Jersey; William Whitehead is appointed Poet Laureate of Great Britain; Jacques Germain Soufflot is inducted into the Royal Academy of Architecture in France. Italian sculptor Antonio Canova is born while deaths in the art field include Italian artists Giuseppe Bibiena and Rosalba Carriera as well as French artist Antoine Pesne. Births in the literary field include British poet and artist William Blake, novelist and dramatist Harriet Lee, German author Karl Philipp Moritz, Swedish poet Bengt Lidner and Polish dramatist Wojciech Boguslawski; deaths in the world of literature include British dramatist Colley Cibber, playwright Edward Moore and French philosopher Bernard Le Bovier de Fontenelle. Other highlights include:

Art: François-Hubert Drouais, *Madame Favart*; Étienne Falconet, *The Bather* (marble); Thomas Gainsborough, *Daughter with Cat*; Jean-Baptiste Greuze, *La Paresseuse Italienne*; William Hogarth, *David Garrick and His Wife*; Pietro Longhi, *The Masked Reception*; Joshua Reynolds, *Dr. Samuel Johnson*; Giovanni Tiepolo, *The Sacrifice of Iphigenia*; Louis Van Loo, *Charles Van Loo and His Family*

Literature: Johann J. Bodmer, *Das Nibelungenlied*; John Brown, *An Estimate of the Manners and Principles of the Times*; Denis Diderot, *Le Fils Naturel*; John Dyer, *The Fleece*; Christian Gellert, *Geistliche Oden und Lieder*; Thomas Gray, *Odes*; David Hume, *The Natural History of Religion*; Friedrich Klopstock, *Geistliche Lieder I*; Tobias George Smollett, *The Reprisal*

MUSICAL EVENTS

A. Births:

Jan 3	Johann A. Sixt (Ger-org)	Jul 12	Christian Danner (Ger-vn)
Jan 28	Antonio Bruni (It-vn-cd)	Nov 6	L. Beffroy de Reigny (Fr-cm)
Feb 17	Antonio Calegari (It-the)	Nov 16	Daniel Read (Am-cm)
Mar 4	George Thomson (Scot-folk)	Nov 20	Giovanni Gaiani (It-org)
Apr	George K. Jackson (Am-cm)	Nov 24	Jacob Eckhard (Ger-org)
Apr 6	Alessandro Rolla (It-vn-cm)	Dec 11	Charles Wesley (Br-org)
Apr 28	Klaus Scholl (Den-cm)		Henry Condell (Br-vn)
Jun 13	Christian Dieter (Ger-vn)		Józef Kozlowski (Pol-cm)
Jun 18	Ignaz Pleyel (Aus-cm-pub)		William Reeve (Br-org)
Jul 8	Richard Wainwright (Br-org)		

B. Deaths:

Jan 11	Louis B. Castel (Fr-the)	Oct 11	Zacharias Hildebrandt
Feb 25	Paolo Bellinzani (It-cm)		(Ger-org.m)
Mar 20	Johann Kunzen (Ger-org)	Oct 13	Nicolo Pasquali (It-vn-cm)
Mar 27	Johann A. Stamitz (Boh-cd-cm)	Nov 21	Johann K. Brandenstein
May 14	Bartolomeo Cordans (It-cm)		(Ger-org.m)
May 30	Michel Forqueray (Fr-org)	Dec 11	Fortunato Chelleri (It-cm)
Jul 4	Jean-Joseph Vadé (Fr-pt-cm)		Emanuele d'Astorga (Sp-cm)
Jul 23	Domenico Scarlatti (It-cm)		Willem de Fesch (Hol-vn-cm)
Aug 11	José Pradas Gallen (Sp-cm)		

C. Debuts:
Other - Madeleine Sophie Arnould (Paris), Angiola Calori (London)

D. New Positions:
Conductors: Gioacchino Cocchi (Haymarket Theater, London), Pascual Fuentes (choral director, Valencia Cathedral), Michael Haydn (kapellmeister, Bishop of Grosswardein), Antonio Soler (maestro de capilla, El Escorial), Matheo Tollis de la Roca (maestro de capilla, Mexico City Cathedral)

Educational: François Francoeur and François Rebel (co-directors, Academie Royale, Paris)

Others: Jean Joseph Boutmy (organ, St. Baaf Cathedral, Ghent), Francois Francoeur (director, Paris Opera), Thomas Alexander Kelly (director, Edinburgh Musical Society), Adolph Carl Kunzen (organ, Marienkirche, Lübeck), Leopold Mozart (court composer, Salzburg), Wilhelm August Roth (music editor, *Der Freund*)

F. Biographical Highlights:
Franz Josef Aumann is ordained a priest at St. Florian; Luigi Boccherini visits Italy before taking a position in the Court Orchestra in Vienna; Johann Gottlob Clemm moves his organ-building business to Bethelem, Pennsylvania; Antonio Duni goes to Russia where he gives private lessons and teaches at the Moscow University; Anton Filtz marries a young English lady, Elisabeth Range; Friedrich William Herschel settles in England and begins teaching music; Francis Hopkinson is a member of the first class to receive a B.A. degree from the University of Pennsylvania; James Nares receives his doctorate from Cambridge University; Johann Gottlieb Naumann goes to Italy with the violinist Anders Wesström and receives instruction from Tartini, Martini and Hasse; Euphrosyne Parepa-Rosa makes her London debut as Elvira in *I Puritani*; Jean-Jacques Rousseau breaks with Diderot and Mme. d'Épinay; David Tannenberg moves to Bethlehem, Pennsylvania, in order to work with Clemm; Luigi Tomasini joins the Esterházy orchestra.

G. Institutional Openings:
Educational: Lord Mornington's Musical Academy (Dublin); Philadelphia Public Concerts

Other: Bolshoy Kamenniÿ Theater (Moscow); Large Stone Theater (St. Petersburg); Teatro Comunale (Bologna); Teatro de Operas y Comedias (Buenos Aires); Theater Royal (Norwich); University Theater (Moscow)

H. Musical Literature:
Agricola, Johann F., *Anleitung zur Singekunst*
Blainville, Charles H., *Histoire générale, critique et philosophique de la musique*
Kirnberger, Johann P., *Der allzeit fertige Polonaisen- und Menuetten-componist*
Marpurg, Friedrich W., *Éléments de la musique*
Martini, Giovanni, *Storia della musica I*
Pasquali, Nicolò, *Thorough-Bass Made Easy*
Rodriguez de Hita, Antonio, *Diapasón instructivo*

Sulzer, Johann G.,   *Pensées sur l'origine des sciences et des Beaux-Arts*

I. Musical Compositions:

Agricola, Johann F.,   *Trauerkantate* (oratorio)
   Psalm 21 for Chorus and Orchestra
Albrechtsberger, Johann,   *Christo Kreutz-Erfindung*
Arne, Thomas,   *Isabella* (incidental music)
Bach, Johann Christian,   *Requiem in F Major*
Bach W. F.,   *Ja, Ja, es hat mein Gott* (cantata)
   Halleluja, wohl diesen volk (cantata)
Bertoni, Ferdinando,   *Antigona* (opera)
   Lucio Vero (opera)
   Sesostri (opera)
Bonno, Giuseppe,   *Colloquio amoroso fra Piramo e Tisbe* (opera)
Boyce, William,   *Ode in Commemoration of Shakespeare*
Ciampi, Vincenzo,   *Catone in Utica* (opera)
   Il clemenza di Tito (opera)
   Il chimico (opera)
Cocchi, Gioacchino,   *Semiramide I* (opera)
   Demetrios (opera)
Duni, Egidio,   *Le peintre amoureux de son modèle* (opera)
Galuppi, Baldassare,   *Ezio* (opera)
   Sesostri (opera)
Gassmann, Florian,   *Merope* (opera)
Giardini, Felice de',   *Rosmira* (opera)
Graun, Carl H.,   *Te Deum Laudemus*
Guglielmi, Pietro,   *Lo solachianello 'mbroglione* (opera)
Handel, George F.,   *The Triumph of Time and Truth* (oratorio)
Holzbauer, Ignaz,   *La clemenza de Tito* (opera)
   6 Symphonies in 4 Parts, Opus 2
   Isacco (oratorio)
Insanguine, Giacomo,   *La Matilde generosa* (opera)
Jommelli, Niccolò,   *Temistocle* (opera)
   Creso (opera)
Pérez, David,   *Solimano* (opera)
Piccinni, Niccolò,   *Caio Mario* (opera)
   L'amante ridicolo deluso (opera)
   La schiava seria (opera)
Porpora, Nicola,   *Salve Regina No. 5*
Rameau, Jean-Philippe,   *Zéphyre* (ballet)
   Anacréon II (ballet)
Reutter, Georg,   *Il sogno* (opera)
Sacchini, Antonio,   *Il giocatore* (opera)
Sammartini, Giovanni,   *6 Concerti grossi, Opus 6*
Scarlatti, Domenico,   *30 Keyboard Sonatas, Volume XIII*
Scarlatti, Giuseppe,   *L'isola disabitata* (opera)
   Il mercato di Malmantile (opera)
Seyfert, Johann,   *Der sterbentag Jesu* (oratorio)
Stamitz, Johann,   *6 Symphonies, Opus 2*
Telemann, Georg P.,   *Passion According to John V*
   Cantata for the Birthday of King Friedrich V
Traetta, Tommaso,   *La Didone abbandonata* (opera)
   La Nitteti (opera)
   Ezio (opera)

1758

World Events:
In the U.S., the French forces under General Montcalm manage to hold off the British at Fort Ticonderoga but suffer the loss of Fort Duquesne which is rebuilt by the English and renamed Fort Pitt; Fort Louisbourg in Nova Scotia also falls to the British; the first Indian Reservation is opened in Burlington County, New Jersey; the first school exclusively for Negroes opens in Philadelphia; future President James Monroe is born. Internationally, the Russians suffer defeat at Zorndorf, the Prussians a defeat at Hochkirch and the French a defeat at Krefeld; Burma becomes an independent state with the capitol at Rangoon; the British take over the Bengal State in India; Halley's Comet is discovered.

Cultural Highlights:
Samuel Johnson begins writing the *Idler* papers for John Newbery's *Universal Chronicle*; the *Annual Register* begins publication; Giovanni Pitoni becomes President of the Venetian Academy of Art; the *Bay Psalm Book* is completely revised and reprinted in England. Births in the field of literature include American lexicographer Noah Webster, German poet and novelist Ludwig Theobul Kosegarten and Danish author Peter Andreas Heiberg; deaths include American preacher and author Jonathan Edwards, British poet John Dyer, author James Hervey and French author Françoise Grafigny. Births in the art world include French artists Pierre-Paul Prud'hon and Antoine Charles (Carle) Vernet, Scotch artist Alexander Nasmyth, British portrait artist John Hoppner and German sculptor Johann Heinrich von Dannecker; deaths include German architect Johann Zimmerman. Other highlights include:

Art: François Boucher, *The Mill at Charenton*; John Copley, *Mary and Elizabeth Royall*; Jacques A. Gabriel, *École Militaire, Paris*; John Greenwood, *American Sea Captains in Surinam*; William Hogarth, *An Election IV*; Alessandro Longhi, *The Pisani Family*; Anton Mengs, *Ceiling of San Eusebius*; Jean-Marc Nattier, *Madame Adélaide de France*; Jean-Baptiste Pigalle, *Love and Friendship*; Joshua Reynolds, *Lady Betty Hamilton*; Louis-François Roubiliac, *William Shakespeare*

Literature: William Collins, *Ode on Popular Superstitions*; Denis Diderot, *Le Père de Famille*; Benjamin Franklin, *The Way of Wealth*; Salomon Gessner, *Der Tod Abels*; Johann Gleim, *Preussische Kriegslieder*; Thomas Gray, *Progress of Poetry*; John Home, *Agis*; James Macpherson, *The Highlander*; Arthur Murphy, *The Upholsterer*; Voltaire, *Candide*; Christoph Wieland, *Lady Johanna Gray*

MUSICAL EVENTS

A. Births:

Jan 24	Johann Drexel(Ger-cm)
Feb 4	Pierre G. Gardel (Fr-bal)
Feb 7	Benedikt Schack (Boh-ten)
Feb 12	Christian Latrobe (It-cd-cm)
Feb 14	François Lays (Fr-ten)
Apr 21	Frédéric Blasius (Fr-cm-cd)
Jul 17	Bohumíl Dlabac (Cz-mus)
Jul 23	Timothy Swan (Am-hymn)
Aug 16	Henri Joseph de Croes (Bel-vn)
Sep 25	Josepha Auernhammer (Aus-pn)
Sep 27	Johann Buchholz (Ger-org.m)
Oct 5	Thomas Greatorex (Br-org)
Dec 3	Josef Gelinex (Boh-cm)
Dec 4	Nicolas Lupot (Fr-vn.m)
Dec 11	Carl F. Zelter (Ger-cm-cd)
	Domingo Arquimbau (Sp-cm)
	Antonio Bianchi (iii) (It-bar)
	Ignaz Böck (Ger-hn)
	Antonio Moreira (Por-cm)
	Louis F. Pique (Fr-vn.m)
	Bernardo Porta (It-cm-cd)
	José M. Aldana (Mex-vn-cm)

B. Deaths:

Feb 5	Bernhard C. Weber (Ger-org)	Oct 4	Giuseppe Brescianello (It-vn)
Mar 22	Richard Leveridge (Br-bs)	Oct 14	Domenico Gizzi (It-cas)
Mar 28	Matteo Palotta (It-cm)	Nov 20	Johan H. Roman (Swe-cm)
Mar 31	Johann B. Köning (Ger-mus)	Nov 24	Johann Tobias (Ger-org.m)
Apr 30	François Dagincour (Fr-org)	Dec 2	Joseph Meck (Ger-vn-cm)
Jun	John Travers (Br-org)	Dec 5	Johann F. Fasch (Ger-cm)
Jun 7	Richard Bridge (Br-org.m)		Domenica Casarini (It-sop)
Oct	Alessandro Toeschi (It-vn)		

C. Debuts:

Other - Marie-Thérèse Laruette (Paris)

D. New Positions:

Conductors: Charles Gauzargues (Master of the Royal Chapel, Paris), Johann Philipp Kirnberger (kapellmeister, Princess Amalie, Berlin), Pierre van Maldere (Brussels Opera), Hermann Friedrich Raupach (kapellmeister, St. Petersburg), Tommaso Michele Francesco Traetta (maestro di cappella, Duke of Parma)

Others: William Boyce (organ, Chapel Royal, London), Laurent Desmazures (organ, Notre Dame, Rouen), Charles-Simon Favart (director, Opéra-Comique, Paris), Pierre C. Fouquet (organ, Chapel Royal, Paris), Jean-Pierre Legrand (organ, St. Germain-des-Près)

E. Prizes and Honors:

Honors: Giovanni Battista Consoni, Giuseppe Antonio Consoni, Giovanni Battista "Padre" Martini and Giovanni Plantanida (Accademia Filarmonica, Bologna), Thomas Dupuis (Royal Society of Musicians)

F. Biographical Highlights:

Carl Friedrich Abel leaves Dresden and moves to London where he settles permanently; Anna Lucia de Amicis makes her Paris debut; Johann Andre, on a business trip to Mannheim, becomes enamoured of the music scene; Jean Audiffren retires from his position at the Marseilles Cathedral; Caterina Gabrieli is forced to leave Padua early due to one of her many scandals; Johann Adam Hiller travels to Leipzig while tutoring the nephew of Count Brühl and decides to settle there, reviving the Liebhaberkonzerte subscription series some time later; Giovanni Battista Lampugnani settles for a time in Milan; Jean Marie Leclair and his wife separate; Antonio Lolli becomes solo violinist in the Court Orchestra of the Duke of Württemberg in Stuttgart; Gian Francesco Majo becomes second organist in Naples; Vincenzo Manfredini goes to Russia for an eleven-year stay in the St. Petersburg Court; Italian castrato Giusto Ferdinando Tenducci is enthusiastically received in London.

G. Institutional Openings:

Other: Accademia Filarmonica (Milan); Louis Balthazard La Chevardiére, Music Publisher (Paris); Crow Street Theater (Dublin); Johann Haffner, Music Publisher (Nuremburg); *Journal de Musique Française, Italienne (Echo)*

H. Musical Literature:

Adlung, Jakob, *Anleitung zu der musikalischen Gelehrtheit*
Baumgarten, Alexander, *Aesthetica*
Bremner, Robert, *Instructions for the Guitar*
Clément, Charles François, *L'Accompagnement du Clavecin*
Corrette, Michel, *Le parfait Maître a chanter*
Geminiani, Francesco, *The Harmonical Miscellany*
Marpurg, Friedrich W., *Anleitung zur Singe-composition*
    Generalbasse und der composition III

Travenol, Louis, *Mémoire sur le sieur Travenol...*

I. Musical Compositions:

Agricola, Johann F., *Die auferstehung des Erlösers* (oratorio)
Arne, Thomas, *The Sultan* (opera)
    The Prophetess (incidental music)
Avison, Charles, *6 Concertos, Opus 6, for Harpsichord and Strings*
Bach, Johann C., *Magnificat in C Major*
Beck, Franz, *6 Overtures, Opus 1*
Boyce, William, *Ode to the New Year*
Dauvergne, Antoine, *Enée et Lavinie* (opera)
    Les fêtes d'Euterpe (ballet)
Duni, Egidio, *Le docteur Sangrado* (opera)
    La fille mal gardée (opera)
    Nina et Lindor (opera)
Ferrandini, Giovanni B., *Demetrio* (opera)
Galuppi, Baldassare, *Adriano in Siria* (opera)
    Ipermestra (opera)
    Demofoonte (opera)
    L'oracolo del Vaticano (cantata)
Gassmann, Florian, *Issipile* (opera)
Gluck, Christoph W., *L'île de Merlin* (opera)
    La fausse esclave (opera)
Gossec, François, *6 Symphonies, Opus 4*
Grétry, André, *6 Small Symphonies*
Guglielmi, Pietro, *Il filosofo burlato* (opera)
Hasse, Johann A., *Demofoonte II* (opera)
    Nitteti (opera)
    Il sogno di Scipione (opera)
Haydn, Franz J., *Der neue krumme Teufel* (opera)
Holzbauer, Ignaz, *Nitteti* (opera)
Jommelli, Niccolò, *L'asilo d'amore* (serenade)
    Ezio III (opera)
    Tito Manlio (opera)
Lampugnani, Giovanni, (opera)
    Le cantatrici (opera)
Majo, Giovan di, *Ricimero re dei Goti* (opera)
Mondonville, Jean de, *Les Israëlites au Mont Oreb* (oratorio)
Piccinni, Niccolò, *Alessandro nelle Indie* (opera)
    La Scaltra letterata (opera)
    Gli uccellatori (opera)
    Madame Arrighetta (opera)
    La Morte di Abele (oratorio)
Reutter, Georg, *Le Grazie vendicate* (opera)
Richter, Franz X., *3 Symphonies, Opus 10*
Rinaldo di Capua, *Adriano in Siria* (opera)
Sacchini, Antonio, *Olimpia tradita* (opera)
Sarti, Giuseppe, *Anagilda* (opera)
Smith, John C., *Judith* (oratorio)
    Paradise Lost (oratorio)
Stamitz, Johann, *4 Symphonies, Opus 4*
Telemann, Georg P., *Passion According to Matthew IV*
Traetta, Tommaso, *Olimpiade* (opera)
    Demofoonte (opera)

1759

World Events:
In the U.S., the British forces take over Fort Niagara by force; Crown Point and Fort Ticonderoga are taken over by the British forces when the French abandon them; both British General James Wolfe and French General Louis Joseph de Montcalm are killed in the Battle of the Plains of Abraham while the British defeat the French and take over the city of Quebec; the first known insurance company in the New World begins business in Philadelphia; George Washington marries the widow Martha Dandridge; the first Jewish synagogue in the New World is built in Newport, Rhode Island. Internationally, in the Seven Years War, the Prussian forces suffer decisive defeats at Kunersdorf and Maxen while the French forces win at Bergen and lose at Minden; the Jesuit Order is expelled from Spain and Portugal and the Jesuit University in Portugal is closed; King Ferdinand VI of Spain is succeeded by King Charles II.

Cultural Highlights:
The magazine *Briefe, die Neueste Literatur Betreffend* begins publication in Berlin; Clodion (Claude Michel) receives the Prix de Rome in Art; German poet Ewald Christian von Kleist is mortally wounded at the Battle of Kunersdorf. British artist Julius Caesar Ibbetson is born while deaths in the art world include French artists Christophe Huet, Philip Mercier and sculptor Lambert Sigisbert Adam as well as British artist Charles Brooking. Births in the literary field include French author François Guillaume Andrieux, Scotch poet Robert (Bobby) Burns, British author Alexander Chalmers, Swedish poet Thomas Thorild, Hungarian author Ferenc Kazinczy and German poet and author Johann Christoph Friedrich von Schiller; deaths in the literary world include British poet William Collins. Other highlights include:

Art: François Boucher, *Madame de Pompadour*; Jean-Baptiste Greuze, *Bookseller Babuti*; Peter Harrison, *Christ Church, Cambridge*; William Hogarth, *The Cockpit*; Alessandro Longhi, *Vincenzo Dona*; Pietro Longhi, *The Tooth-Drawer*; Joshua Reynolds, *The Seventh Earl of Lauderdale*; Giovanni Tiepolo, *St. Thecla Praying for the Plague-Stricken*; Benjamin West, *Thomas Mifflin*

Literature: Denis Diderot, *Les Salons I*; Alexander Gerard, *An Essay on Taste*; Oliver Goldsmith, *The Present State of Polite Learning in Europe*; Samuel Johnson, *History of Rasselas*; Ewald von Kleist, *Cissides und Paches*; Gotthold Lessing, *Philotas*; Charles Macklin, *Love à la Mode*; William Mason, *Caractacus*; Michel Jean Sedaine, *Blaise le Savetier*; Adam Smith, *The Theory of Moral Sentiments*

MUSICAL EVENTS

A. Births:

Jan 4	Maria Rosa Coccia (It-cm)	May 23	António Leite (Por-cm)
Jan 20	Giuseppe Bertini (It-cd)	Jul 10	Sofia M. Westenholz (Ger-pn)
Jan 31	François Devienne (Fr-fl)	Sep 6	Guillaume Villoteau (Fr-mus)
Feb 27	Johann Rellstab (Ger-pub)	Oct 31	Carolus E. Fodor (Hol-hps)
Mar 2	Johann Haeffner (Swe-org)	Nov 27	Franz Krommer (Cz-vn-cm)
Apr 6	Jean Lebrun (Fr-hn)		Charles Albrecht (Am-pn.m)
May 6	Joseph K. Ambrosch (Ger-ten)		Andrew Ashe (Br-fl)
May 16	Jacob Scheller (Boh-vn)		Brigida Banti-Giorgi (It-sop)
May 18	Charles Duquesnoy (Bel-ten)		Salomea Deszner (Pol-sop)
May 22	Gervais Couperin (Fr-org)		Franz Gleissner (Ger-pub)

B. Deaths:

Jan 16	Francisco Manalt (Sp-vn)	Jun 29	Charles Sohier (Fr-vn)
Jan 27	Francesco Senesino (It-cas)	Jul 25	Johann Altnikol (Ger-org)
Mar 28	Ignazio Conti (It-cm)	Aug 8	Carl H. Graun (Ger-cm)
Apr 8	François de La Croix (Fr-cm)	Aug 15	Tobias H. Trost (Ger-org.m)
Apr 14	George F. Handel (Ger-cm)	Sep 4	Girolamo Chili (It-cm-the)
Apr 28	Pietro Mingotti (It-imp)		Giuseppe Valentini (It-vn)
May 4	Heinrich Titz (Ger-org.m)		Gustavus Waltz (Ger-bs)

C. Debuts:

Other - Carl Friedrich Abel (London), Antonia M. Girelli (Venice), Thomas Norris (Oxford)

D. New Positions:

Conductors: Johann Friedrich Agricola (kapellmeister, Berlin), Giovanni Battista Borghi (maestro di cappella, Macerata Cathedral, Naples), Pascal Boyer (maître de chapelle, Nimes), Franz Xaver Brixi (kapellmeister, St. Vitus' Cathedral, Prague), Giacomo Carcani (maestro di cappella, Ravenna Cathedral), Giovanni Battista Casali (maestro di cappela, St. John Lateran, Rome), Karl Höckh (kapellmeister, Zerbst)

Educational: Pasquale Cafaro (director, Naples Conservatory), Johann Ridinger (director, Stuttgart Academy)

Others: Johann Georg Albrechtsberger (organ, Melk Abbey)

E. Prizes and Honors:

Prizes: Carl Friedrich Abel (Chamber Musician to the Queen), Thomas Arne (honorary doctorate, Oxford), John Beard (honorary doctorate, Oxford), François Bédos de Celles (Bordeaux Académie des Sciences), William Boyce (Master of the King's Music), Giovanni B. Cirri (Accademia Filarmonica, Bologna)

F. Biographical Highlights:

John Beard marries his second wife, Charlotte Rich; Christian Cannabich marries Elisabeth de la Motte and moves up to first violin section in the Mannheim Court Orchestra; François Joseph Gossec marries Marie-Elisabeth Georges; André Grétry is sent to Rome on a scholarship to study music; Francis Hopkinson writes *My Days Have Been So Wondrous Free*, the first known song written in the New World; Pietro Locatelli, traveling to Russia with his opera company, introduces comic opera to Moscow audiences for the first time; James Lyon graduates from the College of New Jersey (Princeton) with a degree in theology; Giovanni Paisiello graduates from the Conservatorio di S. Onofrio in Naples and is given a teaching position there for the next four years; Carlo Toeschi becomes concertmaster in the Mannheim Court Orchestra.

G. Institutional Openings:

Other: Michael Hillegas Music Shop (Philadelphia--first known in the New World); *Kritische Briefe über die Tonkunst*; Moscow Opera House

H. Musical Literature:

d'Alembert, Jean, *De la liberté de la musique*
Gianotti, Pietro, *Le guide du compositeur I*
Hardouin, Henri, *Breviarie du Diocese de Reims*
Ludwig, Johann A., *Versuch von den Engenschaften...*
Marpurg, Friedrich W., *Kritische einleitung in die geschichte...der alten Musik*
    Historisch-kritische beyträge IV

I. Musical Compositions:

Abel, Carl, *6 Symphonies in 4 Parts*
Aulette, Pietro, *Didone* (opera)
Bertoni, Ferdinando, *Il Vologeso* (opera)
Bonno, Giuseppe, *Isacco figura del redentore* (oratorio)
Boyce, William, *Harlequin's Invasion* (opera)
Cannabich, Christian, *Ippolito e Aricia* (ballet)
Duni, Egidio, *La veuve indécise* (opera)
Galuppi, Baldassare, *Melite riconosciuto* (opera)
 La ritornata di Londra (opera)
Gassmann, Florian, *Gli uccellatori* (opera)
Gluck, Christoph W., *L'arbre enchante* (opera)
 La Cythere assiégée (opera)
 Le diable à quatre (opera)
Gossec, François, *6 Symphonies, Opus 4*
Grétry, André, *Messe Solennele*
Guglielmi, Pietro, *La ricca locandiera* (opera)
 I capricci di una vedova (opera)
 La moglie imperiosa (opera)
Hasse, Johann A., *Achille in Sciro* (opera)
Haydn, Franz J., *Symphony (No. 16) in B-flat Major*
 Symphony No. 1 in D Major
 6 Divertimentos, Opus 1, for String Quartet
Holzbauer, Ignaz, *Alessandro nell'Indie* (opera)
 Ippolito ed Aricia (opera)
Hopkinson, Francis, *My Days Have Been So Wondrous Free* (song)
Jommelli, Niccolò, *Nitteti* (opera)
 Endimione (opera)
Mondonville, Jean de, *Les fureurs de Saül* (oratorio)
Monsigny, Pierre, *Les aveux indiscrets* (opera)
Orgitano, Vincenzo, *Il finto pastorello* (opera)
Philidor, François, *Blaise le savetier* (opera)
 L'huître et les plaideurs (opera)
Piccinni, Niccolò, *Siroe, ré di Persia* (opera)
 Ciro riconosciuto (opera)
 Le trame per amore (opera)
Porpora, Nicola, *Israel ad Aegyptiis liberatu* (oratorio)
Quantz, Johann J., *6 Flute Duets, Opus 2*
Rameau, Jean P., *Le procureur dupé sans le savoir* (opera)
Rinaldo di Capua, *Le Donne ridicole* (intermezzo)
Sacchini, Antonio, *Il copista burlato* (opera)
Sarti, Giuseppe, *Armida abbandonata* (opera)
 Achille in Sciro (opera)
Scarlatti, Giuseppe, *La serva scaltra* (opera)
Telemann, Georg P., *Miriam und deine Wehmut* (oratorio)
 Das befreite Israel (oratorio)
 Passion According to Mark I
 Die Hirten bei der Krippe zu Bethlehem (oratorio)
Traetta, Tommaso, *Solimano* (opera)
 Ippolito ed Aricia (opera)
 Ifigenia in Aulide (opera)

1760

World Events:
In the U.S., the French give up both Montreal and Detroit; the French troops from Montreal are massacred by Indians on their retreat; Baron Amherst is appointed Governor-General of British North America; New York passes the first law requiring the licensing of physicians and surgeons; probable date of the invention of the rocking chair and bifocal glasses by Benjamin Franklin. Internationally, Berlin is burned by the Russians, Prussia is defeated at Landshut and the Austrians are defeated at Liegnitz and Torgau; George II of England dies and is succeeded by George III; the first school for the deaf and dumb is opened in Scotland.

Cultural Highlights:
The Royal Society of Arts is founded in London; Augustin Pajou is taken into the French Academy; James Macpherson publishes his *Fragments of Ancient Poetry Collected in the Highlands of Scotland*. British artist Lemuel Abbott is born and French artist Louis de Silvestre dies. Births in the literary field include Spanish poet Leandro Fernández de Moratin, German poet Johann Peter Hebel and British novelist William Beckford; deaths include British author Isaac Hawkins Browne and German poet and librettist Christiane von Zeigler. Other highlights include:

Art: Canaletto, *San Marcus Plaza*; Jean-Honoré Fragonard, *Villa d'Este in Tivoli*; Thomas Gainsborough, *Mrs. Philip Thicknesse*; Anton Mengs, *Augustus and Cleopatra*; Joshua Reynolds, *Georgiana*; George Stubbs, *Mares and Foals in Landscape*; Giovanni Tiepolo, *The Finding of Moses*; Carle Van Loo, *Louis XV in State Robes*; Richard Wilson, *Destruction of Niobe's Children*

Literature: James Beattie, *Original Poems and Translations*; George Colman, *Polly Honeycomb*; Gasparo Gozzi, *Il Mondo Morale*; Christian Adolf Klotz, *Genius Saeculi*; Robert Lloyd, *The Actor*; Johann Karl Musäus, *Grandison der Zweite I*; Charles Palissot de Montenoy, *Les Philosophes*; Laurence Sterne, *Tristram Shandy I, II* and *The Sermons of Mr. Yorick*; Voltaire, *L'Ecossaire*

MUSICAL EVENTS

A. Births:

Jan	William Shrubsole (Br-org)	Jun 14	Cándido J. Ruano (Sp-cm)
Jan 10	Johann Zumsteeg (Ger-cm)	Aug 7	William H. Potter (Br-fl)
Jan 13	Jacques Cousineau (Fr-hp)	Aug 11	Karl G. Bellman (Ger-pn.m)
Jan 19	Melchor L. Jiménez (Sp-cm)	Sep 8	Samuel Harrison (Br-ten)
Feb 12	Jan L. Dussek (Boh-cm)	Sep 14	Luigi Cherubini (It-cm)
Feb 15	Jean F. Lesueur (Fr-cm)	Sep 21	Gaetano Valeri (It-org)
Feb 18	Inácio de Almeida (Por-cm)	Oct	Therese Teyber (Aus-sop)
Feb 19	Katharina Cavalieri (Aus-sop)	Oct 9	Pierre Gaveaux (Fr-ten-cm)
Apr	Angelo Farchi (It-cm)	Nov 9	H. P. Gérard (Fr-cm-cd)
Apr	Louis A. Frichot (Fr-inv)	Nov 26	Celeste Coltellini (It-mez)
Apr 12	Franz Bühler (Ger-cm-cd)	Dec 2	Joseph Graetz (Ger-the)
May 18	C. Rouget de Lisle (Fr-cm)		Johann Distler (Aus-vn)
May 19	R. Drouard de Bousset (Fr-org)		Vincenzo Rastrelli (It-cd)

B. Deaths:

Jan 24	Lavinia Fenton (Br-voc)	Apr 24	Michele Mascitti (It-cm)
Jan 25	Louis A. Clicquot (Fr-org.m)	May	Philip Hollister (Ir-org.m)
Feb 14	F. Collin de Blamont (Fr-cm)	May 10	Christoph Graupner (Ger-cm)
Feb 21	Wolf W. Haas (Ger-inst.m)	May 19	R. Drouard de Bousset (Fr-org)
Mar 2	François Bouvard (Fr-cm)	May 27	Giacomo Rampini (i) (It-cm)
Mar 13	Anton Filtz (Boh-cm-cd)	Jun 30	T. Albuzzi-Todeschini (It-alto)
Apr 12	Ernst T. Baron (Ger-lute)	Aug 1	Tommaso Scarlatti (It-ten)

Aug 1	Giuseppe Serassi (It-org.m)		Oct 26	César Clérambault (Fr-cm)
Aug 4	Maria Rosa Negri (It-sop)		Oct 28	Andrea Adolfati (It-cm)
Aug 10	Jean Lebeuf (Fr-mus)		Dec 1	Jean B. Chrétien (Fr-cel)
Aug 12	Annibale Fabri (It-ten)		Dec 6	Rogue Ceruti (It-cm)
Oct	Girolamo Abos (Sp-cm)		Dec 16	Vicente Rodríguez (Sp-org)
Oct 24	Giuseppe Orlandini (It-cm)			Prospero Castrucci (It-vn)

C. Debuts:
Other - Cecilia Grassi (Venice)

D. New Positions:
Conductors: Andrea Adolfati (maestro di cappella, Padua), Paolo Tommaso Alberghi (maestro di cappella, Faenza Cathedral), Quirini Gasparini (maestro di cappella, Turin Cathedral), William Herschel (Durham Militia Band), José de Orejón y Aparicio (maestro de capilla, Lima Cathedral, Peru), Francesco Zanetti (maestro di cappella, Perugia Cathedral)

Educational: Joah Bates (tutor, King's College, Cambridge), Nicola Porpora (voice, Conservatorio di S. Onofrio, Naples)

Others: Theodore Aylward (organ, Oxford Chapel, London), Johann Christian Bach (organ, Milan Cathedral), Pieter Hellendaal (organ, St. Margaret's, Norfolk), William Selby (organ, Holy Sepulchre, London)

E. Prizes and Honors:
Honors: Francois Francoeur (Director of the King's Music, Paris), François Rebel (ennobled), Garret Wellesley (Earl of Mornington)

F. Biographical Highlights:
Carl Friedrich Abel is given royal publication privileges in London; Andrea Adolfati is appointed maestro di cappella at Padua just six months before his death; Johann Christian Bach joins the Catholic faith in order to be able to find a position in Italy; William Billings becomes a tanner's apprentice; Charles Burney, back in London after a nine-year stay in Norfolk, begins to teach music privately; Giuseppe Gazzaniga, following his father's death, goes to Italy to study music with Porpora; François Granier leaves Lyons for a six-year stay in Paris; Johann Adolf Hasse loses his property and his manuscripts in the siege of Dresden; Franz Joseph Haydn marries Anna Marie Keller; John Mainwaring's *Memoirs of the Life of the Late G. F. Handel* is the first musical biography of any composer; Wolfgang Amadeus Mozart begins piano lessons with his father Leopold; Josef Mysliveček begins the serious study of music while still a miller's apprentice; Giusto Ferdinando Tenducci spends time in a debtor's prison.

G. Institutional Openings:
Performing Groups: Musikalische Gesellschaft (Riga)

Festivals: Hampshire Musical Festival (Winchester)

Other: English Horn (by Ferlandis of Bergamo); Gelehrte Clubb (Magdeburg)

H. Musical Literature:
Antoniotto, Giorgio, *Treatise on the Composition of Music*
Boutmy, Jean-Joseph, *Traité Abrége de la basse continue*
Boyce, William, *Cathedral Music I*
Geminiani, Francesco, *The Art of Playing the Guitar*
Kirnberger, Johann P., *Construction der gleichschwebenden Temperatur*
Madan, Martin, *Collection of Psalm and Hymn Tunes*
Nares, James, *A Regular Introduction to Playing on the Harpsichord or Organ*
Quantz, Johann J., *New Church Melodies*

Rameau, Jean-Philippe, *Code de musique pratique*
Tans'ur, William, *The Psalmsinger's Jewel*
West, Benjamin, *Sacra Concerto; or the Voice of Melody*

I. Musical Compositions:

Arne, Thomas, *Thomas and Sally* (opera)
Avison, Charles, *6 Sonatas, Opus 7, for 2 Violins, Cello and Harpsichord*
Boccherini, Luigi, *6 String Trios, Opus 1*
Cannabich, Christian, *Symphony (No. 5) in G Major*
Dauvergne, Antoine, *Canente* (opera)
Duni, Egidio, *La boutique du poète* (opera)
　　L'isle des foux (opera)
Galuppi, Baldassare, *Solimano* (opera)
　　La clemenza di Tito (opera)
　　L'amante di tutte (opera)
Gassmann, Florian, *Filosofia ed amore* (opera)
Giardini, Felice de', *6 String Trios, Opus 2b*
Gluck, Christoph W., *Tetide* (serenade)
　　L'ivrogne corrigé (opera)
Gossec, François, *Messe de morts*
Guglielmi, Pietro, *L'Ottavio* (opera)
Hasse, Johann A., *Artaserse II* (opera)
　　12 Concertos in 6 Parts, Opus 3
Haydn, Franz J., *Symphony No. 2 in C Major*
　　2 Partitas, H. XVI
Haydn, Michael, *Concerto in B-flat Major for Violin and Orchestra*
Holzbauer, Ignaz, *La Betulia Liberata* (oratorio)
Jommelli, Niccolò, *Alessandro nell'Indie* (opera)
　　Caio Fabrizio (opera)
Lampugnani, Giovanni, *Amor contadina* (opera)
　　Giulia (opera)
Logroscino, Nicola, *Il vecchio marito* (opera)
　　Il natale di Achille (opera)
　　Stabat Mater
Monsigny, Pierre, *Le maître en droit* (opera)
Philidor, François, *Le soldat magicien* (opera)
　　Le volage fixé (opera)
Piccinni, Niccolò, *La Cecchina* (opera)
　　Il ré pastore (opera)
　　L'Origille (opera)
Porpora, Nicola, *Il trionfo di Camilla II* (opera)
Rameau, Jean-Philippe, *Les paladins* (opera)
Richter, Franz X., *6 Symphonies, Opus 2*
　　6 Symphonies, Opus 3
Sacchini, Antonio, *Il testaccio* (opera)
　　La vendemmia (opera)
　　I due fratelli Beffati (opera)
Sarti, Giuseppe, *Andromaca* (opera)
　　Il testaccio (opera)
　　Astrea splacata (opera)
Scarlatti, Giuseppe, *L'Issipile* (opera)
　　La clemenza di Tito (opera)
Telemann, Georg P., *The Resurrection and Ascension of Jesus* (oratorio)
　　Passion According to Luke IV
Traetta, Tommaso, *Enea nel Lazio* (opera)
　　I Lindaridi (opera)
Wagenseil, Georg C., *Demetrio* (opera)
　　6 Symphonies, Opus 3

1761

World Events:
In the U.S., the abolition of the unpopular Writs of Assistance giving soldiers freedom to search any house at their will finds an advocate for the colonies in James Otis; the first scientific expedition to observe the transit of Venus is led by John Winthrop; a treaty with the Cherokees eases the Indian troubles in the Carolinas; the first cookbook in the New World is published; the first venetian blinds are introduced in Philadelphia. Internationally, the Russians capture Kolberg while the Austrians take Schweidnitz; Mikhail Lomonosov discovers the existence of an atmosphere on Venus; the A. W. Faber and Co., Pencil Makers, is founded; the Bridgewater Canal, the first viaduct canal, is opened in England.

Cultural Highlights:
Étienne Falconet publishes his *Reflexions sur la sculpture*; Anton Raphael Mengs becomes the Court Painter in the Madrid court; Jean Antoine Houdon wins the Prix de Rome in Art; writer Charles Batteux is inducted into the French Academy; Giovanni Battista Piranesi is taken into the Academia de San Luca; Giovanni Battista Tiepolo is invited to Madrid to decorate the royal palace. Births in the art world include American artist Edward Savage, British artist John Opie and French artist Louis-Leopold Boilly; deaths include French sculptor Francois Balthasar Gaspard Adam. Births in the literary world include German poet Friedrich von Matthisson and dramatist August Friedrich von Kotzebue, Portugese author Jose de Mecedo, French dramatist Francois Just Marie Raynouard and Scottish poet John Hamilton; deaths include British author William Law and novelist Samuel Richardson. Other highlights include:

Art: Francois Boucher, *Girl and Birdcatcher*; Jean-Baptiste Greuze, *The Village Bride*; Peter Harrison, *Brick Market in Newport*; John Hesselius, *Charles Calvert and His Slave*; William Hogarth, *Five Orders of Periwigs*; Anton Mengs, *Parnassus*; Joshua Reynolds, *Garrick between Comedy and Tragedy*; Louis-Francois Roubiliac, *The Tomb of Lady Nightingale*

Literature: Charles Churchill, *Rosciad*; George Colman, *The Jealous Wife*; Gustav Creutz, *Atis och Camilla*; Carlo Goldoni, *Una delle Ultima Serendi Carnevale*; Gasparo Gozzi, *Love of Three Oranges*; Thomas Gray, *The Fatal Sisters*; John Hawkesworth, *Edgar and Emmeline*; Jean François Marmontel, *Contes Moraux*; Jean-Jacques Rousseau, *Julie, ou La Nouvelle Heloise*; Laurence Sterne, *Tristram Shandy III, IV*

MUSICAL EVENTS

A. Births:

Jan 20	Giovanni Perotti (It-cm)	Aug 16	Evstigney Fomin (Rus-cm)
Feb 20	Ludwig Abeille (Ger-org)	Sep 2	Peter N. Petersen (Ger-fl)
Feb 22	Jacob Kimball, Jr. (Am-m.ed)	Sep 12	Georg F. Wolf (Ger-cm-cd)
Jun 13	Anton Wranitzky (Cz-vn-cm)	Sep 24	Friedrich Kunzen (Ger-cm)
Jun 21	Carl Lichnowsky (Pol-pol)		Giovanni Cimadoro (It-cm)
Jul 20	Joseph Lefebvre (Fr-cm)		Ernst Hausler (Ger-cel)
Aug	Pierre Gaveaux (Fr-ten)		

B. Deaths:

Jan 3	Willem de Fesch (Bel-org)	Mar 27	Johann Steiner (Swi-cm)
Jan 25	Frederic Paulin (Fr-org)	Jul 12	Meinrad Spiess (Ger-cm)
Jan 28	Francesco Feo (It-cm)	Aug	Louis Hotteterre (Fr-fl)
Feb 15	Carlo Cecere (It-cm)	Sep	Frederick Hollister (Ir-pn.m)
Mar 7	Antonio Palella (It-cm)	Sep 29	Angelo M. Scaccia (It-vn)
Mar 22	Pierre de Beauchamp (Fr-mus)	Oct 22	Nicolas Forqueray (Fr-org)

Oct 25   Gioacchino Conti, "Gizziello"   François Blanchet (Fr-hps.m)
         (It-cas)   Adam Falckenhagen (Ger-lute)

C. Debuts:
Other - Nicolas Capron (Paris), Jean Dauberval (Paris), Jean Piérre Duport (Paris)

D. New Positions:
Conductors: Esprit Joseph Blanchard (maître de chapelle, Versailles), Michel Richard Delalande (maître de musique, Chartres Cathedral), Egidio Romoaldo Duni (Comédie-Italienne, Paris)

Others: John Beard (manager, Covent Garden), Filippo Gherardeschi (organ, Livorno Cathedral), Feodor G. Volkov (director, Russian Imperial Theater)

E. Prizes and Honors:
Honors: Matthew Dubourq (Master of Her Majesty's Band of Music), Filippo Gherardeschi and Antonio Tozzi (Accademia Filarmonica, Bologna), James Oswald (Chamber Composer to the King).

F. Biographical Highlights:
Johann André begins his association with music by translating various French opera libretti into the German language; Luigi Boccherini begins a two-year stay in Lucca playing cello in the local orchestra; Charles Burney loses his wife; João de Sousa Carvalho enters the Naples Conservatory on a royal grant from the Portugese government; Domenico Cimarosa, having given abundant proof of his musical talent in recital and test, is given free scholarship to enter the Conservatorio di Santa Maria di Loreto; Farinelli leaves Spain and retires to a grand villa he had built near Bologna; Franz Joseph Haydn becomes the second kapellmeister at Esterhazy estate in Eisenstadt; Francis Hopkinson is admitted to the Pennsylvania bar and begins the practice of law; Wolfgang Amadeus Mozart, at age 6, composes his first piece of music; Josef Mysliveček becomes a master miller but still continues his study of music.

G. Institutional Openings:
Performing Groups: Noblemen and Gentlemen's Catch Club (London), St. Cecilia Society of Charleston, South Carolina (first known in the New World);

Other: Glassychord (Glass Harmonica, invented by Benjamin Franklin); Konzertsaal auf dem Kamp (Hamburg); Giovanni Pirenesi Publishing House; Riga Symphony Orchestra; Johannes Zumpe, Piano and Harpsichord Maker (London)

H. Musical Literature:
Albrecht, Johann, *Gründliche einleitung in die anfangslehren der Tonkunst*
Lyon, James, *Urania*
Marpurg, Friedrich W., *Die Kunst das clavier zu spielen II*
Mattheson, Johann, *George Frederick Handel*
Parry, John, *Collection of Welsh, English and Scotch Airs*
Romero de Avila, Manuel, *Arte de canto, llano y órgano*
Saint-Sévin, Joseph (L'Abbé), *Les principes du violon*
Wesley, John, *Select Hymns with Tunes Annext*

I. Musical Compositions:
Adlgasser, Anton C. *Esther* (oratorio)
Arne, Michael, *Edgar and Emmeline* (opera)
Arne, Thomas, *Judith* (oratorio)
    Florizel and Perdita (opera)
Bach, Johann Christian, *Artaserse* (opera)
    Catone in Utica (opera)
Bertoni, Ferdinando, *La bella Cirometta* (opera)

Boccherini, Luigi, *6 String Quartets, Opus 2*
    6 Duets for 2 Violins, Opus 3
Dauvergne, Antoine, *Hercule mourant* (opera)
Duni, Egidio, *La bonne fille* (opera)
    Mazet (opera)
Galuppi, Baldassare, *Li tre amanti ridicoli* (opera)
    Il caffè di campagna (opera)
    Demetrio (opera)
Gassman, Florian, *Catone in Utica* (opera)
Gluck, Christoph W., *Don Juan* (ballet)
    Le cadi dupé (opera)
Gossec, François, *6 Symphonies, Opus 5*
    Le périgourdin (intermezzo)
Hasse, Johann A., *Zenobia* (opera)
Haydn, Franz J., *Symphony No. 6 in D Major, "Le matin"*
    Symphony No. 7 in C Major, " Le midi"
    Symphony No. 8 in G Major, " Le soir"
    Symphony No. 10 in D Major
Jommelli, Niccolò, *L'Olimpiade* (opera)
    L'isola disabitata (opera)
Majo, Giovan di, *L'Almeria* (opera)
Mondonville, Jean de, *Les titans* (oratorio)
Monsigny, Pierre, *Le cadi dupé* (opera)
    On ne s'avise jamais de tout (opera)
Orgitano, Vincenzo, *Le pazzie per amore* (opera)
Pescetti, Giovanni, *Zenobia* (opera)
Philidor, François, *Le maréchal ferrant* (opera)
    Le jardinier et son seigneur (opera)
Piccinni, Niccolò, *Demofoonte* (opera)
    La buona figliuola maritata (opera)
    Lo gli stravaganti (opera)
    La schiavitù per amore (opera)
Sacchini, Antonio, *Andromaca* (opera)
    La finta contessa (opera)
    Gesù presentato al tempio (oratorio)
Sarti, Giuseppe, *Nitteti* (opera)
    Issipile (opera)
Schmid, Johann M., *Tod und Begräbnis Jesu* (oratorio)
Smith, John C., *Medea* (unfinished opera)
Tartini, Giuseppe, *6 Sonatas, Opus 9, for Violin, Cello and Cembalo*
Telemann, Georg P., *Passion According to John VI*
    Resurrection (oratorio)
    Don Quichotte der Löwenritter (opera)
Traetta, Tommaso, *Enea e Lavinia* (opera)
    Armida (opera)
Vachon, Pierre, *6 Symphonies, Opus 2*

1762

World Events:
In the U.S., the Louisiana Territory is secretly ceded to Spain by the French via the Treaty of Fontainebleau in order to prevent the British from taking over the French territory during the fighting; the Ethan Allen ironworks are founded in Salisbury, Connecticut; the first known printing press in the New World is set up in Georgia. Internationally, newly-crowned Czar Peter III is assassinated and is succeeded by his wife, Catherine the Great, Empress of Russia; Russia concludes an alliance with Prussia and drops out of the war; Sweden and Prussia sign the Treaty of Hamburg; England temporarily seizes Cuba and the Phillipines from Spain; the Austrians suffer defeats at Burkersdorf and Freiberg; the Marine Chronometer is built by John Harrison.

Cultural Highlights:
The Sorbonne Library for the Arts opens its doors in Paris; the first two volumes of Horace Walpole's *Anecdotes of Painting in England* are published in London; Anton Raphael Mengs publishes his study on *Beauty and Taste in Painting*; Étienne N. Boullée is inducted into the Royal Academy of Architecture in Paris; Charles André (Carle) Van Loo is appointed Painter to the King in Paris. Births in the literary field include British poet and dramatist Joanna Baillie, clergyman and poet William Lisle Bowles, dramatist George Colman, Jr., and French poet André Marie de Chénier; deaths in the literary field include American-born author James Ralph, French poet Crébillon (Prosper Jolyot) and German philosopher Alexander Gottlieb Baumgartner. Births in the art world include French architect Pierre François Fontaine; deaths in the art field include French sculptors Edmé Bouchardon and Louis-François Roubiliac and Austrian artist Paul Troger. Other highlights include:

Art: Étienne Falconet, *Christ in Gethsemane*; William Hogarth, *The Times I*; Pietro Longhi, *Lion House*; Giovanni Pannini, *Trevi Fountain* (Rome); Allan Ramsay, *Mary Jane Coke*; Louis-François Roubiliac, *Handel Monument, Westminster Abbey*; George Stubbs, *Horses Exercising at Richmond*; Louis Tocqué, *Jean Marc Nattier*; Richard Wilson, *Thames near Twickenham*; Johann Zoffany, *Garrick in "Farmer's Return"*

Literature: Elizabeth Carter, *Poems on Several Occasions*; William Falconer, *The Shipwreck*; Oliver Goldsmith, *Citizen of the World*; James Macpherson, *Fingal*; Hannah More, *The Search after Happiness*; Jean-Jacques Rousseau, *Social Contract*; Tobias George Smollett, *Adventures of Sir Lancelot Greaves*; Laurence Sterne, *Tristram Shandy V, VI*; William Whitehead, *School for Lovers*

MUSICAL EVENTS

A. Births:

Jan 1	Marchese de Villarosa (It-mus)	May 22	Georg C. Müller (Ger-cm)
Jan 20	Jérôme J. Momigny (Bel-cm-the)	Jun 16	Carl C. Agthe (Ger-org)
Jan 29	Giuseppe Nicolini (It-cm)	Jul 4	Marco Santucci (It-cm)
Feb 2	Girolamo Crescentini (It-cas)	Aug 10	Santiago Ferrer (Sp-cm)
Feb 19	Friedrich Hurka (Cz-ten-cm)	Oct 15	Samuel Holyoke (Am-cm)
Mar 22	Andrew Adgate (Am-voc)	Nov 4	Carlo Gervasoni (It-the)
Mar 24	Marcos de Portugal (Por-cm)	Dec 25	Michel Kelly (Ir-ten)
Mar 24	Ferdinand Waldstein (Boh-pat)	Dec 26	Franz Tausch (Ger-cl)
Mar 25	Francisco Pollini (It-pn)		Feliks Janiewicz (Pol-vn)
Apr 4	Stephen Storace (Br-cm)		James Leach (Br-ten)
Apr 26	Pierre J. Garat (Fr-ten)		Theobald Monzani (It-fl)
May 18	Johann C. Till (Am-org)		William T. Parke (Br-ob)

B. Deaths:

Feb 11	Johann T. Krebs (Ger-org)	Jun 19	Johann E. Eberlin (Ger-cm)
Feb 12	Laurent Belissen (Fr-cm)	Jul	Johann V. Görner (Ger-cm)
Mar 30	Vincenzo Ciampi (It-cm)	Jul 5	Jakob Adlung (Ger-org-mus)
Apr 7	Pietro Guarneri (It-vn.m)	Jul 20	Christoph Nichelmann (Ger-cm)
Apr 23	Johann S. Endler (Ger-cm)	Aug 8	Jean Audiffren (Fr-cm)
May 5	Johann Klemm (Ger-org.m)	Sep 17	Francesco Geminiani (It-cm)
May 16	Ernst C. Hesse (Ger-vla)	Oct 6	Francisco Manfredini (It-cm)
May 24	Joseph Umstatt (Aus-cm)	Nov 26	Jacques Naudot (Fr-fl)
Jun	Giovanni Giorgi (It-cm)	Dec 5	A. de la Pouplinière (Fr-pat)

C. Debuts:

Other - Josef Valentin Adamberger (Italy--stage name of Adamonti), Antonio Bernasconi (Munich), Anne Catley (London), Polly Young (London)

D. New Positions:

Conductors: Antoine Dauvergne (Concerts Spirituels, Paris), Ignazio Fiorillo (kapellmeister, Kassel), Baldassare Galuppi (maestro di cappella, St. Mark's, Venice), Pietro Gnocchi (at age 82, maestro di cappella, Brescia Cathedral), Michael Haydn (kapellmeister, Salzburg), William Herschel (Leeds Concerts), Johann Schwanenberg (kapellmeister, Brunswick)

Others: Rafael Anglés (organ, Valencia Cathedral), Benjamin Cooke (organ, Westminster Abbey), Henry Delamain (organ, Christ Church, Oxford), Johann Christian Kittel (organ, Predigerkirche, Erfurt), Pierre van Maldere (director, Brussel's Grand Theater), Giovanni Pescetti (organ, St. Mark's, Venice)

E. Prizes and Honors:

Honors: Giovanni Rutini (Accademia Filarmonica, Bologna)

F. Biographical Highlights:

Anna Lucia de Amicis makes her London debut; Johann Christian Bach leaves Italy and moves permanently to London; Wilhelm Friedemann Bach is offered a post at Darmstadt but loses it by his inaction; Robert Bremner moves his publishing headquarters to London; Jaime de Casellas retires due to illness; Daniel Dal Barba becomes temporary maestro di cappella at Verona Cathedral; Antoine Dauvergne, besides conducting the Concerts Spirituels, also becomes co-director of the Paris Opera; Filippo Finazzi marries Gertrud Steinmetz; Franz Joseph Haydn is kept on as kapellmeister by the new Prince, Nikolaus Esterházy; James Lyon is licensed to preach by the Presbyterian Synod in New Jersey; Wolfgang Amadeus Mozart and his sister are taken on their first performance tour by their father, Leopold; Pietro Nardini becomes solo violinist with the Stuttgart Court Orchestra; Jean-Jacques Rousseau flees Paris after the government condemns his *Social Contract*; Antonio Sacchini is granted leave to go to Naples for the performance of his *Semiramide*.

G. Institutional Openings:

Performing Groups: Band of the Royal Regiment of Artillery (oldest permanent musical organization in England)

Other: Bremner Publishers, London Branch; Harp Pedal System (by Michael K. Oginski); *Journal de Clavecin*; St. Cecilia Hall (Edinburgh); Welcker Music Publishers (London)

H. Musical Literature:

Bach, C. P. E., *The Proper Method of Playing Keyboard Instruments II*
Beattie, James, *On Poetry and Music*
Clément, Charles, *Essai sur la basse fondamentale*
Hardouin, Henri, *Méthode nouvelle pour apprendre le plain-chant*

Ludwig, Johann A., *Gedanken über die grossen Orgeln*
Potter, John, *Observations on the Present State of Music and Musicians*
Soler, Antonio, *Llave de la modulación*
    Antiquedades de la musica

I. Musical Compositions:

Abel, Carl F., *6 Overtures in 8 Parts, Opus 4*
Arne, Thomas, *Artaxerxes* (opera)
    Love in a Village (opera)
    Beauty and Virtue (serenade)
Bach, C. P. E., *Harpsichord Sonata in B Minor*
Bach, Johann Christian, *Alessandro nell'Indie* (opera)
Bach, Wilhelm F., *Lobe den Herrn in seinem Heiligtum* (cantata)
Boccherini, Luigi, *Sonata in C Major for 2 Cellos*
Cannabich, Christian, *Symphony No. 25 in C Major*
Dauvergne, Antoine, *Alphée et Aréthuse* (ballet)
Galuppi, Baldassare, *Viriate* (opera)
    Il marchese villano (opera)
    L'orfana onorata (intermezzo)
Gassmann, Florian, *Un pazzo ne fa Cento* (opera)
Gluck, Christoph, W., *Orfeo ed Euricice* (opera)
Gossec, François, *6 Symphonies, Opus 6*
Hasse, Johann A., *Il trionfo di Clelia* (opera)
Haydn, Franz J., *Symphonies No. 3-5*
    Symphony No. 9 in C Major
    4 Divertimentos, Opus 2
    Concerto No. 1 for Horn and Orchestra
    La vedova (opera)
    Il dottore (opera)
    Il scanarello (opera)
    La Marchesa Nespola (opera)
    Acide (opera)
Logroschino, Nicola, *La viaggiatrice de bell'umore* (opera)
Manfredini, Vincenzo, *Olimpiade* (opera)
    Amour et Psyché (ballet)
Mondonville, Jean de, *Psyché* (opera)
    Les Fêtes de Paphos (opera)
Monsigny, Pierre, *Le roi et le fermier* (opera)
Mozart, Wolfgang A., *Minuet and Trio in G Major, K. 1*
Philidor, François, *Sancho Pança* (opera)
Piccinni, Niccolò, *Artaserse* (opera)
    Antigono (opera)
    Amor senza malizia (opera)
Sacchini, Antonio, *I due bari* (opera)
    L'amore in campo (opera)
Sarti, Giuseppe, *Semiramide* (opera)
    Didone abbandonata (opera)
    6 Clavier Sonatas
Schwanenberg, Johann, *Solimano* (opera)
    Adriano in Siria (opera)
Telemann, Georg P., *The Day of Judgment* (oratorio)
    Passion According to Matthew V
Toeschi, Carlo G., *Télémaque* (ballet)
    6 Symphonies, Opus 1
Traetta, Tommaso, *Sofonisba* (opera)
    Zenobia (opera)
    Alessandro nelle Indie (opera)
Wagenseil, Georg C., *Prometeo Assoluto* (serenade)

1763

World Events:
In the U.S., Chief Pontiac of the Ottawa Indians leads a confederation against the settlement of the Ohio Territory and destroys all forts except Fort Pitt and Fort Detroit; France loses all of her New World holdings east of the Mississippi River in the Treaty of Paris; the Proclamation Line limits settlements west of the Appalachians; the first steam boat, the *William Henry*, is unsuccessful in its trial run; the first medical society is formed in Connecticut. Internationally, the Peace of Paris ending the Seven Years War gives the British Canada and Florida as well as complete control in India; the Treaty of Hubertusburg is signed by Austria and Prussia; Frederick the Great establishes village schools in Prussia; Augustus III of Poland dies and is succeeded by Stanislaus II; Rio de Janeiro becomes the capitol of Brazil; excavations begin at Pompeii and Herculaneum in Italy.

Cultural Highlights:
Jean François Marmontel is taken into the French Academy and publishes his *Poétique Française*; Catherine Macauley publishes the first volume of *The History of England from the Accession of James I to that of the Brunswick Line*; Charles André (Carle) Van Loo becomes director of the French Academy of Fine Arts. Births in the art field include American architect Charles Bulfinch, British artist George Morland and French artist Jean Germain Drouais; deaths include Swiss artist Franz A. Bustelli. Births in the literary world include British poet Samuel Rogers, German author Jean Paul Richter and Hungarian poet János Bacsányi; deaths include French author Pierre Carlet de Marivaux,novelist Antoine François Prévost d'Exiles, British poet William Shenstone, poet and humorist William King, Swedish historian and poet Olof von Dalin and poet Hedvig Charlotta Nordenflycht. Other highlights include:

Art: Lambert Adam, *Prometheus Chained* (marble); Thomas Banks, *Death of Epaminondas*; Étienne Falconet, *Pygmalion and Galatea*; Jean-Baptiste Greuze, *Paralytic Tended by His Children*; Francesco Guardi, *Election of the Doge*; George Romney, *Death of General Wolfe*; Carle Van Loo, *Venus and Cupid*; Pietro A. Lorenzoni, *Wolfgang A. Mozart*; Luigi Vanvitelli, *Forum Carolino* (Naples)

Literature: Charles Churchill, *The Duellist*; Richard Glover, *Medea*; Gotthold Lessing, *Minna von Barnhelm*; James Macpherson, *Temora*; Moses Mendelssohn, *Abhandlung über die Evidenz in den Metaphysischen Wissenschaften*; Francis Sheridan, *The Discovery*; Christopher Smart, *A Song to David*; Emanuel Swedenborg, *Life for the New Jerusalem*; Voltaire, *Treatise on Tolerance*

MUSICAL EVENTS

A. Births:

Jan 9	Karl G. Umbreit (Ger-cm)	Jun 22	Etienne Méhul (Fr-cm)
Jan 27	Gottfried Härtel (Ger-pub)	Jun 29	Johann S. Demar (Ger-org)
Feb 5	Charles Incledon (Br-ten)	Jul 2	Peter Ritter (Ger-cm)
Feb 20	Adalbert Gyrowetz (Boh-cm)	Sep 18	Thomas Wright (Br-org)
Mar 6	Jean X. Lefèvre (Swi-cl)	Nov 28	Matthäus Fischer (Ger-cm)
Apr 2	Giacomo G. Ferrari (It-the)	Dec 23	John Davy (Br-cm)
Apr 10	Domenico Dragonetti (It-cb)		Johannes A. Amon (Ger-cd)
Apr 20	Anna Marie Crouch (Br-sop)		Dorothea Bussani (Aus-sop)
May 15	Franz Danzi (Ger-cm)		John Relfe (Br-cm-the)
Jun 14	Johann S. Mayr (Ger-cm)		

B. Deaths:

Jan 11	Giovanni Platti (It-cm)	Mar 20	Maximilian Hellmann (Aus-cm)
Feb 17	Christoph Schaffrath (Ger-hps)	Apr 3	Richard Mudge (Br-cm)
Mar 8	Christian Müller (Ger-org.m)	Jun 1	Johann C. Vogler (Ger-cm)

Jun 20   James Heseltine (Br-org)
Jul 16   Jacques Hotteterre (Fr-fl)
Jul 20   Louis A. Lefebvre (Fr-org)
Aug 14   Giovanni B. Somis (It-vn)

Oct 10   Claude Pellegrin (Fr-cm)
         Anton Dulcken (Bel-hps.m)
         Johann Janitsch (Ger-cm)
         Giuseppe Paganelli (It-cm)

C. Debuts:

Other - Francesco Bussani (Rome), Simon Leduc (Paris), Thomas Linley, Jr. (Bristol)

D. New Positions:

Conductors: Carlo Antonio Campioni (maestro di cappella, Florence), Filippo Maria Gherardeschi (maestro di cappella, Volterra), Orazio Mei (maestro di capella, Livorno Cathedral)

Others: François Bainville (organ, Cathedral of St. Maurice, Angers), Thomas Ebdon (organ, Durham Cathedral), Friedrich Wilhelm Marpurg (director, Berlin Lottery), Christian Friedrich Schale (organ, Berlin Cathedral), Jean François Tapray (organ, Besançon Cathedral), Ernst Wilhelm Wolf (organ, Weimar Court)

E. Prizes and Honors:

Honors: Paolo Morellati (Accademia Filarmonica, Bologna)

F. Biographical Highlights:

Pasquale Anfossi has his first opera production, *La serva spiritosa*, in Rome; Cristoforo Babbi is sent to Faenza to study violin with Alberghi; Luigi Boccherini leaves Lucca for Vienna; Bartolomeo Campagnoli is sent by his father to Modena for further violin study; Anna Lucia De Amicis makes the move to serious opera in London; Carl Ditters von Dittersdorf accompanies Christoph Willibald Gluck on his trip to Italy; Florian Leopold Gassmann is called to Vienna to be a theater conductor; Johann Adolf Hasse and his wife, Faustina Bordoni, are dismissed from Dresden and move to Vienna; Wolfgang Amadeus Mozart has his first pieces published; Gottlieb Muffat is retired on a pension from his Vienna posts; Josef Mysliveček leaves for Venice to study composition with Pescetti; Johann Gottlieb Naumann becomes composer of sacred music at the Dresden Court; Joseph Boulogne Saint-Georges begins music study with Leclair and Gossec; Georg "Abbe" Vogler enrolls in the University of Würzburg to study theology and law.

G. Institutional Openings:

Performing Groups: Leipzig Subscription (Leibhaber) Concerts (revived by Johann Hiller)

Educational: Bremner School of Music (Philadelphia)

Other: *Frusta Litteraria*; Johann Hartknoch, Publisher (Mitau)

H. Musical Literature:

Brown, John, *The Rise, Union and Power, the Progressions, Separations and Corruptions of Poetry and Music*
Hopkinson, Francis, *A Collection of Psalm Tunes...*
Lambert, Johann H., *Sur quelques instruments acoustiques*
Marpurg, Friedrich W., *Anleitung zur Musik überhaupt und zur Singkunst besonders*
Meyer, Philippe J., *La vraie manière de jouer de la Harpe*
Serre, Jean-Adam, *Observations sur les principes de l'harmonie*
Sorge, Georg A., *Kurze erklärung des Canonis Harmonici*
Williams, Aaron, *The Universal Psalmist*

I. Musical Compositions:

Anfossi, Pasquale, *La serva spiritosa* (opera)
　　Lo sposo di tre e marito di nessuna (opera)
Arne, Thomas, *The Birth of Hercules* (opera)
Bach, Johann Christian, *Zanaida* (opera)
　　Orione (opera)
　　Symphony in B-flat Major, Opus 9, No. 3
　　Symphony in E-flat Major, Opus 18, No. 1
　　6 Clavecin Concertos, Opus 1
　　6 Trios, Opus 2, for Violin, Cello and Harpsichord
Bernasconi, Andrea, *Artaserse* (opera)
Boccherini, Luigi, *3 Cello Sonatas*
Bonno, Giuseppe, *Il sogno di Scipione* (opera)
Cannabich, Christian, *Symphony No. 26 in F Major*
　　Ceyx et Alcyone (ballet)
Dauvergne, Antoine, *Polyxène* (opera)
Dittersdorf, Carl von, *Concerto in E Minor for Flute and Orchestra*
Duni, Egidio, *Le rendez-vous* (opera)
　　Les deux chasseurs et la laitière (opera)
Furlanetto, Bonaventura, *La sposa de' sacri cantici* (oratorio)
Galuppi, Baldassare, *Maria Magdalena* (oratorio)
　　Arianna e Teseo (opera)
　　Il re alla caccia (opera)
　　La donna di governo (opera)
Giardini, Felice de', *Siroe* (opera)
Gluck, Christoph W., *Il trionfo di Clelia* (opera)
Guglielmi, Pietro, *Tito Manlio* (opera)
　　La francese brillante (opera)
　　L'Olimpiade (opera)
Hasse, Johann A., *Requiem in C Major*
Haydn, Franz J., *Symphonies No. 12-16*
Jommelli, Niccolò, *La pastorella illustre* (pastorale)
　　Il trionfo d'amore (pastorale)
　　Didone abbandonata (opera)
Lampugnani, Giovanni, *Enea in Italia* (opera)
Manfredini, Vincenzo, *Carlo Magno* (opera)
　　Pygmalion (ballet)
Monsigny, Pierre, *Le nouveau monde* (opera)
Philidor, François, *Le bûcheron* (opera)
　　Les fêtes de la paix (opera)
Piccinni, Niccolò, *Il cavaliere per amore* (opera)
　　Le contadine bizzarre (opera)
　　Le donne vendicate (intermezzo)
Porpora, Nicola, *Ouverture Royale in D Major*
Richter, Franz X., *Simphonie Periodique No. 49*
　　Sinfonias (No. 12-14) a piu stromenti obbligati
　　6 Sonatas for Harpsichord, Set II
Sacchini, Antonio, *Olimpiade* (opera)
　　Alessandro nell'Indie (opera)
Sarti, Giuseppe, *Cesare in Egitto* (opera)
　　Il Narciso (opera)
Scarlatti, Giuseppe, *Pelopida* (opera)
Toeschi, Carlo G., *4 Flute Concertos*
　　Feste del seraglio (ballet)
Traetta, Tommaso, *Ifigenia in Tauride* (opera)

1764

World Events:
In the U.S., the Currency Act and the Sugar Act, passed by the British Parliament to raise money to pay war debts, brings on protests from the colonists; St. Louis is founded on the Mississippi River by French fur traders; Rhode Island College (Brown University) is founded; the *Connecticut Courant* (*Hartford Courant* in 1837) begins weekly publication; James Otis publishes his *The Rights of the British Colonies Asserted and Proved*. Internationally, the Russian government confiscates all lands belonging to the Russian Orthodox Church; France expels the Jesuit order from its borders; Stanislaus II is made king in Poland but Russian and Prussia control the politics; Madame Pompadour dies; the British begin the system of numbering houses along each street; James Hargreaves of England invents the Spinning Jenny.

Cultural Highlights:
The Literary Club is founded in London by Samuel Johnson and Joshua Reynolds; the Leipzig Art Academy is founded with Adam Friedrich Öser as director; Giovanni B. Bettino Cignaroli founds the Academy of Verona; Giovanni Battista Casanova becomes director of the Dresden Academy of Art; Johann Joachim Winckelmann publishes his *History of Ancient Art*. Births in the field of art include British architect Benjamin Henry Latrobe and German sculptor Johann Gottfried Schadow; British artist William Hogarth dies. Births in the literary field include Danish poet Jens Immanuel Baggesen, British novelist Ann Radcliffe, Spanish poet Nicasio Alvarez de Cienfuegos, French dramatist André Marie de Chénier and playwright Gabriel Marie Legouvé; deaths include German poet and librettist Christian Friedrich Henrici and British poet and satirist Charles Churchill and poet Robert Dodsley. Other highlights include:

Art: John Copley, *John Sparhawk*; William Hogarth, *Finis, or the Bathos*; Jean-Antoine Houdon, *St. Bruno*; Joshua Reynolds, *Mrs. Hale as Euphrosyne*; George Stubbs, *Cheetah with Two Indians* and *Mares and Foals by a Stream*; Giovanni Tiepolo, *Apotheosis of Spain*; John Trumbull, *The Oath of Brutus*; Carle Van Loo, *The Magic Lantern*

Literature: Cesare Beccaria, *Essays on Crime and Punishment*; Thomas Chatterton, *Apostate's Will*; Charles Churchill, *The Candidate*; Oliver Goldsmith, *The Traveler*; James Grainger, *The Sugar Cane*; Imanuel Kant, *Observations on the Sense of the Beautiful and the Sublime*; Anna Luise Karschin, *Selected Poems*; Friedrich Klopstock, *Solomon*; Robert Lloyd, *The Capricious Lovers*; Voltaire, *Dictionnaire Philosophique*

MUSICAL EVENTS

A. Births:

Jan 7	William Forster, Jr., (Br-vn.m)	Jul 1	Georg Grosheim (Ger-cm)
Jan 13	Franz Lauska (Ger-pn)	Jul 5	János Lavotta (Hun-vn)
Jan 25	Felix J. Lipowsky (Ger-mus)	Sep 11	Valentino Fioravanti (It-cm)
Feb 21	Franz X. Glöggl (Aus-mus)	Sep 13	Richard Mount-Edgcumbe
Feb 22	Alexander Campbell (Scot-cm)		(Br-cm)
Mar 1	Jeremiah Ingalls (Am-cm)	Oct 14	Charles Plantade (Fr-cm)
Mar 5	Johann Grenser (Ger-ww.m)	Oct 21	János Behari (Hun-vn)
Apr 18	Bernhard A. Weber (Ger-pn-cd)	Nov 30	Franz X. Gerl (Aus-bs)
May 25	Matthew Camidge (Br-org)	Dec 9	Jeanne Saint-Aubin (Fr-sop)
May 29	Jean Levasseur (Fr-cel)	Dec 10	Louis S. Lebrun (Fr-ten)

B. Deaths:

Mar 11	Charles Levens (Fr-org)	Apr 17	Johann Matteson (Ger-the)
Mar 30	Pietro Locatelli (It-vn-cm)	Apr 27	Jaime de Casellas (Sp-cm)
Apr 13	Nicola Fiorenza (It-vn)	May 3	Francesco Algarotti (It-cri)

May 3	Robert Wass (Br-bs)	Oct 22	Jean Marie Leclair (Fr-cm)
Jun	Musgrave Heighington (Br-org)	Nov 13	Johann Nauss (Ger-org)
Sep 2	John Reading (Br-org)	Dec	Lorenzo Zavateri (It-vn)
Sep 10	Giovanni A. Giai (It-cm)		Angelo Monticelli (It-cas)
Sep 12	Jean P. Rameau (Fr-cm-the)		Wilhelm Pachelbel (Ger-cm)
Oct 13	Daniel Sullivan (Ir-c.ten)		

C. Debuts:

Other - Lucrezia Aguiari (Florence), Joseph Legros (Paris), Corona Schröter (Leipzig), Antoine Trial (Paris), Frederica Weichsell (London)

D. New Positions:

Conductors: Edmund Ayrton (Chapel Royal, London), Carlo Antonio Campioni (maestro di cappella, Florence), Carl Ditters von Dittersdorf (kapellmeister, Grosswardein), Johann Gottlieb Görner (Leipzig Gelehrtenkonzert), Esteban Salas y Castro (maestro de capilla, Santiago de Cuba)

Educational: Garrett Colley Mornington (professor, Dublin University)

Others: Edmund Broderip (organ, Mayor's Chapel, Bristol), Cornelius Heinrich Dretzel (organ, St. Sebald, Nuremberg), August Bernhard Herbing (organ, Magdeburg Cathedral), David Traugott Nicolai (organ, Hauptkirche, Leipzig), Johann Siebenkäs (organ, St. Lorenz, Nuremberg)

E. Prizes and Honors:

Honors: Carl Friedrich Abel and Johann Christian Bach (Chamber Musicians to Queen Charlotte), Charles Burney (Royal Society of Arts)

F. Biographical Highlights:

Carl Friedrich Abel, with Johann Christian Bach, begins a twenty-year concert series in London; Anton Cajetan Adlgasser is sent by the Archbishop of Salzburg for a year's study in Italy; Angelo Amorevoli retires from the stage but continues to sing at the Dresden court; Domenico Annibali is retired with a pension; Jacob Anthony, maker of woodwinds, arrives in Philadelphia; Samuel Arnold begins playing harpsichord in the Covent Garden orchestra; Wilhelm Friedemann Bach leaves Halle and begins teaching privately; Charles Burney and his family move to Paris in order to provide the type of education they wish for their daughters; Christian Cannabich makes his first visit to Paris in the retinue of Duke Christian IV; Martin Gerbert is appointed Prince-Abbot of St. Blasien; Christoph Willibald Gluck leaves the Vienna Court and travels to Paris and in Germany; Jean Marie Leclair is murdered in his own home; Antonio Lolli makes his Paris debut; James Lyon accepts a pastorate in Nova Scotia; Gian Francesco Majo leaves Naples for Vienna; Wolfgang Amadeus Mozart plays for Louis XV and meets Johann Christian Bach while in London.

G. Institutional Openings:

Performing Groups: Giuseppe Bustelli Opera Co. (Prague); Philadelphia Subscription Concerts (by Frances Hopkinson and Robert Bremner)

Educational: University of Dublin Chair of Music

Other: Bratislava Theater; Dublin Rotunda; *Journal de Musique Française et Italienne*

H. Musical Literature:

Albrecht, Johann, *Abhandlung über die Frage: Ob die Musik beim Gottesdienst zu dulden sei oder nicht*

Camidge, John, *Six Easy Lessons for the Harpsichord*

Euler, Leonhard, *Conjecture sur la raison de quelques dissonances...*

Flagg, Josiah, *Collection of the Best Psalm Tunes*

Gianotti, Pietro, *Méthode abrégée d'accompagnement à la harpe e au clavecin*

Hiller, Johann A., *Anekdoten zur lebensgeschichte französischer, teutscher, italienischer...*
Ludwig, Johann A., *Den unverschämten Entehrern der Orgeln*
Roel del Rio, Antonio, *Reparos musicos*
Roussier, Pierre, *Traité des accords, et de leur succession*
Solano, Francisco, *Nova instrucção musical*

I. Musical Compositions:
Anfossi, Pasquale, *Il finto medico* (opera)
Arne, Thomas, *The Guardian Outwitted* (opera)
    The Arcadian Nuptials (opera)
Avison, Charles, *6 Sonatas, Opus 8, for 2 Violins, Cello and Harpsichord*
Bernasconi, Andrea, *Olimpiade* (opera)
Cannabich, Christian, *Le jugement de Paris* (opera)
Galuppi, Baldassare, *Sofonisba* (opera)
    Cajo Mario (opera)
    La partenza il ritorno de' marinari (opera)
    Sacrificium Abraham (oratorio)
Gassmann, Florian, *L'Olimpiade* (opera)
Giardini, Felice de', *Enea e Lavinia* (opera)
Giraud, François, *Acanthe et Cydippe* (pastorale)
Gluck, Christoph W., *La rencontre imprévue* (opera)
    Alessandro (ballet)
Guglielmi, Pietro, *Siroe re de Persia* (opera)
    Li rivali placati (opera)
Hasse, Johann A., *Egeria* (opera)
Haydn, Franz J., *Symphonies No. 18*
    Symphonies No. 21-24
    6 String Quartets, Opus 3
Hiller, Johann A., *Die verwandelter weiber* (opera)
Jommelli, Niccolò, *Demofoonte* (opera)
    Il ré pastore (opera)
Monsigny, Pierre, *Rose et Colas* (opera)
    Le bouquet de Thalie (opera)
Mozart, Wolfgang A., *Symphony No. 1 in E-flat Major, K. 16*
    10 Violin Sonatas, K. 6-15
Mysliveček, Josef, *Medea* (opera)
Naumann, Johann, *Il creduti spiriti* (opera)
Paisiello, Giovanni, *Il bagno d'Abano* (opera)
    I Francesi brillanti (opera)
Philidor, François, *Le sorcier* (opera)
Piccinni, Niccolò, *Berenice* (opera)
    L'equívoco (opera)
    Il nuovo Orlando (opera)
    La villeggiatura (opera)
Rameau, Jean P., *Abaris* (opera)
Richter, Franz X., *6 Sonatas, Opus 3, for 2 Violins and Cello*
    Sinfonia Périodique No. 61
    6 Sonatas da Camera (cembalo, flute, violin, cello)
Rinaldo di Capua, *Il caffè di campagna* (opera)
Sacchini, Antonio, *Semiramide* (opera)
    Lucio Vero (opera)
    Il gran Cidde (opera)
    Eumene (opera)
Sarti, Giuseppe, *Il gran Tamerlano* (opera)
    Il naufragio di Cipro (opera)
Telemann, Georg P., *Passion According to Luke V*
Tessarini, Carlo, *6 Grand Overtures for String Quartet, Opus 18*
Traetta, Tommaso, *Antigono* (opera)

1765

World Events:

In the U.S., more discontent and unrest is caused by the British Parliament passing the Stamp Act and especially the Quartering Act which seeks to force colonists to put up troops in their homes at their expense; the Declaration of Rights and Grievances is issued by the Stamp Act Congress meeting in New York City and sent to the British Parliament; Chief Pontiac and the Ottawa Confederation is defeated; the first medical school at the College of Philadelphia is opened; Thomas Hutchinson publishes his *History of the Colony of Massachusetts Bay*. Internationally, Joseph II becomes the Holy Roman Emperor and co-ruler of Austria with Maria Theresa; King George III of England suffers his first bout with mental illness; James Watt perfects his steam engine; the Chinese invade Burma; William Blackstone publishes his *Commentaries on the Laws of England*.

Cultural Highlights:

The Cliosophic Society at Princeton becomes the first college literary society in the New World; the Society of Artists is chartered in London; Thomas Godfrey's *The Prince of Parthia* is the first play to be written by a native American; François Boucher becomes the director of the French Academy of Fine Arts as well as First Painter to the King; David Hume becomes a part of the British Embassy in Paris; Thomas Percy publishes his *Reliques of Ancient English Poetry*; Samuel Johnson brings out his *First Easy Rudiments of Grammar*. Births in the literary field include American novelist William H. Brown, German author Friederike Sophie Christiane Brun, Portugese poet Manuel Maria du Bocage and Scottish poet James Grahame; deaths include British poet and author Edward Young and Italian poet and librettist Antonio Rolli. American inventor and artist Robert Fulton is born while Belgian artist Charles André (Carle) Van Loo and British artist George Lambert pass away. Other highlights include:

Art: Canaletto, *Church of the Convento della Carita*; Jean Baptiste Chardin, *Attributes of the Arts...and Music*; John Copley, *Boy with Squirrel*; Jean-Honoré Fragonard, *Corèsus and Callirrhoé* and *The Bathers*; Jean-Baptiste Greuze, *La Bonne Mère*; Joshua Reynolds, *Lady Bunbury Sacrificing*; Émile-Jean Vernet, *Ports of France XV*; Richard Wilson, *View of Rome from Villa Madama*

Literature: Alicia Cockburn, *Flowers of the Forest*; Dormont de Belloy, *Le Siège de Calais*; Henry Brooke, *The Fool of Quality*; Samuel Foote, *The Commissary*; Thomas Godfrey, *The Prince of Parthia*; Oliver Goldsmith, *Essays*; Giuseppe Parini, *Il Giorno*; Michel Sedaine, *The Duel*; Laurence Sterne, *Tristram Shandy VII, VIII*; Horace Walpole, *The Castle of Otranto*

MUSICAL EVENTS

A. Births:

Feb 8	Joseph von Eybler (Aus-cm)	Oct 25	Karl G. Hering (Ger-the)
Feb 23	Charles L. André (Bel-cm)	Oct 26	Jan Jakub Ryba (Cz-cm)
May 28	Jean B. Cartier (Fr-vn)	Oct 27	Ann S. Storace (Br-sop)
Jun 13	Anton Franz Eberl (Aus-cm)	Nov 20	Friedrich Himmel (Ger-pn)
Jun 19	Pietro Gianotti (It-cb-cm)	Nov 23	Thomas Attwood (Br-org)
Jul 14	Friedrich Seidel (Ger-org)	Nov 27	Bernard Sarrette (Fr-ed)
Sep 7	Michel C. Oginski (Pol-cm)	Dec 25	Joseph Mazzinghi (Br-pn)
Sep 18	Oliver Holden (Am-cm)	Dec 27	Elizabeth Billington (Br-sop)
Oct 16	Frédéric Duvernoy (Fr-hn)		Charles Dignum (Br-ten)
Oct 22	Daniel Steibelt (Ger-pn)		Pietro Terziani (It-cm)

B. Deaths:

Jan 12	Johann M. Molter (Gr-cd-cm)	Aug 23	Michel G. Besson (Fr-vn-cm)
Jan 15	Karlmann Kolb (Ger-org)	Sep 5	Christophe Ballard (Fr-pub)
Jan 19	Johan J. Agrell (Swe-vn-cm)	Sep 5	Claude P. Caylus (Fr-mus)
Feb 9	Elisabetta Gambarini (Br-sop)	Oct 8	Rosalie Levasseur (Fr-sop)
Mar 7	Giuseppe A Consoni (It-cm)	Dec 25	Antonio Tonelli (It-cm)
Apr 20	Wilhelm A. Roth (Ger-org)		Francesco Ciampi (It-vn)
May	José de Orejón (Peru-org)		Nicola Logroscino (It-cm)
Jun 19	Pietro Gianotti (It-cm-the)		Pietro Nacchini (It-org.m)

C. Debuts:

Other - Venanzio Rauzzini (Rome)

D. New Positions:

Conductors: Georg W. Gruber (kapellmeister, Nuremberg), Julien-Amable Mathieu (maître de chapelle, Versailles), Raynor Taylor (Sadler's Wells)

Educational: Tommaso Traetta (director, Conservatorio dell'Ospedaletto, Venice)

Others: Pieter van den Bosch (organ, Antwerp Cathedral), Richard Woodward (organ, Christ Church Cathedral, Dublin)

E. Prizes and Honors:

Honors: Giovanni Fioroni and Bernardo Ottani (Accademia Filarmonica, Bologna)

F. Biographical Highlights:

Johann Georg Albrechtsberger leaves the Melk Abbey and goes to Silesia; Hyacinthe Azaïs becomes music master at a small college in Sorèze; Maxim Berezovsky is sent by the Russian government to Bologna for further music study with Padre Martini; Antonia Bernasconi makes her Vienna debut; Matthew Dubourg leaves Dublin to return to London; Jan Ladislav Dussek, at age five, begins piano study; Baldassare Galuppi becomes chief conductor of Italian Opera in the Court of Catherine the Great in Russia and also introduces Italian contrapuntal style into the Russian liturgical music; Wolfgang Amadeus Mozart and his father spend time in England and Holland on a concert tour; Johann Gottlieb Naumann begins a three-years stay in Italy conducting several of his operas; Antonio Salieri is left an orphan by the death of his father; Giuseppe Sarti is sent by the King of Denmark to Italy to recruit singers for the re-opening of the Italian Opera; David Tannenberg continues his organ building career in Lititz, Pennsylvania; Giuseppe Tartini gives up his position at St. Anthony's in Padua.

G. Institutional Openings:

Performing Groups: Bach-Abel Subscription Concerts (London); Bergen Harmonice Society; Società Filarmonica (Pisana)

Educational: Allgemeine Deutsche Bibliothek

Other: Ackermann Theater (Hamburg); Giovanni Artaria and Co., Publishers (Mainz-Vienna); Sadler's Wells Music House II (London); Theater of the Estates (Ljuljana)

H. Musical Literature:

Albrecht, Johann L., *Vom Hasse der Musik*
Arnold, John, *Church Music Reformed*
Löhlein, Georg S., *Clavier-Schule I*
Paolucci, Giuseppe, *Arte pratica de contrappunto*
Scheibe, Johann A., *Abhandlung über das recitativ*
Tessarini, Carlo, *Grammatica di musica*
    An Accurate Method to...Playing the Violin
Wesley, John, *Sacred Melody*

I. Musical Compositions:

Arne, Thomas, *Bacchus and Ariadne* (opera)
Bach, Johann Christian, *Adriano in Siria* (opera)
    The Maid of the Mill (opera)
    6 Symphonies, Opus 3
    6 Canzonettes, Opus 4
Benda, George A., *Xindo riconnosciuto* (opera)
Boccherini, Luigi, *La Confederazioni dei Sabini con Roma* (cantata)
Cannabich, Christian, *Ulisse et Circée* (ballet)
    Les amours de Télémaque (ballet)
Duni, Egidio, *L'école de la jeunesse* (opera)
Galuppi, Baldassare, *La virtù liberata* (cantata)
    Triumphus divini amoris (oratorio)
Gassmann, Florian, *Il trionfo d'amore* (opera)
Giardini, Felice de', *Il re pastore* (opera)
    Ruth (oratorio)
Giordani, Tommaso, *The Enchanter* (opera)
    Love in Disguise (opera)
    Don Fulminone (opera)
Gluck, Christoph W., *Alessandro* (ballet)
    Semiramis (ballet)
    La corona (opera)
    Telemaco (opera)
Gossec, François, *3 Grand Symphonies, Opus 8*
    Le faux lord (opera)
Grétry, André, *La vendemmiatrice* (intermezzo)
Hasse, Johann A., *Romolo ed Ersilia* (opera)
Haydn, Franz J., *Symphonies No. 25-32*
    Concertos No. 1 and 2, for Violin and Orchestra
    Concerto No. 1 in C for Cello and Orchestra
    Concerto in D Major for Flute and Orchestra
    Concerto No. 1 for Horn and Orchestra
    Concerto in D Major for Contrabass and Orchestra
    Cembalo Concerto No. 3
    Keyboard Sonata No. 12 in A Major
    Te Deum in C Major
Insanguine, Giacomo, *La vedova capricciosa* (opera)
    Il nuovo Belisario (opera)
Jommelli, Niccolò, *Imeneo in Atene* (pastorale)
Logroscino, Nicola, *La gelosia* (opera)
    Il tempo dell' onore (opera)
Mondonville, Jean de, *Thésée* (opera)
Mozart, Wolfgang A., *Symphonies No. 4 and 5, K. 19 and 22*
    Motet, "God is Our Refuge"
Paisiello, Giovanni, *Artaserse* (opera)
    Demetrio (opera)
    L'amore in ballo (opera)
Philidor, François, *Tom Jones* (opera)
Piccinni, Niccolò, *La buona moglie* (opera)
    Il barone di Torreforte (opera)
Richter, Franz X., *6 Symphonies, Opus 4*
Sacchini, Antonio, *Il Creso* (opera)
    La contadina in Corte (opera)
Sarti, Giuseppe, *Mithridate* (opera)
Schobert, Johann, *Le Garde-chase et le braconnier* (singspiel)
Tessarini, Carlo, *6 Grande Overtures, Opus 20, for String Quartet*
Toeschi, Carlo G., *6 Symphonies, Opus 3*
Traetta, Tommaso, *Semiramide* (opera)

1766

World Events:

In the U.S., the hated Stamp Act is repealed by the British Parliament but only because of the loss of trade by English businesses; in its place, Parliament passes the Declaratory Act claiming that Parliament in the mother country has the right to control the colonies; Benjamin Franklin becomes the American representative to Parliament and publishes his *Examination before the House of Commons*; Richard Bland publishes his *Inquiry into the Rights of the British Colonies;* the Mason-Dixon Line between Maryland and Pennsylvania is established; Queens College (Rutgers University) is founded in New Jersey; the Philadelphia Medical Society is formed; peace is established with the Indians under Chief Pontiac. Internationally, Catherine the Great grants freedom of worship to all Russians; Frederick V of Denmark dies and is succeeded by Christian VII; India experiences a great famine.

Cultural Highlights:

James Christie, famous Art Auctioneer, begins plying his trade in London; the Dresden Academy of Art is founded; Bristol's Theater Royal, the oldest theater in London still in use today, is opened; Francis Hayman becomes President of the Society of Artists; artist Hubert Robert is inducted into the French Academy; Denis Diderot publishes his *Essay on Painting*; Heinrich Wilhelm von Gerstenberg publishes the first volume of his *Briefe uber Merkwurdigkeiten der Literatur.* In the art world, German artist Wilhelm von Kobell is born; deaths include French artists Jacques Andre Aved and Jean Marc Nattier, German architect Dominikus Zimmerman as well as Italian artist Claudio F. Beaumont. Births in the literary field include American dramatist and painter William Dunlap, German philosopher Friedrich Bouterwek, French author Mme. de Stael, British poet Robert Bloomfield and author Isaac d'Israeli; German poet and philosopher Johann Christoph Gottsched dies. Other highlights include:

Art: Pompeo Batoni, *General Gordon*; John Singleton Copley, *Mrs. Thomas Boylston*; Etienne Falconet, *Monument to Peter the Great*; Jean-Honore Fragonard, *The Swing*; Thomas Gainsborough, *The Harvest Wagon*; Alessandro Longhi, *Painter Urbani*; Michel B. Ollivier, *Mozart Playing Afternoon Tea*; Benjamin West, *Pylades and Orestes*; Joseph Wright, *Orrery*

Literature: George Colman and David Garrick, *The Clandestine Marriage*; Johannes Ewald, *Elegies*; Denis Fonvizin, *The Brigadier*; Oliver Goldsmith, *The Vicar of Wakefield*; Gotthold Lessing, *Laocoon*; Tobias Smollett, *Travels through France and Italy*; Christoph Wieland, *The Story of Agathon*; Anna Williams, *Miscellanies in Prose and Verse*

MUSICAL EVENTS

A. Births:

Jan 10	Louis Massonneau (Ger-vn)	Oct 9	Dionys Weber (Boh-cm-the)
Feb 21	Vincenzo Lavigna (It-cm)	Oct 21	Francesco Ruggi (It-cm)
Feb 24	Samuel Wesley (Br-org)	Nov 16	Rodolphe Kreutzer (Fr-vn-cm)
Mar 28	Joseph Weigl (Aus-cm)	Nov 20	John W. Callcott (Br-org)
Jul 3	J. M. Beauvarlet-Charpentier (Fr-org)		John Addison (Br-cb-cm)
			Stephan Degtyaroff (Rus-cm)
Jul 16	Johann Doring (Ger-bs)		Feodor P. Lvov (Rus-cd)
Aug 1	Ignaz A. Ladurner (Fr-pn)		James Power (Ir-pub)
Aug 16	Carolina Nairne (Scot-pt-cm)		Franz X. Sussmayr (Aus-cm)
Sep 4	Luigi Bassi (It-bar)		

B. Deaths:

Jan 30	Susanna M. Cibber (Br-sop-act)	Jul 17	Barthold Fritz (Ger-org.m)
Feb 13	Luis Misón (Sp-fl-cm)	Sep 23	John Brown (Br-rel-mus)
Feb 26	August B. Herbing (Ger-org)	Sep 24	Johann Hencke (Aus-org.m)
Mar 3	Gregor J. Werner (Aus-cm-cd)	Oct 7	André Chéron (Fr-org-cd)
Mar 20	Giovanni Pescetti (It-cm)	Dec 15	Carlo Tessarini (It-vn-cm)
Mar 25	Johannes Ritschel (Ger-vn)		François Blanchet, fils
Jun 23	Thomas Roseingrave (Br-org)		(Fr-hps.m)

C. Debuts:

Other - Tommaso Guarducci (London), Rosalie Levasseur (Paris), Marie Jeanne Trial (Paris)

D. New Positions:

Conductors: Pedro Aranaz y Vidés (maestro de capilla, Saragossa Cathedral), Giuseppe Colla (maestro di cappella, Parma), Domenico Fischietti (kapellmeister, Dresden), Filippo Gherardeschi (maestro di cappella, Chiesa Conventuale di S. Stefano, Pisa), Feodor L'vov (Imperial Chapel, St. Petersburg), Giovanni M. Rutini (maestro di cappella, Modena), Anton Schweitzer (kapellmeister, Hildburghausen)

Others: Muzio Clementi (organ, St.Lorenzo, Damaso), William Herschel (organ, Octagon Chapel, Bath), Thomas Norris (organ, St. John's College)

E. Prizes and Honors:

Honors: Joseph Dall'Abaco (baronet)

F. Biographical Highlights:

Leopold Abel becomes concert-master of the orchestra at Brandenburg-Schwedt; John Alcock, Sr., receives his doctorate from Oxford; Michael Arne marries singer Elizabeth Wright; Luigi Boccherini goes on a concert tour of France with Manfredini; Charlotte Brent marries conductor Thomas Pinto; Muzio Clementi is taken to Dorset for further music study by the British patron Beckford; Johann Nikolaus Forkel leaves Lüneburg for a year in Schwerin; André Grétry goes to Geneva as a teacher and meets Voltaire who encourages him to seek his musical fortune in Paris; Franz Joseph Haydn is promoted to full kapellmeister at the Esterhházy estate; Wolfgang Amadeus Mozart visits Paris and returns to Salzburg by way of Switzerland and Munich; Giovanni Paisiello settles in Naples; Antonio Salieri becomes the student and protegé of Florian Gassmann; Jan Václav Stich (Giovanni Punto) and four colleagues run away from their court positions to Prussia; Giovanni Battista Viotti is taken into the house of Prince Alfonso of Turin and given music lessons.

G. Institutional Openings:

Performing Groups: Anacreontic Society of London; Musikalische Gesellschaft (Kassel); Société de Musique (Beauvais)

Other: Drottningholm Palace Theater II (Stockholm); Leipziger Schauspielhaus (Stadttheater); Southwark Theater (Philadelphia); Wöchentliche Nachrichten und Anmerkungen

H. Musical Literature:

Bédos de Celles, François, L'Art du facteur d'orgues I
Blainville, Charles H., Harmonie théoretico-pratique
Dubreuil, Jean, Dictionnaire lyrique portatif
Flagg, Josiah, 16 Anthems to Which is Added a Few Psalm Tunes
Heck, John, The Art of Fingering
Lacassagne, Joseph, Traité général des elemens du chant
Lingke, Georg F., Die Sitze der musikalischen Haupt-Sätze in einer harten un weichen Tonart

Trydell, John, *2 Essays on the Theory and Practice of Music*

I. Musical Compositions:
Anfossi, Pasquale, *Fiammetta generosa* (opera)
Arnold, Samuel, *Harlequin Dr. Faustus* (opera)
Avison, Charles, *12 Concertos in 4 Parts, Opus 9*
Bach, Johann Christian, *6 Sinfonias, Opus 6*
Benda, George A., *Il buon marito* (opera)
Boccherini, Luigi, *6 String Trios, Opus 4*
    4 Cello Sonatas
Cannabich, Christian, *6 Symphonies, Opus 4*
    6 Symphonies for Large Orchestra
    6 Trio Sonatas, Opus 3
    L'amour espagnol (ballet)
    L'amour jardinier (ballet
Dittersdorf, Carl von, *6 Symphonies, Opus 1*
    Symphony in E-flat Major, Opus 8, No. 1
    4 Concertos for Violin and Orchestra
Duni, Egidio, *La clochette* (opera)
Galuppi, Baldassare, *La cameriera spiritosa* (opera)
    La pace tra la Virtù e la Bellezza (cantata)
Gassmann, Florian, *Achille in Sciro* (opera)
    Il viaggiatori ridicolo (opera)
    6 String Quintets
Giordani, Tommaso, *L'eroe cinese* (opera)
Gossec, François, *Les pêcheurs* (opera)
    6 String Trios, Opus 9
Haydn, Franz J., *Symphonies No. 16-20*
    Keyboard Concertos No. 2, 6, 7 and 9
    Divertimentos No. 8, 12-14
    Keyboard Sonatas No. 9-11
    La Canterina (opera)
    Cäcilienmesse in C Major
Haydn, Michael, *Rebekka als Braut* (opera)
Hiller, Johann A., *Der Teufel ist los* (singspiel)
Holzbauer, Ignaz, *Il guidizio di Salomone* (oratorio)
Insanguine, Giacomo, *Le quattro mal maritate* (opera)
Jommelli, Niccolò, *Vologeso* (opera)
    La critica (opera)
    Il matrimonio per concorso (opera)
    Mass in D Major
Monsigny, Pierre, *Aline, reine de Golconde* (opera)
Mozart, Wolfgang A., *6 Sonatas, K. 26-31, for Violin and Keyboard*
    Stabat Mater, K. 33c
    Kyrie in F Major, K. 33
Philidor, François, *Le nozze disturbate* (opera)
Piccinni, Niccolò, *La pescatrice* (opera)
    Il gran Cid (opera)
    La Molinarella (opera)
Richter, Franz X., *Concerto in G Major for Cello and Orchestra*
Sacchini, Antonio, *L'isola d'amore* (opera)
    La contadine Byarre (opera)
Sarti, Giuseppe, *Ipermestra* (opera)
Scarlatti, Giuseppe, *Armida* (opera)
Traetta, Tommaso, *Le serve rivali* (opera)
    Rex Salomone (oratorio)
Trial, Jean-Claude, *Ésopé à Cythère* (opera)

1767

World Events:
In the U.S., the New York Assembly is disbanded by the British Parliament for refusing to quarter British troops in private homes under the Quartering Act; the British Parliament also passes the Townshend Acts imposing new revenues on almost all importations to the colonies; the colonists retaliate by invoking a policy of non-importation of British goods; Daniel Boone makes his first exploration trip west of the Appalachian Mountains; the first planetarium in the New World is built in Philadelphia by David Rittenhouse; the second medical school in the New World is opened at King's College in New York; future President John Quincy Adams is born as is the popular general and future President Andrew Jackson. Internationally, the first Mysore War breaks out in India with the British forces fighting against the ruler of the Indian state of Mysore; the Jesuits and their Inquisition are expelled from the island of Sicily and from Spain; the Austrian government begins large-scale educational reforms, especially for the young; Burma invades Thailand, destroying its capitol.

Cultural Highlights:
The Düsseldorf Academy of Art is founded; the Italian Royal Academy of Science and Letters is founded in Mantua; Allan Ramsay becomes painter to King George III; Giambattista Piranesi is knighted by the Pope; Johann Gottfried von Herder publishes his *Fragmente über die neuere Deutsche Literatur*; Jean François Marmontel publishes his *Eléments de Littérature*. Births in the literary field include British novelist Maria Edgeworth, Dutch poet Jan Frederik Helmers, German poet and critic August Wilhelm von Schlegel and French novelist Benjamin Constant; deaths in the field of literature include British author Robert Paltock and Scottish poet Michael Bruce. Births in the world of art include French artists Anne Louis Girodet-Trioson and Jean Baptiste Isabey as well as Swiss artist Jacques Laurent Agasse; deaths include Italian artist Giovanni Battista Pittoni and French artist Hubert Drouais. Other highlights include:

Art: Daniel Nikolaus Chodowiecki, *Parting of Calas from His Dog*; John Singleton Copley, *Girl with Bird and Dog*; Thomas Gainsborough, *The Duke of Argyll*; Jean-Antoine Houdon, *St. Bruno*; Jean Baptiste Lemoyne, *Montesquieu*; Joshua Reynolds, *Lady Mary Bruce*; Joseph-Marie Vien, *Greek Girl at the Bath*; Benjamin West, *The Departure of Regulus*

Literature: John Dickinson, *Letter from a Farmer in Pennsylvania to...the British Colonies*; Hugh Kelly, *Memoirs of a Magdalen*; Johann Kasper Lavater, *Schweizer-lieder*; Jean François Marmontel, *Bélisaire*; Moses Mendelssohn, *Phädon*; Louis Sébastien Mercier, *L'Homme Sauvage*; Joseph Priestley, *History and Present State of Electricity*; Laurence Sterne, *Letters of Yorick to Eliza*; Johann J. Winckelmann, *Monumenti Antichi Inediti*

MUSICAL EVENTS

A. Births:

Feb 2	Franz Volkert (Boh-org)		Sep 8	Karl Lichtenstein (Ger-imp)
Feb 3	Francesco Basili (It-cm)		Sep 17	Henri M. Berton (Fr-cm)
Mar 13	Heinrich Domnich (Ger-hn)		Sep 20	José Nunes García (Bra-cm)
Apr 27	Andreas Romberg (Ger-cel)		Sep 26	Wenzel Müller (Aus-cm-cd)
May 25	Friedrich Eck (Ger-vn)		Oct 6	Gottlieb Graupner (Ger-cm)
May 25	Ferdinand Fränzl (Ger-vn)		Oct 21	Francesco Ruggi (It-cm)
May 26	Martin J. Adrien (Bel-bs)		Nov 11	Bernhard Romberg (Ger-cel)
Jul 31	Amélie Candeille (Fr-sop)		Dec 13	August E. Müller (Ger-org)
Aug 30	Christian Schwencke (Ger-cm)			Luigi Ascoli (It-ten)

B. Deaths:

Jan 3	Luca Antonio Predieri (It-cm)	Jun 25	George P. Telemann (Ger-cm)
Jan 9	Francesca Bertolli (It-alto)	Jul 3	Matthew Dubourg (Br-vn-cd)
Jan 25	Johann C. Ritter (Ger-org)	Aug 9	Per Brant (Swe-vn-cm)
Mar 18	Thaddäus F. Lipowsky (Ger-cm)	Aug 28	Johann Schobert (Ger-hps)
Apr 5	James Grassineau (Br-mus)	Sep 2	Juan F. de Iribarren (Sp-cm)
May 8	Thomas Johnston (Am-org.m)	Oct 22	Johann Haffner (Ger-pub)
Jun 24	Johan Freithoff (Nor-vn)		

C. Debuts:

Other - Louise Rosalie Dugazon (Berlin--as ballerina), Elizabeth Ann Linley (London), Gertrud Mara (Dresden)

D. New Positions:

Conductors: Louis Joseph Francoeur (Paris Opera), Antonio Gaetano Pampari (maestro di cappella, Urbina Cathedral), Gaetano Pugnani (King's Theater, London), Luigi A. Sabbatini (maestro di cappella, S. Barnaba, Marino), Jean-Claude Trial (Paris Opera), Francesco Uttini (Stockholm Opera)

Others: Pierre Montan Berton (manager, Paris Opera), Christian Weinlig (organ, Leipzig)

E. Prizes and Honors:

Honors: Francesco A. Uttini (Master of the King's Music, Sweden)

F. Biographical Highlights:

Felice Alessandri marries singer Maria Lavinia Guadagni; Thomas Arne begins work with the Noblemen and Gentlemen's Catch Club in London; John Beard retires from active music life because of increasing deafness; Charles Burney marries his second wife; João de Sousa Carvalho joins the Brotherhood of St. Cecilia; Jean Baptiste Davaux goes to Paris and takes on several non-musical positions including one with the government; Johann Nikolaus Forkel begins two years of study at Göttingen; Giuseppe Gazzaniga studies with Piccinni; André Grétry arrives in Paris to seek his musical fortune; Pietro Alessandro Guglielmi goes to England for a five-year stay of writing and conducting operas; Wolfgang Amadeus Mozart visits Vienna where he and his sister contract small pox; Jean Jacques Rousseau returns to Paris; Johann Schobert and his family all die from eating poisonous mushrooms.

G. Institutional Openings:

Performing Groups: Opera Velha (Rio de Janeiro); St. Cecilia Society of Ratisbon; Venice Opera Co.

Other: Longman and Broderip, Music Publishers (London); Old American Co. (N.Y.); Joshua Shudi, Harpsichord Maker (London)

H. Musical Literature:

Arnold, John, *The Essex Harmony*
Blainville, Charles, *Histoire générale, critique et philologique de la musique*
Dressler, Ernst, *Fragmente einiger Gedanken des musikalischen Zuschauers*
Dubreuil, Jean, *Manuel harmonique*
Hopkinson, Francis, *The Psalms of David*
Petri, Johann S., *Anleitung zur praktischen Musik*
Rousseau, Jean-Jacques, *Dictionnaire de Musique*
Sorge, Georg A., *Anleitung zur Fantasie*
Tartini, Giuseppe, *De' principi dell'armonia musicale contenuta nel diatonico genere*
Testori, Carlo G., *La musica raggionata*
Viale, Giuseppe, *L'arbre généalogique de l'harmonie*

I. Musical Compositions:

Abel, Carl F., *6 Symphonies, Opus 7*
Adlgasser, Anton, *La Nitteti* (opera)
Alessandri, Felice, *Ezio* (opera)
    Il matrimonio per concorso (opera)
Anfossi, Pasquale, *I matrimonio per dispetto* (opera)
Arne, Michael, *Cymon* (opera)
Arnold, Samuel, *The Cure of Saul* (oratorio)
Bach, Johann Christian, *Carattaco* (opera)
Cannabich, Christian, *6 Symphonies, Opus 4*
    Mirtil et Amarilis (ballet)
    L'enlèvement de Prosperine (ballet)
Dittersdorf, Carl von, *6 Symphonies, Opus 4*
    Symphony in B-flat Major, Opus 8, No. 2
    Das Reich der toten (opera)
Gassmann, Florian, *L'amore artigiano* (opera)
    Amore e Psyche (opera)
Giordani, Tommaso, *Phyllis at Court* (opera)
    Isaac (oratorio)
Gluck, Christoph W., *Alceste* (opera)
    Il prologo (opera)
Gossec, François, *Toinon et Toinette* (opera)
    Le double déguisement (opera)
Grétry, André, *Isabelle et Gertrude* (opera)
Hasse, Johann A., *Partenope* (opera)
Haydn, Franz J., *Symphony No. 35 in B-flat Major*
    Keyboard Concerto No. 5 in G Major
    Divertimento In E-flat Major for Horn, Violin and Cello
    Stabat Mater in G Minor
Hiller, Johann A., *Die Muse* (singspiel)
    Lottchen am Hofe (opera)
Jommelli, Niccolò, *La Semiramide in Bernesco* (opera)
Mozart, Wolfgang A., *Symphony No. 6 and 7, K. 43 and 45*
    Symphony (No. 43) in F Major, K. 76
    6 Divertimentos, K. 41a
    Piano Concertos No. 1-4 (based on previous works)
    Organ Sonatas No. 1-3
    Grabmusik, K. 42 (cantata)
    Die Schuldigkeit des ersten Gebots (sacred drama)
    Apollo et Hyacinthus (intermezzo)
Mysliveček, Josef, *Farnace* (opera)
    Il Bellerofonte (opera)
    Il trionfo di Clelia (opera)
Naumann, Johann G., *L'Achille in Sciro* (opera)
    Alessandro nelle Indie (opera)
Paisiello, Giovanni, *L'idolo cinese* (opera)
    Lucio Papirio dittatore (opera)
    Il marchese Tulipano (opera)
Philidor, François, *Ernelinde* (opera)
Piccinni, Niccolò, *La finta baronessa* (opera)
Richter, Franz X., *6 Symphonies, Opus 7*
    Periodic Overture No. 18
Sacchini, Antonio, *L'Olimpiade* (opera)
Talon, Pierre, *6 Symphonies, Opus 5*
Telemann, Georg P., *Passion According to St. Mark II*
Tozzi, Antonio, *Il re pastore* (opera)
Traetta, Tommaso, *Siroe re di Persia* (opera)

1768

World Events:
In the U.S., the Regulator Movement seeking tax reform from the British Parliament is founded in North Carolina while unrest continues to mount in all of the colonies against the Townshend Acts; the Massachusetts Assembly is dismissed en masse by the British Parliament for ignoring the tax collections required by Parliament and for refusing to honor the Quartering Act; a treaty concluded between the British and the Cherokee Indians pushes the Virginia Territory westward; the first medical students graduate from the Philadelphia College Medical School; the New York Chamber of Commerce becomes the first in the New World. Internationally, Turkey declares war on Russia to begin a century of on-and-off warfare between the two powers, primarily over control of the Dardanelles; Russia sends in its troops to crush a Polish bid for independence; France buys the island of Corsica from Genoa; Captain James Cook begins the first of his world voyages.

Cultural Highlights:
The Royal Academy of Art is founded in London with Joshua Reynolds as its first President; Thomas Gray begins the teaching of history at the University of Cambridge; Étienne Bonnot de Condillac is inducted into the French Academy while Benjamin West, Richard Wilson, Johann Zoffany and Francesco Zuccarelli are inducted into the Royal Academy in London; Tobias Smollet leaves England for health reasons and decides to settle in Italy. Births in the field of literature include German author Johannes Daniel Falk and poet Zacharias Werner as well as French author François René de Chateaubriand; deaths in the literary field include British novelists Sarah Fielding and Laurence Sterne, Dutch poet Willem van Haren and Italian poet and librettist Carlo Innocenzo Frugoni. Births in the art world include German artist Joseph Anton Koch and sculptor Konrad Eberhard, Spanish sculptor José Álvarez y Cubero and British artist John Crome; deaths in the art field include Scottish artist John Runciman, Italian artist (Antonio) Canaletto, German artist Johann Joachim Winckelmann and French architect François de Cuvilliés. Other highlights include:

Art: Jacques A. Gabriel, *Petit Trianon* (Versailles); Anton Mengs, *Lamentation* (Madrid); Joshua Reynolds, *David Garrick as Kiteley*; Hubert Robert, *Temple and Obelisk*; Alexander Roslin, *Lady with the Veil*; Benjamin West, *Agrippina Landing at Brindisium* and *Venus Lamenting Adonis' Death*; Joseph Wright, *Experiment with the Air Pump*; Francesco Zuccarelli, *The Finding of Moses*

Literature: James Boswell, *Account of Corsica*; Louis Carmontelle, *Proverbes dramatiques I*; Oliver Goldsmith, *The Good-Natured Man*; Thomas Gray, *Poems*; Hugh Kelly, *False Delicacy*; Michel Jean Sedaine, *Gageure Imprévue*; Laurence Sterne, *Sentimental Journey*; Alexander Sumarokov, *The Usurer*; Horatio Walpole, *Mysterious Mother*; Christoph Wieland, *Idris und Zenide*

MUSICAL EVENTS

A. Births:

Feb 15 Sebastian Friedl (Ger-cel)	Sep 21 Louis E. Jadin (Fr-pn)
Feb 24 Jean Blaise Martin (Fr-ten)	Oct 20 Gaetano Crivelli (It-ten)
Mar 4 Johann F. Kind (Ger-lib)	Nov 24 Jean E. Pauwels (Bel-vn-cd)
Apr 12 Carolus A. Fodor (Hol-pn-cd)	Dec 6 Johann Henneberg (Aus-org-cd)
Apr 26 Pascal Fuentes (Sp-cm)	Francisco Cabo (Sp-org)
May 21 Guillaume Kennis (Bel-vn)	Margarethe Danzi (Ger-sop)
Jul 6 Johann G. Backofen (Ger-hp)	Xavier Desargus (Fr-hp)
Aug 10 Johann M. Vogl (Aus-bar)	Friedrich Hiller (Ger-vn)
Sep 12 Benjamin Carr (Br-cm)	

B. Deaths:

Jan 2	Gregorio Babbi (It-ten)	Jun 6	Gregor Schreyer (Ger-cm)
Jan 28	John Wainwright (Br-hymn)	Jul 6	Johann Beissel (Ger-cm)
Mar 3	Nicola Porpora (It-cm)	Jul 11	José de Nebra (Sp-cm)
Mar 14	Vigilio Faitello (It-cm)	Oct 8	Pierre de Fournier (Fr-org)
Apr 2	Georg Donberger (Aus-org)	Oct 28	Michel Blavet (Fr-fl-cm)
Apr 7	Michel Mathieu (Fr-vn-cm)	Oct 31	Francisco Veracini (It-vn-cm)
Apr 26	Pascual Fuentes (Sp-cm)	Nov 1	Pierre van Maldere (Bel-vn)
Apr 27	Nicolas Bergison (Fr-cm)	Nov 29	Johann Albrecht (Ger-mus)
May 22	Joseph Majer (Ger-org)		

C. Debuts:

Other - Johann E. Dauer, Jean-Louis Duport (Paris)

D. New Positions:

Conductors: Carl Philipp Emanuel Bach (cantor, Johanneum and music director, Hamburg churches), Filippo Gherardeschi (kapellmeister, Duke of Tuscany), Johann Peter E. Hartmann (Copenhagen Royal Orchestra), Antonio Ripa (maestro de capilla, Seville Cathedral), Tommaso Traetta (kapellmeister, St. Petersburg), Ernst Wilhelm Wolf (kapellmeister, Weimar)

Educational: Antonio Sacchini (director, Conservatorio dell' Ospedaletto, Venice)

Others: Carlo Monza (organ, Milan Court), Paolo Morellati (organ, Vicenza Cathedral), Christian Schubart (organ, Ludwigsburg), Robert Wainwright (organ, Collegiate Church, Manchester)

E. Prizes and Honors:

Honors: Lucrezia Aguiari (Court Virtuoso, Parma), Carlo Monza (Accademia dei Pugni)

F. Biographical Highlights:

Johann Georg Albrechtsberger settles in Vienna; Elizabeth Anspach marries William Craven; Johann Baptist Baumgartner begins his career as a concert cellist; William Boyce resigns due to his increasing deafness and retires to Kensington; Anna Lucia De Amicis marries doctor Francesco Buonsollazzi and re-enters the opera stage; Egidio Duni along with Favart is pensioned off by the Comédie-Italienne in Paris; Karl Friberth marries soprano Maria Spangler; Baldassare Galuppi leaves Russia and returns to Venice to resume his position at St. Mark's; Tommaso Giordani moves back to London; Christoph Willibald Gluck buys a home in the Rennweg; Franz Joseph Haydn loses much of his music in a fire at the Esterházy estate; Michael Haydn marries Maria Lipp; José Mauricio begins theological studies at Coimbra University; Pierre-Alexandre Monsigny enters the service of the Duke of Orléans as majordomo; Wolfgang Amadeus Mozart again visits Vienna and receives from Joseph II a commission for *La Finta Semplice*; Alessio Prati goes to Naples for music study; Giuseppe Sarti returns to Copenhagen and resumes his duties as kapellmeister at the court; Giuseppe Tartini suffers a mild stroke; Giovanni Battista Viotti begins music study with Pugnani.

G. Institutional Openings:

Performing Groups: Helvetische Konkordiagesellschaft

Festivals: Birmingham Music Festival (England)

Other: Esterházy Opera House; Johann Götz, Music Publisher (Mannheim)

H. Musical Literature:

Adlung/Agricola, *Musica mechanica organoedi*
Adlung/Albrecht, *Musikalisches siebengestirn*

Davy, Charles, *Essay upon the Principles and Powers of Vocal and Instrumental Music*
Hayes, William, *Ancecdotes of the Five Music Meetings*
Heck, John, *A Complete System of Harmony*
Lambert, Johann H., *Sur la vitesse du son*

I. Musical Compositions:
Albrechtsberger, Johann, *Symphonies No. 1 and 2*
Alessandri, Felice, *L'Argentino* (opera)
    Arianna e Teseo (opera)
Arnold, Samuel, *The Royal Garland* (opera)
Bach, Johann Christian, *6 Keyboard Sonatas, Opus 5*
Bach, Johann C. F., *Symphonies No. 1-3*
Boccherini, Luigi, *6 Violin Sonatas, Opus 5*
Cannabich, Christian, *Acis et Galathée* (ballet)
    Roland furieux (ballet)
    Les filets de Vulcain (ballet)
Cimarosa, Domenico, *Mass in F Major*
Duni, Egidio, *Les moissonneurs* (opera)
    Les sabots (opera)
Galuppi, Baldassare. *Ifigenia in Tauride* (opera)
Gassmann, Florian, *La notte critica* (opera)
Giordani, Tommaso, *The Elopement* (opera)
Gossec, François, *Les agréments d'Hylas et Silvie* (pastorale)
Grétry, André, *Le huron* (opera)
Hasse, Johann A., *Piramo e Tisbe* (opera)
Haydn, Franz J., *Symphony No. 49, "La passione"*
    Cassations No. 8 and 9
    Keyboard Sonata No. 46 in A-flat Major
    Piano Trio (No. 14) in F Major
    Stabat Mater
    Lo speziale (opera)
Haydn, Michael, *Die hochzeit auf der Alm* (singspiel)
Hiller, Johann A., *Die liebe auf dem lande* (singspiel)
Holzbauer, Ignaz, *Adriano in Siria* (opera)
Jommelli, Niccolò, *Fetonte* (opera)
    La schiava liberata (opera)
    L'unione coronata (serenade)
Mozart, Wolfgang A., *Symphonies No. 7 and 8, K. 45 and 48*
    2 Symphonies, K. 45
    Missa Brevis, K. 49
    Bastien und Bastienne, K. 50 (operetta)
    La finta semplice, K. 51 (opera)
Paisiello, Giovanni, *Olimpia* (opera)
Philidor, François, *Le jardinier de Sion* (opera)
Piccinni, Niccolò, *Lo sposo burlato* (opera)
    La locandiera di spirito (opera)
    Il Napoletani in America (opera)
Richter, Franz X., *6 String Quartets, Opus 5*
Rodriguez de Hita, Antonio, *Briseida* (opera)
    Las Segadoras de Vallecas (zarzuela)
Sacchini, Antonio, *Artaserse* (opera)
Sarti, Giuseppe, *La giardiniera brillante* (opera)
    La calzolaia di Strasburg (opera)
Schwanenberg, Johann, *Antigono* (opera)
Traetta, Tommaso, *L'isola disabitata* (serenade)
    Amor in trappola (opera)
Uttini, Francesco, *Violin Trios, Opus 1*
Zingarelli, Nicolò, *I quattro pazzi* (intermezzo)

1769

World Events:
In the U.S., George Washington introduces the Virginia Resolves to the Virginia Assembly--the Colonial Governor retaliates by dissolving the entire Virginia Assembly; explorer Daniel Boone enters into the Kentucky Territory for the first time; San Francisco Bay is discovered by the Spanish in their exploration of California; Padre Crespi names their new Spanish colony in lower California Nuestra Señora la Rena de Los Angeles; Dartmouth College is founded in New Hampshire. Internationally, Poland is partitioned off by the super powers Prussia and Austria; the French forces take over control on the island of Corsica; N. J. Cugnot builds a steam driven vehicle; Richard Arkwright patents his Water Frame; the Wedgwood Ware Factory is founded; future French general and emperor Napoleon Bonaparte is born.

Cultural Highlights:
The Cignoroli School of Painting (the Academy of Verona) is founded with Giovanni Baptiste Cignaroli as its director; Jean Baptiste Pigalle receives the Order of St. Michael; portrait painter Joshua Reynolds is given an honorary doctorate by Oxford University; Jean Baptiste Huet is inducted into the French Academy. Births in the world of art include British artists Thomas Barker and Thomas Lawrence as well as French sculptor François Joseph Bosio; deaths in the field include German artist Johann Elias Ridinger and Italian artist Giuseppe Bazzani. Births in the literary world include German critic and author Johann F. Rochlitz, poet Christian August Eberhard and historian Ernst Moritz Arndt, French dramatist Louis Benoit Picard and poet Charles Julien de Chénedollé and Austrian novelist Karoline Pichler; deaths include British poet William Falconer and German poet Christian Fürchtegott Gellert. Other highlights include:

Art: Pompeo Batoni, *Joseph II and Leopold of Tuscany*; Jacques-Louis David, *Jacques Buron and Wife*; Jean-Honoré Fragonard, *The Study* and *The Love Letter*; Thomas Gainsborough, *Isabella, Countess of Sefton*; Jean-Baptiste Greuze, *Offering to Love*; Joshua Reynolds, *Miss Morris as Hope*; George Stubbs, *Lion Attacking a Horse*; Benjamin West, *Self-Portrait*; Joseph Wright, *An Academy by Lamplight*

Literature: Samuel Adams, et al, *An Appeal to the World*; Thomas Chatterton, *Elinoure and Juga*; Richard Cumberland, *The Brothers*; Johannes Ewald, *Adam and Eve*; Denis Fonvizin, *The Brigadier*; Johann von Herder, *Kritische Wälder*; Friedrich Klopstock, *Hermanns Schlacht*; Charlotte Lennox, *The Sister*; Gotthold Lessing, *Wie die Alten den Tod Gebildet*; Tobias Smollett, *Adventures of an Atom*

MUSICAL EVENTS

A. Births:

Mar 7	Josef A. Ladurner (Aus-cm)	Jun 24	Alexei Titov (Rus-cm)
Mar 13	Christian F. Wilke (Ger-org.m)	Jul 4	Louis de Persius (Fr-cm-cd)
Apr 12	Giovanni A. Perotti (It-cm)	Aug 30	Bonifacio Asioli (It-cm)
May 4	Charles Hague (Br-vn)	Oct 14	Friedrich Dulon (Ger-fl)
May 7	Giuseppe Farinelli (It-cm)		Maria Bland (Br-sop)
May 14	Johann C. Voigt (Ger-org)		Pietro Casella (It-cm)
May 30	Benedikt Hacker (Ger-cm)		Francesco Gnecco (It-cm)
Jun 1	Józef A. Elsner (Pol-cm)		Jean Jacques Grasset (Fr-vn)
Jun 14	Dominique Della Maria (Fr-cm)		Hyacinthe Jadin (Fr-pn-cm)
Jun 14	Jean Elleviou (Fr-ten)		Daniil Kashin (Rus-cm)

B. Deaths:

Oct 9	Marianus Königsperger (Ger-org)		Chevalier d'Herbain (Fr-cm)
Dec 6	William Felton (Br-org)		James Oswald (Scot-cm-pub)

C. Debuts:
Other - Francesco Benucci (Pistoia), Magdelena Heroux (Mannheim)

D. New Positions:
Conductors: Pedro Aranaz y Vidés (maestro de capilla, Cuenca Cathedral), Carl Ditters von Dittersdorf (kapellmeister, Johannisberg), François Giroust (maître de musique, Saint Innocents, Paris), Bernardo Ottani (maestro di cappella, S. Giovanni, Monte), Franz Xaver Richter (kapellmeister, Strasbourg Cathedral), Ignaz Vitzthumb (Grand Théâtre, Brussels).

Others: Antoine Dauvergne (co-director, Paris Opera)

E. Prizes and Honors:
Honors: Jean Baptiste Huet (French Academy)

F. Biographical Highlights:
Anton Cajeton Adlgasser marries his third wife, Maria Anna Fesemayr, a singer at the Salzburg Court; Esteban de Arteaga abandons the Society of Jesus in hopes of obtaining a position with Charles III of Spain; Isidore Bertheaume withdraws from active music life for six years; William Billings begins teaching choral singing in Boston; Luigi Boccherini moves to Madrid and becomes virtuoso to the Infante Luis; Dmitri Bortniansky receives a scholarship for study in Italy where he begins studying with Galuppi and other teachers; William Boyce is forced by increasing deafness to retire from active music life; Charles Burney receives his doctorate as well as his B.M. degree from Oxford; Jan Ladislav Dussek begins studying organ while studying in the Jesuit College in Iglau; Franz Joseph Haydn has his first music published; Niccolò Jommelli returns to Italy when the Stuttgart Court orchestra disbands; Vincenzo Manfredini leaves Russia to return to Italy; Wolfgang Amadeus Mozart leaves on a two-year Italian journey with his father; Pietro Nardini returns to Padua to care for an ailing Tartini; Christian Gottlob Neefe studies law at the University of Leipzig while carrying on with his music writing and study; Johann Baptist Vanhal accompanies Baron Riesch to Italy and begins a two-year stay; Joseph Franz Weigl moves to Vienna and begins playing in the Court Opera.

G. Institutional Openings:
Performing Groups: Composers Concerts (by Giovanni Gualdo in Philadelphia--first known series in the New World); Concerts de la Loge Olympique (Paris); Concerts des Amateurs (Paris)

Educational: Regia Scuola de Canto (Parma)

Other: Hôtel de Musique (Berne); Polytonal Clavichord (by J. A. Stein); Teatro Accademico (Mantua)

H. Musical Literature:
Altenburg, Johann, *Lebens-Umstände des Organisten Altenburg*
Bayly, A., *A Collection of Anthems Used in His Majesty's Chapel Royal*
Gibert, Paul-César, *Solfèges ou leçons de musique*
Gluck, Christoph W., *Preface to Alceste*
Martini, Giovanni, *Compendio della teoria de' numeri per uso del musico*
Trydell, John, *Analogy of Harmony*
Webb, Daniel, *Observations on the Correspondance between Poetry and Music*

I. Musical Compositions:
Alessandri, Felice, *Il re alla caccia* (opera)
Avison, Charles, *6 Concertos in 7 Parts, Opus 10*
Bach, Johann C. F., *Symphony No. 4 in E Major*
   Der Tod Jesu (oratorio)
Boccherini, Luigi, *6 String Trios, Opus 6*

      6 String Quartets, Opus 8
Cannabich, Christian, *6 Symphonia Concertantes, Opus 7*
      Céphale set Procrid (ballet)
      Renaud et Armide (ballet)
Cimarosa, Domenico, *Magnificat*
      Gloria patri
Dittersdorf, Carl von, *3 Symphonies, Opus 5*
Galuppi, Baldassare, *Il villano geloso* (opera)
      Tres Mariae ad sepulchrum Christi (oratorio)
      Flora, Apollo, Medoaco (cantata)
Gassmann, Florian, *L'opera seria* (opera)
      6 Quartets, Opus 1 (flute and strings)
Gatti, Luigi, *Virgilio e Manto* (cantata)
Giardini, Felice de', *Italian Hymn* (Come, Thou Almighty King)
Giordani, Tommaso, *The Castle Ode*
Gluck, Christoph W., *Le feste d'Apollo* (opera)
Gossec, François, *6 Symphonies for Large Orchestra, Opus 12*
      6 String Quartets, Opus 14
Graf, Christian, *6 Symphonies, Opus 9*
Grétry, André, *Lucile* (opera)
      Le tableau parlant (opera)
Guglielmi, Pietro, *Ruggiero* (opera)
      L'impresa d'opera (opera)
Haydn, Franz J., *6 Divertimentos, Opus 9, for String Quartet*
      Concerto No. 4 in G Major for Violin and Orchestra
      Symphonies No. 36 and 38
Holzbauer, Ignaz, *6 Symphonies in 8 Parts, Opus 3e*
Insanguine, Giacomo, *La finta semplice* (opera)
Monsigny, Pierre, *Le déserteur* (opera)
      La rosière de Salency (opera)
Mozart, Wolfgang A., *3 Symphonies, K. 66 (unnumbered)*
      Serenade No. 1 in D Major, K. 100
      4 Cassations No. 1 and 2, K. 62 and 63
      Missa Brevis in D Major, K. 65
      Mass in C Major, K. 66, "Dominicus"
      Te Deum in C Major, K. 141
      40 Minuets, K. 61g,h, 64, 103-105
      March in D Major, K. 62
Mysliveček, Josef, *L'Ipermestra* (opera)
      Il Demofoonte (opera)
Naumann, Johann, *La clemenza di Tito* (opera)
      La passione di Gesù Christo (oratorio)
Paisiello, Giovanni, *La serva padrona* (opera)
      Don Chisciotte della Mancia (opera)
Philidor, François, *L'amant déguisé* (opera)
Piccinni, Niccolò, *Demetrio* (opera)
      La finta ciarlatana (opera)
      l'innocenza riconosciuta (opera)
      Sara (oratorio)
Pugnani, Gaetano, *Nanetta e Lubino* (opera)
Rutini, Giovanni M., *La Nitteti* (opera)
Sacchini, Antonio, *Nicoraste* (opera)
Sarti, Giuseppe, *L'asile de l'amour* (opera)
Toeschi, Carlo, *6 Symphonies, Opus 6*
      3 Grandes Symphonies, Opus 8
      Concerto in B-flat Major for Violin and Orchestra

1770

World Events:

In the U.S., the so-called Boston Massacre takes place March 5--the British, under provocation, kill several colonists; Carpenter's Hall, a landmark in Philadelphia, is constructed; the first municipal college, the College of Charleston, is founded in South Carolina; the first mental institution in the colonies opens in Williamsburg, Virginia; the estimated population of the colonies is about 2,000,000; the first volume of Benjamin Franklin's *Autobiography* appears. Internationally, the Townshend Acts against the colonists are repealed by the British Parliament and Lord North becomes British Prime Minister; Edmund Burke publishes his *Thoughts on the Causes of the Present Discontents*; Austria reforms its elementary school system; Captain Cook explores New Zealand and Australia; the Russian Navy defeats the Turkish fleet; Marie Antoinette marries the French Dauphin.

Cultural Highlights:

John Trumbull publishes his *Essay on the Uses and Advantages of the Fine Arts*; John and William Langhorne publish their translation of Plutarch's *Lives*; Johann Wolfgang von Goethe enters the University of Strasbourg to continue law study; Gotthold Ephraim Lessing becomes librarian at the Wolfenbüttel Library; sculptor Thomas Banks is inducted into the Royal Academy in London. Births in the art world include American artist Henry Sargent, Danish sculptor Bertel Thorvaldsen and French artist François Gérard; deaths include Belgian sculptor John Rysbrack, Italian artists Giovanni Bettino Cignaroli and Giovanni Battista Tiepolo, French artist François Boucher, German sculptor Joseph Feuchtmayer, British artist Francis Cotes and Japanese artist Harunobu Suzuki. Births in the literary world include German philosopher Georg Wilhelm Friedrich Hegel and poet Johann Friedrich Hölderlin, British poet William Wordsworth, French author Étienne Pivert de Sénancour and Scotch poet James Hogg; deaths include British poet Thomas Chatterton and Portugese poet Domingo dos Reis Quita. Other highlights include:

Art: Saverio Dalla Rosa, *Mozart at the Keyboard*; Thomas Gainsborough, *Blue Boy*; Francisco de Goya, *The Flight into Egypt*; Pietro Longhi, *Bison*; Paul Revere, *Bloody Massacre*; Joshua Reynolds, *Lord Sydney and Colonel Dyke*; Giovanni Tiepolo, *St. Francis Receiving the Stigmata*; Benjamin West, *Artist's Wife and Son*; Johann Zoffany, *Bransby, Parsons and Watkins in "Lethe"*

Literature: James Beattie, *The Nature and Immutability of Truth...*; Michael Bruce, *Poems on Several Occasions*; Sébastien Chamfort, *Le Marchand de Smyrne*; Thomas Chatterton, *The Revenge*; Johannes Ewald, *Rolf Krage*; Oliver Goldsmith, *The Deserted Village*; Hugh Kelly, *A Word to the Wise*; Louis Sébastien Mercier, *L'An 2440*; Thomas Percy, *Northern Antiquities*

MUSICAL EVENTS

A. Births:

Feb 2	Giuseppe Naldi (It-bs)	Jun 4	James Hewitt (Br-cm)
Feb 10	Ferdinando Carulli (It-gui)	Jun 27	Aloys Mooser (Swe-org.m)
Feb 18	Johann C. Rinck (Ger-org)	Jun 27	José Virués (Sp-the)
Feb 19	Josef Bähr (Aus-cl)	Nov 8	Friedrich Witt (Ger-cel)
Feb 26	Anton Reicha (Cz-cm-the)	Nov 29	Peter Hänsel (Aus-vn)
Mar 15	William Gardiner (Br-mus)	Dec 16	Ludwig van Beethoven (Ger-cm)
Mar 23	Jan A. Vitásek (Boh-pn-cm)		Thomas Bellamy (Br-bs)
Mar 25	Karl F. Ebers (Ger-cm)		Charles H. Blainville (Fr-the)
Apr 19	Georg Schneider (Ger-hn)		Marie Dickens (Br-sop)
May 19	Antoine Glachant (Fr-vn)		August Duranowski (Pol-vn)
May 24	Ferdinand Fränzl (Ger-vn)		Samuel Webbe, Jr. (Br-cm)

B. Deaths:

Jan 10	Charles Dallery (Fr-org.m)		Oct 1	Louis Guillemain (Fr-vn)
Feb 26	Giuseppe Tartini (It-vn-cm)		Nov 17	Gian Francisco Majo (It-cm)
Apr	Pasquale Bini (It-vn)		Dec 10	Gottlieb Muffat (Aus-org)
Apr 19	Esprit J. Blanchard (Fr-cm)		Dec 30	John Broderip (Br-org)
Apr 20	Marie Camargo (Bel-bal)			Francesco Araja (It-cm-cd)
May 4	Christian Krause (Ger-cm)			Francesca Cuzzoni (It-sop)
May 10	Charles Avison (Br-cm-cri)			Jean Dumas (Fr-the)

C. Debuts:

Other - Maddalena Allegranti (Venice), Jean-Jerome Imbault (Paris), Pierre Leduc (Paris), Mary Ann Pownall (London), Luiza Rosa Todi (Lisbon)

D. New Positions:

Conductors: Daniel Dal Barba (maestro di cappella, Verona Cathedral), Antonio Boroni (kapellmeister, Stuttgart), Carl Ditters von Dittersdorf (kapellmeister, Johannisberg), Pierre Lahoussaye (Italian Opera, London), Stanisleo Mattei (maestro di cappella, S. Francesco, Bologna), Pietro Nardini (maestro di cappella, Florence), Gaetano Pugnani (Teatro Regio, Turin), Giuseppe Sarti (Danish Court Theater, second term)

Others: Nicolas Framery (editor, *Journal de Musique*)

E. Prizes and Honors:

Honors: Armand-Louis Couperin (Organist to the King, Paris), Carl Ditters von Dittersdorf and Wolfgang Amadeus Mozart (Knight of the Golden Spur)

F. Biographical Highlights:

Wilhelm Friedemann Bach moves his family from Halle to Brunswick; Anton Bemetzrieder moves to Paris and begins teaching music; Charles Burney begins his continental travels gathering material for his books; František Dussek settles in Prague and begins music teaching; Wolfgang Amadeus Mozart writes out Allegri's *Misere* from memory after hearing it performed at the Vatican and also gets to study with Padre Martini; Gaetano Pugnani returns to Turin to take up the concertmaster's position in the local orchestra; Jean Jacques Rousseau, back in Paris, takes up music copy work; Carl and Anton Stamitz go to Paris; William Tuckey conducts the first performance of Handel's *Messiah* in the New World; Giovanni Battista Viotti begins studying violin with Pugnani in Turin; Ignaz Vitzthumb and Louis Despièrrière licensed as co-directors of the Grand Théâtre in Brussels.

G. Institutional Openings:

Performing Groups: Liebhaber Konzerte (Berlin)

Festivals: Norwich Festival (England)

Other: Alessandri and Scattaglia, Music Publishers (Venice); Luigi Marescalchi, Music Publisher (Venice); B. Schotts Söhne, Music Publisher (Mainz), Jean Georges Sieber, Music Publisher (Paris); George Smart, Music Publisher (London)

H. Musical Literature:

Billings/Revere, *New England Psalmsinger*
Binns, John, *Dictionary of Musical Terms*
Daube, Johann F., *Der musikalische dillettant I*
Hawkins, John, *An Account of the Institution and Progress of the Academy of Ancient Music*
Heck, John C., *The Art of Playing the Harpsichord*
Holden, John, *An Essay towards a Rational System of Music*
Martini, Giovanni, *Storia della Musica II*
Roussier, Pierre, *Mémoire sur la musique des anciens*
Sacchi, Giovenale, *Della divisione del tempo nella musica nel ballo e nella poesia*

Williams, Aaron, *The Psalmody*

I. Musical Compositions:
Albrechtsberger, Johann, *Symphony No. 3 in D Major*
Anfossi, Pasquale, *Armida* (opera)
    Cajo Mario (opera)
Arne, Thomas, *The Ladies' Frolick* (operetta)
Bach, Johann Christian, *6 Symphonies, Opus 6*
    Gioas, rè di Guida (oratorio)
    Orfeo ed Euridice (opera)
Bach, Johann C. F., *Symphony No. 6 in C Major*
Boccherini, Luigi, *6 String Quartets, Opus 9*
    Cello Concerto in C Major
Cannabich, Christian, *Bacchus et Ariadne* (ballet)
    Angélique et Médor (ballet)
Clementi, Muzio, *6 Keyboard Sonatas, Opus 1*
    3 Keyboard Sonatas, Opus 2d
Dauvergne, Antoine, *La tour enchantée* (ballet)
Dittersdorf, Carl von, *3 Symphonies, Opus 5*
    3 Symphonies, Opus 6
    Il viaggiatore americano in Joannesberg (opera)
    Davidde penitente (oratorio)
Duni, Egidio, *Thémire* (opera)
Galuppi, Baldassare, *Amor lunatico* (opera)
Gassmann, Florian, *Ezio* (opera)
    La contessina (opera)
Giardini, Felice de', *6 Quintets, Opus 11, for Cembalo and Strings*
Giordani, Tommaso, *Il Padre e il figlio rivali* (opera)
Gluck, Christoph W., *Paride ed Elena* (opera)
Grétry, André, *Les deux avares* (opera)
    Silvain (opera)
    L'amitié à l'épreuve (opera)
Haydn, Franz J., *Keyboard Concerto No. 8 in G Major*
    Concerto No. 3 in A Major for Violin and Orchestra
    Keyboard Sonata No. 18 in B-flat Major
    Le pescatrici (opera)
Hiller, Johann A., *La Didone abbandonata* (opera)
    Cantata Profana
Insanguine, Giacomo, *Die Jagd* (singspiel)
    Der dorfbarbier (singspiel)
Jommelli, Niccolò, *Armida abbandonata* (opera)
Manfredini, Vincenzo, *Armida* (opera)
Mozart, Wolfgang A., *Symphonies No. 10 and 11, K. 74 and 84*
    Symphonies (No. 44, 45, 47), K. 81, 95 and 97
    String Quartet No. 1 in G Major, K. 80
    Mitridate (opera)
    Miserere in A Minor, K. 85
Mysliveček, Josef, *La Nitteti* (opera)
Piccinni, Niccolò, *Catone in Utica* (opera)
    Cesare e Cleopatra (opera)
Rinaldo di Capua, *I finti pazzi per amore* (opera)
Sacchini, Antonio, *Calliroe* (opera)
    L'eroe cinese (opera)
Salieri, Antonio, *Le donne letterate* (opera)
    L'amore innocente (opera)
Sarti, Giuseppe, *Soliman II* (opera)
Toeschi, Carlo, *Concerto in D Major for Violin and Orchestra*
    6 Concertos for German Flute and Orchestra

1771

World Events:

In the U.S., the North Carolina "Regulators" comprised of farmers from the backwoods do battle with the British troops over what they consider to be repressive taxes, under-representation in the councils and unjust laws but they are suppressed. Internationally, James Cook completes the first of his round-the-world voyages; Russia conquers the Crimea to the alarm of Prussia and Austria; Adolphus Frederick of Sweden dies and is succeeded by Gustavus II; Oliver Goldsmith publishes his masterwork *A History of England* and the first edition of the *Encyclopedia Britannica* goes on sale.

Cultural Highlights:

Johann Peter Wagner becomes court sculptor at Würzburg; Richard Cosway is taken into the Royal Academy in London; Johann Wolfgang von Goethe receives a license to practice law; Jacques Louis David wins the Second Prix de Rome in Art; Horace Walpole publishes his Volume 4 of his *Anecdotes of Painting*. Births in the literary field include American novelist Charles Brockden Brown, British novelist Walter Scott and poet James Montgomery, French poet and dramatist Louis Jean Lemercier and German poet Siegfried August Mahlmann; deaths include British poets Thomas Gray and Christopher Smart, French author Jean Baptiste d'Argens, Scottish novelist Tobias George Smollett and German author Christian Adolf Klotz. Births in the art world include French artist Antoine Jean Gros; deaths include Belgian artist Louis Michel Van Loo. Other highlights include:

Art: Jean Baptiste Chardin, *Self-Portrait*; Daniel Chodowiecki, *The Artist's Studio*; Jacques Louis David, *The Combat of Mars and Minerva*; Jean Honoré Fragonard, *The Progress of Love*; Ignaz Günther, *Pallas and Mars*; Joshua Reynolds, *Mrs. Abington as Miss Prue*; George Romney, *Mrs. Yates as the Tragic Muse*; Benjamin West, *Penn's Treaty with the Indians*; Johann Zoffany, *Life School of the Royal Academy*

Literature: Dormant de Belloy, *Gaston et Bayard*; José Cadalso y Vázquez, *Sancho García, Conde de Castilla*; Richard Cumberland, *The West Indian*; Friedrich Klopstock, *Oden*; Henry Mackenzie, *The Man of Feeling*; Thomas Percy, *The Hermit of Warkworth*; Jean Pompignan, *Odes Chrétiennes et Philosophique*; Tobias Smollett, *Expedition of Humphrey Clinker*; Phillis Wheatley, *Poems on Various Subjects*

MUSICAL EVENTS

A. Births:

Feb 24	Johann B. Cramer (Ger-pn)
Mar 1	Armand Trial (Fr-cm)
Apr 19	Gioseffo Catrufo (It-cm)
Apr 29	Matthaeus Stegmayer (Aus-lib)
Jun 1	Ferdinando Paër (It-cm)
Jun 17	August Bergt (Ger-cm)
Aug 22	Jan J. Rösler (Hun-cm)
Sep 5	Antonio Benelli (It-ten)
Sep 17	Johann A. Apel (Ger-mus)
Oct 1	Pierre M. Baillot (Fr-vn-cm)
Oct 21	Alexandre Choron (Fr-the)
	Giuseppe Festa (It-vn-cd)
	Francis Linley (Br-org)

B. Deaths:

Jan 23	Martin Berteau (Fr-cel)
Feb 20	Giovanni B. Mastini (It-org)
Mar 1	Isfrid Kayser (Ger-cm)
Mar 30	Anton J. Hampel (Ger-hn)
Jun 23	Jean Claude Trial (Fr-cm)
Jun 27	Antoine Fel (Fr-bs)
Sep	Pietro Auletta (It-cm)
Sep 4	Pietro Gnocchi (It-cm)
Oct 14	Franz X. Brixi (Cz-org)
Oct 27	Johann G. Graun (Ger-cm)
Nov 8	Joseph Gabler (Ger-org.m)
Nov 18	Giuseppe de Majo (It-cm)
Dec 20	Giovanni Gualdo (It-cm)
	Blasius Ugolinus (It-the)

C. Debuts:
   Other - Luigi Marchesi (Rome), Giovanni Battista Rubinelli (Stuttgart)

D. New Positions:
   Conductors: Hyacinthe Azaïs (Concert de Marseilles), Anton Laube (choirmaster, St. Vitus Cathedral, Prague), Jan Stefani (kapellmeister, Warsaw Court)

   Educational: Theodore Aylward (Gresham Professor of Music, Oxford), Charles Broche (organ, Académie des Beaux Arts, Lyons), Pasquale Cafaro (director, Conservatorio della Pietà, Naples)

   Others: Joseph-Lazare Audiffren (organ, St. Victor, Marseilles), Francesco Corbisieri (organ, Naples Royal Chapel), Justin Heinrich Knecht (organ and music director, Biberach), Johann von Königslow (organ, Marienkirche, Lübeck)

E. Prizes and Honors:
   Honors: Maxim Berezovsky, Carlo Monza and Josef Myslivecek (Accademia Filarmonica, Bologna), John Hawkins (knighted), Richard Woodward (honorary doctorate, Trinity College, Dublin)

F. Biographical Highlights:
   Maddalena Allegranti joins the Mannheim Court Opera; Franz Benda is appointed concertmaster of the orchestra of Frederick the Great of Prussia; Domenico Cimarosa leaves the Conservatory and studies with Piccinni; Giovanni Guadagnini moves his violin business to Turin; Johann Gottfried von Herder joins the Bückeburg Court and works with Johann Christoph Friedrich Bach on several of his operas; Antonio Lolli tours Italy and meets Mozart; Gertrud Mara leaves the Dresden Opera and joins the Berlin Court Opera of Frederick the Great; Marcos Antonio da Portugal enters the Seminário Patriarchal in Lisbon and studies music with Carvalho; William Selby moves to the U.S. and settles in Boston where he becomes organist at various churches including the King's Chapel; Johann Baptist Vanhal suffers from mental problems which causes him to lose his post in Dresden; Johann Baptist Wendling makes his first concert tour in Europe.

G. Institutional Openings:
   Performing Groups: Österreichischers Bundesverlag

   Educational: Johann A. Hiller Singing School (Leipzig); Swedish Royal Academy of Music

   Other: Accademia Filarmonica Modenese; Bath Assembly Rooms ("The Upper Room")

H. Musical Literature:
   Bayly, Anselm, *The Sacred Singer*
   Beattie, James, *The Minstrel I*
   Bemetzrieder, Anton, *Leçons de Clavecin et principes d'harmonie*
   Burney, Charles, *Present State of Music in France and Italy*
   Daube, Johann F., *Der musikalische Dillettant II*
   Ferandiere, Fernando, *Prontuario Músico para el instrumentista de Violín y Cantar*
   Hawkins, John, *General History of the Science and Practice of Music I*
   Kirnberger, Johann P., *Die Kunst des reinen satzes in der Musik...I*
   Tans'ur, William, *Melodia Sacra*

I. Musical Compositions:
   Anfossi, Pasquale, *Quinto Fabio (opera)*
      Il barone di Rocca Antica (opera)
   Arne, Thomas, *The Fairy Prince* (opera)
   Arnold, Samuel, *The Magnet* (opera)
   Boccherini, Luigi, *6 String Quintets, Opus 10*

   6 String Quintets, Opus 11
   6 Symphonies, Opus 12
   Cello Concerto in B-flat Major
Dauvergne, Antoine, *Le prix de la valeur* (ballet)
Dittersdorf, Carl von, *L'amore disprezzato* (opera)
Furlanetto, Bonaventura, *Moyses in Nilo* (oratorio)
Galuppi, Baldassare, *L'inimico delle donne* (opera)
   Nuptiae Rachelis (oratorio)
   Dialogus sacer (oratorio)
   Adam (oratorio)
Gassmann, Florian, *Il filosofo inamorato* (opera)
   Le pescatrici (opera)
Gazzaniga, Giuseppe, *Il Calandrino* (opera)
   La locanda (opera)
Giordani, Giuseppe, *L'astuto in imbroglio* (opera)
Giordani, Tommaso, *6 Quintets, Opus 1, for Harpsichord and Strings*
Grétry, André, *Zémire et Azor* (ballet)
   L'ami de la maison (opera)
Guglielmi, Pietro, *Le pazzie di Orlando* (opera)
Hasse, Johann A., *Ruggiero* (opera)
Haydn, Franz J., *Symphonies No. 42 and 43*
   6 Divertimentos, Opus 17, for String Quartet
   Salve Regina in G Minor
Haydn, Michael, *Requiem in C Minor*
Jommelli, Niccolò, *Ifigenia in Tauride* (opera)
   Achille in Sciro (opera)
Mondonville, Jean de, *Les projects de l'Amour* (opera)
Monsigny, Pierre, *Le faucon* (opera)
Mozart, Wolfgang A., *Symphonies No. 12-14*
   Symphony in B-flat Major (No. 42), K. 75
   Symphony in C Major (No. 46), K. 96
   Divertimento in E-flat Major, K. 113
   De Profundis Clamavi, K. 93
   Regina Coeli in C Major, K. 108
   Litany in B-flat Major, K. 109
   La Betulia liberata, K. 118
   Ascanio in Alba (opera)
Mysliveček, Josef, *Montezuma* (opera)
   I gran Tamerlano (opera)
   Adamo ed Eva (oratorio)
Neefe, Christian, *Die Apotheke* (opera)
Paisiello, Giovanni, *Artaserse* (opera)
   Gli scherzi d'amore e fortuna (opera)
Piccinni, Niccolò, *La Corsala* (opera)
   Le finte gemelle (opera)
   La donna di bell'umore (opera)
Pugnani, Gaetano, *Issea* (pastorale)
Rinaldo di Capua, *La donna vendicativa* (opera)
Sacchini, Antonio, *Ezio* (opera)
   Adriano in Siria (opera)
   Jephtes Sacrificium (oratorio)
Salieri, Antonio, *Armida* (opera)
   La moda (opera)
   Don Chisciotte alle nozze di Gamace (opera)
Sarti, Giuseppe, *La clemenza di Tito* (opera)
   La contadina fedele (opera)

1772

World Events:
In the U.S., Samuel Adams in Massachusetts forms the Committees of Correspondance with the sole intent of fomenting revolution within the colonies; financial control of the Government of Massachusetts is taken over by the Crown; the British revenue cutter *Gaspee* is burned by the colonists after it runs aground; Philip Freneau publishes his *Rising Glories in America*; Internationally, the Partition of Poland takes place between Russia, Prussia and Austria; the Papal Inquisition is abolished in France; James Cook begins his second round-the-world voyage; scientists D. Rutherford and J. Priestley, both working independently, discover the existence of the gas Nitrogen.

Cultural Highlights:
Benjamin West is made Painter to the King in London; Giovanni Domenico Tiepolo is taken into the Venetian Academy; Joseph Franciscus Nollekens is inducted into the Royal Academy in London; Joshua Reynolds becomes the Mayor of Plympton; Francesco Zuccarelli becomes the President of the Venetian Academy of Arts; Johann Zoffany is sent by King George III to Florence to study. In the field of art, British artist Edward Bird is born while French artist Louis Tocqué and German sculptor Johann M. Feuchtmayr die. Births in the literary world include German philosopher and poet Friedrich von Schlegel and poet Friedrich von Hardenburg (Novalis), Finnish poet Frans Mikael Franzen, Hungarian poet Sándor Kisfaludy, Irish poet Mary Tighe, British poet Samuel Taylor Coleridge and Greek poet Athanasios Christopoulos; deaths include American religious author John Woolman and Portugese poet Pedro Antonio Joaquim Correa Garção. Other highlights include:

Art: Louis Boilly, *St. Roche Healing the Plague-Stricken*; Jacques Louis David, *Apollo, Diana and the Children of Niobe*; Francisco de Goya, *Allegory of the Trinity*; Pietro Longhi, *Gentlemen in Green*; Charles W. Peale, *George Washington*; Joshua Reynolds, *Dr. Samuel Johnson*; George Romney, *Mr. and Mrs. Lindow*; Johann Zoffany, *Academicians of the Royal Academy*

Literature: Dormont de Belloy, *Pierre le Cruel*; Jacques Cazotte, *Le Diable Amoureux*; Hester Chapone, *Letters on the Improvement of the Mind*; Samuel Foote, *The Nabob*; Richard Graves, *The Spiritual Quixote*; Johann von Herder, *On the Origin of Language*; Barthélemy Imbert, *The Judgment of Paris*; Friedrich Klopstock, *David*; Gotthold Lessing, *Emilia Galotti*; Christoph Wieland, *Der Goldene Spiegel*

MUSICAL EVENTS

A. Births:

Jan 21	Franz von Destouches (Ger-cm)	Jul 25	Gottlob B. Bierey (Ger-cm)
Feb 3	Maurice Artôt (Fr-hn-cd)	Aug 15	Johannes Maelzel (Ger-inv)
Feb 22	Karl J. Wagner (Ger-ob-cd)	Sep 3	Nicola Tacchinardi (It-ten)
Feb 26	Casper Fürstenau (Ger-fl)	Oct 4	François L. Perne (Fr-mus)
Mar 27	Giovanni Liverati (It-ten)	Nov 21	Josef Triebensee (Boh-ob)
Mar 30	Jan Willem Wilms (Hol-cm)		Franz Cramer (Ger-vn)
Apr 1	Ignaz F. Mosels (Aus-mus)		Stephen Jenks (Am-cm)
May 11	Henri Jean Rigel (Fr-cm)		Giuseppe Mosca (It-cm)
Jul 11	Domenico Ronconi (It-ten)		John Pratt (Br-org)

B. Deaths:

Feb 13	Pierre C. Fouquet (Fr-org)	Apr 21	Marie J. Favart (Fr-sop)
Mar 11	Georg Reutter (Aus-cm)	Jun 15	Louis C. Daquin (Fr-org)
Apr 13	Giovanni Dreyer (It-cas)	Jul 24	Johann P. Möller (Ger-org.m)
Apr 19	Johann P. Kellner (Ger-org)	Aug 21	Alessandro Felici (It-hps)

Aug 21	Johann Giulini (Ger-cm)	Francesco Barsanti (It-cm)
Oct 8	Jean de Mondonville (Fr-vn)	Giulia Frasi (It-sop)
Dec 1	Jean A. Bérard (Fr-c.ten)	

C. Debuts:

Other - Franz Christian Hartig (Mannheim), Franziska Lebrun (Schwetzingen), John Mahon (London), Matteo Rauzzini (Munich), Joseph Boulogne Saint-Georges (Paris), Carl David Stegmann (Breslau)

D. New Positions:

Conductors: Domenico Fischietti (kapellmeister, Salzburg), Florian Leopold Gassmann (kapellmeister, Vienna), Friedrich Graf (kapellmeister, Augsburg Protestant Church and St. Anne's Gymnasium), Leopold Hofmann (kapellmeister, St. Stephen's, Vienna), Josef Schuster (kapellmeister, Dresden), Ernst Wilhelm Wolf (kapellmeister, Weimar)

Others: Johann Georg Albrechtsberger (organ and choir, St. Joseph's, Vienna), Pietro Maria Crispi (organ, S. Luigi dei Francesi, Rome), Johann Rose (organ, Quedlinburg Cathedral), Nicolas Séjan (organ, Notre Dame, Paris), Georg Joseph "Abbe" Vogler (chaplain, Mannheim Court)

E. Prizes and Honors:

Honors: Antonio Bianchi (ii) (Accademia Filarmonica, Bologna), Michael Esser (Knight of the Golden Spur)

F. Biographical Highlights:

Olof Ahlström enters the Academy of Music in Stockholm; Maddelena Allegranti begins a long career with the Mannheim Opera; Johann Christian Bach visits the Mannheim court; Charles Burney, traveling in the Low Countries, meets Christoph Willibald Gluck; Gioacchino Cocchi retires to Venice; Hieronymus Colloredo becomes the Archbishop of Salzburg; Wilhelm Cramer, after a great success in London, decides to settle there; Carl Ditters von Dittersdorf marries Nicolina Trink; Thomas Greatorex studies organ with Dr. Benjamin Cooke; Pietro Alessandro Guglielmi leaves London after five years and returns to Italy; Johann Adolf Hasse retires to Vienna; James Lyon accepts a pastorate in Maine; Etienne Méhul, at age ten, becomes the organist at the convent in Givet; Wolfgang Amadeus Mozart, after a brief Salzburg visit, returns to Italy; Ignaz Pleyel begins music studies with Haydn at Eisenstadt; Antonio Sacchini moves to London; Daniel Gottlob Türk enters the University of Leipzig; Nicola Antonio Zingarelli graduates from Naples Conservatory.

G. Institutional Openings:

Performing Groups: St. Petersburg Music Club; Wiener Tonkünstler-Sozietät (Haydn Sozietät in 1826)

Educational: Kerzelli Music College (Moscow)

Other: Barrel Organ (by Flight and Kelly); Celestina (patented by A. Walker); C. G. Ghera, Music Publisher (Lyons); Lemoine Music Publishers (France); Lyceum Theater (London); Melodika (by Johann Andeas Stein); William Napier, Music Publisher (London); Teatro dei Nobili Fratelli Prini (Pisa)

H. Musical Literature:

Corrette, Michel, *Method for Mandolins*
Francoeur, Louis J., *Diapason général de tous les instruments à vent*
Hiller, Johann A., *Anekdoten zur lebensgeschichte grosser Regenten und berühmter Staatsmänner*
Schröter, Christoph G., *Deutliche answeisung zum generalbass*
Tans'ur, William, *The Elements of Music Displayed*
Tiraboschi, Girolamo, *Storia della letteratura italiana*

I. Musical Compositions:

Albrechtsberger, Johann, *Symphony No. 4 in D Major*
Anfossi, Pasquale, *Alessandro nell'Indie* (opera)
    L'amante confuso (opera)
Arne, Thomas, *The Cooper* (operetta)
Bach, Johann Christian, *Themistocle* (opera)
    Endimione (cantata)
Bach, J. C. F., *Symphony No. 10 in E-flat Major*
Boccherini, Luigi, *6 String Quintets, Opus 13*
    6 String Trios, Opus 14
    6 String Quartets, Opus 15
Cannabich, Christian, *Les mariages de Samnites* (ballet)
    Medée et Jason (ballet)
Cimarosa, Domenico, *Le Stravaganze del Conte* (opera)
Dezède, Nicolas, *Julie* (opera)
Galuppi, Baldassare, *Montezuma* (opera)
    Gl'intrighi amorosi (opera)
    Debbora prophetissa (oratorio)
Gassmann, Florian, *I Rovinati* (opera)
    6 String Quartets, Opus 1
Giordani, Tommaso, *Artaserse* (opera)
Gossec, François, *6 String Quartets, Opus 15*
Haydn, Franz J., *Symphonies No. 44-47*
    6 Divertimentos, Opus 20, for String Quartet
    Missa St. Nicolai in G Major
Hiller, Johann A., *Der Krieg* (singspiel)
Insanguine, Giacomo, *Didone abbandonata* (opera)
Jommelli, Niccolò, *Cerere placata* (opera)
    Le avventure di Cleomede (opera)
    Mass in D Major
Manfredini, Vincenzo, *Artaserse* (opera)
Mozart, Wolfgang A., *Symphonies No. 15-21*
    3 Divertimentos, K. 131-133
    3 String Quartets, K. 155-157
    Piano Sonata in D Major, K. 381, for 4 Hands
    3 Church Sonatas, K. 67-69
    6 Minuets, K. 164
    Il sogno di Scipione (opera)
    Lucio Silla, K. 135 (opera)
    Litany in B-flat Major, K. 125
    Regina Coeli in B-flat Major, K. 127
Naumann, Johann, *Isacco, Figura del Redentore* (oratorio)
Neefe, Christian G., *Amors guckkasten* (operetta)
    Der einspruch (opera)
Paisiello, Giovanni, *Montezuma* (opera)
    La Dardane (opera)
Piccinni, Niccolò, *Ipermestra* (opera)
    Scipione in Cartagena (opera)
Pugnani, Gaetano, *Tamas Kouli-Kan nell'India* (opera)
Rodriguez de Hita, Antonio, *Missa del Pange Lingua*
Sacchini, Antonio, *Armida e Rinaldo* (opera)
    Vologeso (opera)
    Nuptiae Ruth (oratorio)
Salieri, Antonio, *La fiera de Venezia* (opera)
    La secchia rapita (opera)
    6 String Quartets, Opus 20
Sarti, Giuseppe, *Deucalion og Pyrrha* (opera)
Traetta, Tommaso, *Antigona* (opera)

1773

World Events:
In the U.S., the Tea Act is the latest tax to be passed by the British Parliament in April along with the so-called Coercive Acts; colonial reaction to the Tea Tax results in the "Boston Tea Party" in December when Massachusetts colonists dump British tea into Boston bay; the Virginia Congress joins the Committes of Correspondance in raising colonial resistance to perceived British injustices; Benjamin Franklin publishes his *Rules by Which a Great Empire May Be Reduced to a Small One*; George Rogers Clark begins laying out the city plans for Louisville, Kentucky; future President William Henry Harrison is born; Boston installs the first large scale street lighting system. Internationally, the British Parliament passes the Regulating Act to reform the British East India Company; the Jesuit order along with its Inquisition is expelled from the Holy Roman Empire and is temporarily dissolved by Clement XIV; several unsuccessful peasant revolts occur in Russia; future Austrian political figure Klemens von Metternich is born.

Cultural Highlights:
The Philadelphia Museum and the Charleston Museum of Natural History open their doors as does the Charleston Theater, the largest in the New World; James Barry enters the Royal Academy in London; James Boswell is taken into the London Literary Club; Claude Michel (Clodion) is admitted to the French Academy; Samuel Arnold receives a doctorate from Oxford; Johann Gottfried von Herder publishes his *Von Deutscher Art und Kunst.* James Monboddo publishes his *Origin and Progress of Language.* Births in the literary field include German poet Johann Ludwig Tieck, author Heinrich Wilhelm Wackenroder and Hungarian poet Mihály C. Vitéz; deaths include British authors Philip S. Chesterfield, John Hawkesworth and George Lyttelton and French poet and dramatist Alexis Piron. French sculptor François Frédéric Lemot is born while French artist Hubert François Gravelot and Italian architect Bartolomeo Francesco Rastrelli die. Other highlights include:

Art: Antonio Canova, *Eurydice*; John Copley, *Governor and Mrs. Thomas Mifflin*; Jacques Louis David, *The Death of Seneca*; Jean-Honoré Fragonard, *The Rendezvous*; Jean Baptiste Greuze, *The Broken Pitcher*; Jean-Antoine Houdon, *Catherine II of Russia*; Joshua Reynolds, *The Graces Decorating Hymen*; Giovanni Tiepolo, *Abraham and the Angels*; John Trumbull, *Rebekeh at the Well*

Literature: Gottfried A. Bürger, *Lenore*; John Byrom, *Collected Poems*; Philip Stanhope Chesterfield, *Letters to His Son*; Thomas Day, *The Dying Negro*; Johann Wolfgang von Goethe, *Götz von Berlichingen* and *Urfaust*; Oliver Goldsmith, *She Stoops to Conquer*; Albrecht von Haller, *Alfred*; John Home, *Alonzo*; Barthélemy Imbert, *Fables*; Friedrich Klopstock, *Messias IV*; John Trumbull, *The Progress of Dullness I*

MUSICAL EVENTS

A. Births:

Feb 1	Johann G. Arnold (Ger-cel)	Jun 3	Michael G. Fischer (Ger-cm)
Feb 15	Johann P. Schulz (Ger-cd)	Jun 10	Charles S. Catel (Fr-the)
Mar 7	Tommaso Marchesi (It-cd-cm)	Jul 23	Karl F. L. Hellwig (Ger-cm)
Mar 14	Pierre Hus-Deforges (Fr-cel)	Aug 29	Raphael Kiesewetter (Ger-mus)
Mar 15	François R. Gebauer (Fr-bn)	Oct 23	Pietro Generali (It-cm)
Mar 29	Charles N. Baudiot (Fr-cel)	Dec 7	Franz J. Lobkowitz (Hun-pat)
Apr 9	Arthur T. Corfe (Br-org)	Dec 24	Joseph Wölfl (Ger-pn-cm)
Apr 18	Josephina Grassini (It-alto)		Charles J. Ashley (Br-cel)
Apr 26	Margarete Schick (Ger-sop)		Matthew P. King (Br-cm)
May 21	August F. Donati (Ger-org.m)		

B. Deaths:

Apr 11   Carlo P. Grua (It-cm)
Apr 19   Florian J. Deller (Aus-vn)
Jul 12   Johann J. Quantz (Ger-cm)
Aug 19   Burkat Shudi (Swi-hps.m)

Nov 25   Carl Höckh (Ger-vn-cm)
Nov 30   Louis A. Legrand (Fr-org)
Johann L. Albrecht (Ger-cm)

C. Debuts:

Other - Giacomo Davide (Milan); Giovanni Giornovichi (Paris), Marie-Alexandre Guénin (Paris), Manuela Guerrero (Madrid), Martin Marsick (Paris), Carl Stenborg (Stockholm)

D. New Positions:

Conductors: Francois Joseph Gossec (Concerts Spirituels, Paris), Joseph Boulogne St. Georges (Concerts de Amateurs, Paris)

Others: John Alcock, Jr. (organ, St. Matthew's, Walsall), Charles Burney (organ, Oxford Chapel), Pierre Gaviniés (director, Concert Spirituels, Paris), Johann Wilhelm von Königslow (organ, Marienkirche, Lübeck), Johann Gottfried Vierling (organ, Stadtkirche, Schmalkalden), Christoph Martin Wieland (editor, *Der Teutsche Merkur*)

E. Prizes and Honors:

Honors: Ferdinando Bertoni (Accademia Filarmonica, Bologna), Jean Baptiste Cupis (baronet), Carl Ditters von Dittersdorf (ennobled by the Empress Maria Theresa in Vienna)

F. Biographical Highlights:

Pedro Aranaz y Vidés is ordained a priest; Jean Pierre Duport, at the invitation of Frederick the Great, moves to Berlin; Christoph Willibald Gluck moves with his family to Paris; Johann Adolf Hasse and his wife, mezzo-soprano Faustina Bordoni, leave Vienna and settle in Venice; Franz Joseph Haydn writes and performs his *Symphony No. 48* for the Empress Maria Theresa during her visit to the Esterhazy estate; Antonio Lolli goes to the Court of Catherine the Great in St. Petersburg where he soon becomes a favorite of the Empress; Wolfgang Amadeus Mozart tries for a position at the Viennese Court but fails to obtain it; George Joseph "Abbe" Vogler, sent by the Elector of Mannheim to study music in Italy, takes Holy Orders while in Rome.

G. Institutional Openings:

Performing Groups: New York Harmonic Society; Swedish National Opera (Stockholm)

Other: Innsbruck Redoutengebäude; Swedish National Theater (Stockholm); Teatro della Nobile Academia del Casino (Perugia); *Der Teutsche Merkur*; Christian Ludwig Weber, Music Publisher (St. Petersburg)

H. Musical Literature:

Bayley, Daniel, *New Universal Harmony*
Burney, Charles, *The Present State of Music in Germany, the Netherlands and the United Provinces*
Corrette, Michel, *Method for the Doublebass*
Daube, Johann F., *Der musikalische Dillettant III*
Hiller, Johann A., *Anweisung zur Singekunst...*
Kirnberger, Johann P., *Die wahren Grundsätze zum Gebrauch der Harmonie*
Scheibe, Johann A., *Über die musikalische Composition I*
Telemann, Georg M., *Unterricht in Generalbass-Spielen*
Watts, John, *Psalms of David Imitated*

I. Musical Compositions:

Abel, Carl F., *6 Symphonies, Opus 10*

Andre, Johann, *Der Töpfer* (singspiel)
Anfossi, Pasquale, *L'incognita perseguitata* (opera)
    Demofoonte (opera)
    Antigono (opera)
Bach, Johann C. F., *Die Kindheit Jesu* (oratorio)
    Die Auferstehung und Himmelfahrt Jesu (oratorio)
Boccherini, Luigi, *6 Flute Sextets, Opus 16*
    6 Flute Quintets, Opus 17
Cimarosa, Domenico, *La finta parigina* (opera)
Clementi, Muzio, *6 Keyboard Sonatas, Opus 2*
Dezède, Nicolas, *L'erreur d'un moment* (opera)
Dittersdorf, Carl von, *4 Symphonies, Opus 7*
    Symphony in E-flat Major, Opus 8, No. 3
    Harpsichord Concerto in B-flat Major
Galuppi, Baldassare, *La serva per amore* (opera)
Gassmann, Florian, *6 String Quartets, Opus 2*
    5 Trios for Flute, Violin and Bass
Gossec, François, *3 Symphonies for Large Orchestra*
Grétry, André, *Le magnifique* (opera)
    Céphale et Procris (opera)
Haydn, Franz J., *Symphony No. 50 in C Minor*
    Symphony No. 65 in A Major
    Piano Sonatas No. 19-24
    L'infedeltà delusa (burletta)
    Philemon und Baucis (opera)
    Acide II (opera)
Hiller, Johann A., *Die Jubelhochzeit* (singspiel)
Insanguine, Giacomo, *Arianna e Teseo* (opera)
    Merope (opera)
    Adriano in Siria (opera)
Monsigny, Pierre, *La belle Arsène* (opera)
Mozart, Wolfgang A., *Symphonies No. 22-27*
    Divertimento in D Major, K. 205
    Serenade in D Major, K. 185
    Concerto No. 5, K. 175, for Piano and Orchestra
    String Quartets No. 5-12, K157-160, 169-173
    String Quintet in B-flat Major, K. 174
    Mass in C Major, K. 167, "Trinitatis"
    Motet in F, K. 165, "Exultate, Jubilate"
    Missa Brevis in G Major, K. 140
Mysliveček, Josef, *Il Demetrio* (opera)
    Romolo ed Ersilias (opera)
Naumann, Johann, *Armida* (opera)
    Solimano (opera)
Neefe, Christian G., *12 Piano Sonatas I*
Paisiello, Giovanni, *Alessandro nell' Indie* (opera)
Philidor, François, *Le bon fils* (opera)
    Zémire et Mélide (opera)
Piccinni, Niccolò, *Il vagabondo fortunato* (opera)
Reichardt, Johann, *Amors Guckkasten* (operetta)
    Hänschen und Gretschen (operetta)
Sacchini, Antonio, *Tamerlano* (opera)
Saint-Georges, Joseph, *6 String Quartets, Opus 1*
Salieri, Antonio, *La locandiera* (opera)
Toeschi, Carlo, *6 Symphonies, Opus 7*
    3 Symphonies, Opus 10
Traetta, Tommaso, *Amore e Psyche* (opera)
Uttini, Francesco, *Thetis och Pelée* (opera)

1774

World Events:
In the U.S., the First Continental Congress meets in Philadelphia and draws up a Petition of Grievances to be sent to the London Parliament who in turn passes the "Intolerable Acts" to punish the colonists; Thomas Jefferson brings out his *Summary View of the Rights of British America*; the Port of Boston is closed and General Gage is appointed Governor of Massachusetts; colonial militia break into Fort William and Mary and carry off arms and ammunition; the Battle of Point Pleasant opens the Shawnee Territory in Ohio to exploitation by the colonists; the Quebec Act pushes the Canadian border down to the Ohio River causing concern on the part of several colonies who also claim the land. Internationally, the Treaty between Russia and Turkey gives Russia free use of the Black Sea and the Dardanelles; the British appoint a Governor-General for India; Louis XV of France dies and is succeeded by Louis XVI; Joseph Priestley isolates "dephlogisticated air" (oxygen) while Carl W. Scheele discovers the existence of chlorine.

Cultural Highlights:
Jacques Louis David receives the Prix de Rome in Art; François Xavier de Feller becomes editor of the *Journal Historique et Littéraire*; John Singleton Copley and Thomas Gainsborough both settle permanently in London; Thomas Warton publishes the first volume of his *History of English Poetry*. Births in the art world include German artist Casper David Friedrich and French artist Pierre Narcisse Guérin; deaths include French architect Jacques François Blondel and sculptor Jean-Baptiste Lemoyne and German artist Christian Wilhelm Dietrich. Births in the literary field include German poet and author Friedrich Wilhelm Riemer and British poet Robert Southey; deaths include British poet Oliver Goldsmith and Scottish poet Robert Fergusson. Other highlights include:

Art: Clodion, *St. Cecilia* (marble); Jacques Louis David, *Antiochus and Stratonice*; Henry Fuseli, *The Death of Cardinal Beaufort*; Francisco de Goya, *The Count of Miranda*; Ignaz Günther, *Pietà* (Nenningen); Carl G. Langhans, *Hatzfeld Palace* (Breslau); Pietro Longhi, *The Elephant*; Edward Penny, *The Virtuous Comforted* and *The Profligate Punished*; Joshua Reynolds, *Joseph Baretti*

Literature: Pierre Beaumarchais, *Mémoires*; Henry Brooke, *Juliet Grenville*; Charles Dibdin, *The Waterman*; Louise Épinay, *Les Conversations d'Émilie*; Johann von Goethe, *The Sorrows of Young Werther*; Friedrich Klopstock, *Die Deutsche Gelehrtenrepublik*; John Trumbull, *An Elegy on the Times*; William Whitehead, *Poems II*; Christoph Wieland, *Story of the Abderites*; John Woolman, *Journal*

MUSICAL EVENTS

A. Births:

Jan 24	Karl Möser (Ger-vn-cd)	Jun 18	Marc A. Cerin (It-vn.m)
Feb 16	Pierre Rode (Fr-vn-cm)	Oct 21	Friedrich P. Barth (Ger-ob)
Feb 24	Archibald Constable (Scot-pub)	Nov 12	Bernhard C. Natorp (Ger-m.ed)
Mar 5	Christoph Weyse (Den-cm)	Nov 14	Gaspare Spontini (It-cm)
Mar 20	John Braham (Br-ten)	Nov 15	William Horsley (Fr-org)
Apr 15	François Fayolle (Fr-mus)	Dec 20	Guillaume Gatayes (Fr-gui)
Apr 17	Václav Tomašek (Boh-pn-cm)		Franz Eck (Ger-vn)

B. Deaths:

Jan 20	Florian L. Gassmann (Boh-cm)	Aug 25	Niccolò Jommelli (It-cm)
Jan 30	Jean-Pierre Guignon (It-vn)	Oct 20	Charles LeClerc (Fr-vn-pub)
Jan 30	Franz I. Tuma (Boh-cm)	Dec 2	Johann F. Agricola (Ger-cm)
May	Joseph Baildon (Br-cm)		John Byfield, Jr. (Br-org.m)

C. Debuts:

Other - Louise Rosalie Dugazon (Paris--as soprano), William Mahon (London)

D. New Positions:

Conductors: Giuseppe Bonno (kapellmeister, Vienna), Carl F. C. Fasch (Berlin Court Opera), André da Silva Gomes (mestre de capela, São Paulo Cathedral), Andrea Lucchesi (kapellmeister, Bonn), Antonio Salieri (Italian Opera, Vienna), Antonio Tozzi (kapellmeister, Munich), Daniel Gottlob Türk (kantor, Ulrichskirche, Halle), Giovanni Zanotti (maestro di cappella, S. Petronio, Bologna)

Others: Johann Michael Demmler (organ, Augsburg Cathedral), James Hook (organ, Vauxhall Gardens), Pascal Taskin (Keeper of the King's Instruments, Paris)

E. Prizes and Honors:

Honors: Christoforo Bartolomeo Babbi (Accademia Filarmonica, Bologna), Christoph Willibald Gluck (Court Composer, Vienna), Georg Joseph "Abbe" Vogler (Knight of the Golden Spur)

F. Biographical Highlights:

Benedetta Emilia Agricola, following the death of her husband, is dismissed from the Berlin Court Opera Company; Wilhelm Friedemann Bach leaves Halle and decides to try his luck in Berlin; Franz Chrismann installs the new organ at St. Florian; Nicholas Marie Dalayrac is appointed a member of the elite Guard of Honor at Versailles but continues taking music lessons from Honoré François Langlé and André Grétry; Johannes Simon Mayr is admitted to the Jesuit College at Ingolstadt; Wolfgang Amadeus Mozart travels to Munich for the premiere of his *La finta giardiniera* and becomes acquainted with the music of Haydn; Venanzio Rauzzini makes his London debut; Johann Baptist Toeschi becomes concertmaster in the Mannheim Orchestra; Robert Wainwright receives his doctorate in music from Oxford University.

G. Institutional Openings:

Performing Groups: Pantheon Concerts (London)

Other: Johann André Publishing Co. (Offenbach); *Deutsche Chronik* (Augsburg); Christopher Ganer, Piano Maker (London); *Gentleman and Lady's Musical Companion*; Gray and Davison, Organ Builders (London); *The New Musical and Universal Magazine*; New Street Theater (Birmingham, England); John Preston and Son, Violin Maker and Publishers (London); Späth und Schmahl, Piano and Organ Builders (Regensburg); Tannenberg Organ (Holy Trinity Church, Lancaster, Pennsylvania)

H. Musical Literature:

Euler, Leonhard, *Lettres à une princess d'Allemagne*
Eximeno, Antonio, *Dell'origine e delle regole della musica...*
Gerbert, Martin, *De cantu et musica sacra*
Hiller, Johann A., *Anweisung zum musikalisch-richtigen Gesang*
Lambert, Johann H., *Remarques sur le Temperament*
Langdon, Richard, *Divine Harmony*
Löhlein, Georg S., *Violinschule*
Mancini, Giambattista, *Pensieri e riflessioni pratiche sopra il canto figurato*
Martini, Giovanni, *Esemplare ossia Saggio fondamentale pratico de contrappunto I*
Reichardt, Johann F., *Über die deutsche komische oper*
Tarade, Théodore, *Nouveaux principes de musique...*

I. Musical Compositions:
Alessandri, Felice, *Creso* (opera)
    La cameriera per amore (opera)
Anfossi, Pasquale, *Lucio Silla* (opera)
    La finta giardiniera (opera)
    Olimpiade (opera)
Bach, Johann Christian, *Lucio Silla* (opera)
    Amor vincitore (cantata)
Bach, Johann C. F., *Brutus* (opera)
Boccherini, Luigi, *6 String Quintets, Opus 20*
    6 Flute Quintets, Opus 19
Bonno, Giuseppe, *Il Giuseppe riconosciuto* (oratorio)
Cannabich, Christian, *Achille reconnu* (ballet)
    La fête marine (ballet)
Dittersdorf, Carl von, *Il tribunale di Giove* (opera)
Galuppi, Baldassare, *Tres pueri hebraei in captivitate Babylonis* (oratorio)
Giardini, Felice de', *Elfrida* (incidental music)
Giordani, Tommaso, *Antigono* (opera--adapted from Hasse)
Gluck, Christoph W., *Iphigénie en Aulide* (opera)
Gossec, François, *Sabinus* (opera)
    Symphony in F Major, "Tobias"
    La nativité (oratorio)
Haydn, Franz J., *Symphonies No. 51 and 52*
    Symphonies No. 54-58
    Symphony No. 60 in C Major
    Piano Sonatas No. 25-30
    The Return of Tobias (oratorio)
    Missa Sancti Josephi in E-flat Major
    Der Zerstreute (incidental music)
Haydn, Michael, *Divertimento in B-flat Major, Opus 92*
    Titus (opera)
Jommelli, Niccolò, *Il trionfo di Clelia* (opera)
    Miserere
Monsigny, Pierre, *Le rendez-vous bien employé* (opera)
Mozart, Wolfgang A., *Symphonies No. 28-30*
    Serenade in D Major, K. 203
    Concerto, K. 191, for Bassoon and Orchestra
    Dixit Dominus, Magnificat, K. 193
    Missa Brevis in F Major, K. 192
    Missa Brevis in D Major, K. 194
    Litany in D Major, K. 195
Mysliveček, Josef, *Antigona* (opera)
    Artaserse (opera)
Naumann, Johann, *Ipermestra* (opera)
    Le nozze disturbate (opera)
    Mass in A Major
Neefe, Christian G., *6 Piano Sonatas II*
Paisiello, Giovanni, *La frascatana* (opera)
    Il credulo deluso (opera)
    Andromeda (opera)
Piccinni, Niccolò, *Alessandro nelle Indie* (opera)
    Gli amanti mascherati (opera)
Sacchini, Antonio, *Nitetti* (opera)
Saint-Georges, Joseph, *2 Violin Concertos, Opus 3*
    Concerto, Opus 4, for Violin and Orchestra
Salieri, Antonio, *La Calamita de' Cuori* (opera)
Traetta, Tommaso, *Lucio Vero* (opera)

1775

World Events:
In the U.S., the Second Continental Congress meets in Philadelphia and Patrick Henry makes a speech against British tyranny and concludes with his famous statement, "Give me liberty or give me death"; the American Revolution begins with the Battles of Lexington and Concord and Bunker (Breed's) Hill and the capture of Fort Ticonderoga by American forces under Ethan Allen; the Congress appoints George Washington Commander-in-Chief of the colonial forces; Washington defeats the Britsh at Princeton but suffers defeat at Brandywine; the Congress approves a Navy and a force of Continental Marines; Benjamin Franklin is appointed first Postmaster General of the colonies; Daniel Boone leads the first settlers into the Kentucky territory; the Continental Congress approves the design for a U.S. flag. Internationally, the British Parliament imposes the New England Restraining Act on the colonies; the Peasant's Revolt over servitude takes place in Bohemia; Edmund Burke publishes his *Conciliation with America*.

Cultural Highlights:
Pierre Antoine Tassaert is made Court Sculptor to the court of Frederick the Great; Johann Heinrich Voss becomes editor of the *Musensalmanach*; Johann Wolfgang von Goethe, at the invitation of the Duke Carl Augustus, settles in Weimar; Francisco José de Goya is hired to design tapestries for the Madrid palace; George Crabbe begins the practice of surgery; John Ash publishes his *New and Complete Dictionary of the English Language*; Births in the art world include American artist John Vanderlyn, British artists Thomas Girtin, Joseph Mallard Turner and sculptor Richard Westmacott and French artist François Marius Granet; deaths include German sculptors Ignaz Günther and Johann J. Kändler, French artist François-Hubert Drouais and British architect Peter Harrison. Births in the literary field include British novelists Jane Austen, Matthew Gregory Lewis essayist and critic Charles Lamb and poet Walter Savage Landor, Scotch poet and author John Leyden, Italian poet Carlo Porta and German philosopher Friedrich Wilhelm Joseph von Schelling; dead is French dramatist Pierre Dormont de Belloy. Other highlights include:

Art: Jean Baptiste Chardin, *Self-Portrait with Eye Shade*; Clodion, *Satyr and Bacchante*; John Copley, *Mr. and Mrs. Ralph Izzard*; Nathaniel Hone, *The Conjurer*; Jean-Antoine Houdon, *Christoph Willibald Gluck*; Joshua Reynolds, *Miss Bowles and Her Dog*; George Romney, *Mrs Carwardine and Her Son*; Benjamin West, *Colonel Guy Johnson*; Johann Zoffany, *Self-Portrait*

Literature: Vittorio Alfieri, *Cleopatra*; Pierre Beaumarchais, *The Barber of Seville*; John Burgoyne, *The Maid of the Oak*; Louis Carmontelle, *Théâtre de Campagne*; George Crabbe, *Inebriety*; Charles Dibdin, *The Quaker*; Samuel Johnson, *A Journey to the Western Isles of Scotland*; Friedrich Müller, *Die Schafschur*; Richard Sheridan, *The Duenna* and *The Rivals*; John Trumbull, *M'Fingal I*; Mercy Warren, *The Group*

MUSICAL EVENTS

A. Births:

Jan 21	Manuel García (Sp-ten)	Oct 21	Giuseppe Baini (It-cd-mus)
Feb 19	Moritz Dietrichstein (Aus-cm)	Oct 27	Traugott Eberwein (Ger-vn)
Jun 13	Antoni Radziwill (Ger-pat)	Oct 30	Catterino Cavos (It-cm)
Jul 5	William Crotch (Br-org)	Dec 6	Nicolas Isouard (Fr-cm)
Aug 17	Felipe Libon (Sp-vn)	Dec 16	François Boieldieu (Fr-cm)
Aug 28	Edmeé Sophie Gail (Fr-voc)	Dec 28	João Bomtempo (Por-pn-cd)
Oct 6	Johann A. André (Ger-cm)		Richard G. Ashley (Br-vla)
Oct 15	Bernhard Crusell (Fin-cl)		Luigi Mosca (It-cm)
			Felice Radicati (It-vn)

B. Deaths:

Jan 15 Giovanni Sammartini (It-cm)
May 5 Karl J. Riepp (Ger-org.m)
May 7 Cornelius Dretzel (Ger-org)
May 9 Vittoria Tesi (It-alto)
Jun 11 Egidio R. Duni (It-cm)
Aug 6 Heinrich N. Gerber (Ger-org)

Sep 7 Johann Holzbogen (Ger-vn)
Nov 7 Johann Hildebrandt (Ger-org.m)
Nov 7 François Rebel (Fr-vn-cd)
Nov 27 Samuel Powell (Ir-pub)
Nov 29 Lorenzo G. Somis (It-vn)
Jean Dubreuil (Fr-pn)

C. Debuts:

Other - Harriett Adams (London), Katarina Cavalieri (Vienna), Louis J. Guichard (Paris), Vincenzo Righini (Parma)

D. New Positions:

Conductors: Christoforo Bartolomeo Babbi (Teatro Comunale, Bologna), Christian Cannabich (Mannheim Orchestra), Carlo Monza (maestro di cappella, Milan), Johann Friedrich Reichardt (kapellmeister, Berlin), Friedrich Wilhelm Rust (kapellmeister, Dessau), Paolo Scalabrini (kapellmeister, Copenhagen)

Educational: Giovanni Furno (theory, Naples Conservatory), Giuseppe Sarti (director, Conservatorio dell'Ospedaletto, Venice)

Others: Pierre-Montan Berton (general director, Paris Opera), Ernst Ludwig Gerber (organ, Sondershausen), Johann Siebenkäs (organ, St. Sebald, Nuremburg), Richard Wainwright (organ, Collegiate Church, Manchester), Robert Wainwright (organ, St. Peter's, Liverpool)

F. Biographical Highlights:

Thomas Attwood at age nine joins the Chapel Royal as a chorister; Ludwig van Beethoven receives his first music lessons from his father; John Behrent builds the first known piano in the New World; Maximus Berezovsky leaves Italy for Russia only to find all the good positions filled by Italians; Francesco Bianchi takes a job at the Italian Theater in Paris; Benjamin Cooke receives his doctorate from Cambridge; Caterina Gabrieli makes her London debut; Christoph Willibald Gluck goes to Paris for an opera production and returns to Vienna; Franz Joseph Haydn performs for the Archduke Ferdinand; Alessio Prati leaves Italy and takes up a composing career in Paris; Tommaso Traetta, in ill health, leaves Russia and goes to London; Georg Joseph "Abbe" Vogler returns to Mannheim and becomes vice-kapellmeister as well as spiritual advisor to the Elector.

G. Institutional Openings:

Performing Groups: Musikübende Gesellschaft (Leipzig)

Educational: Mannheimer Tonschule

Other: Gotha Court Theater; Hanover Square Concert Hall (London); Simon et Pierre Leduc, Music Publishers (Paris); Keith Prowse and Co. (London); John Snetzler, Organ Builder (London Branch); Robert Stodart Piano Co. (London)

H. Musical Literature:

Engramelle, Marie, *La Tonotechnie*
Gianotti, Pietro, *Le guide du compositeur II*
Gibert, Paul-César, *Mélange musical: premier recueil*
Lambert, Johann H., *Observations sur les sons des flûtes*
Laporte, Joseph de, *Anecdotes Dramatiques*
Manfredini, Vincenzo, *Regolo armoniche*
Martini, Giovanni, *Saggio fondamentale pratico di comtrappunto II*
Reichardt, Johann F., *Schreiben über die berlinische musik*
Roussier, Pierre, *L'harmonie pratique*
Sulzer, Johann G., *Allgemeine theorie der schönen künste*

I. Musical Compositions:
Alessandri, Felice, *La Novità* (opera)
  Alcina e Ruggero (opera)
André, Johann, *Erwin und Elmire* (singspiel)
Anfossi, Pasquale, *L'avaro* (opera)
  Didone abbandonata (opera)
Arne, Thomas, *Caractacus* (opera)
Bach, C. P. E., *The Israelites in the Wilderness* (oratorio)
Bach, Johann Christian, *6 Keyboard Sonatas, Opus 7*
  6 Quartets, Opus 8
  3 Symphonies, Opus 9
  6 Violin Sonatas, Opus 10
Bach, J. C. F., *Michaels Sieg* (cantata)
Benda, George A., *Medea* (opera)
  Ariadne auf Naxos (opera)
Boccherini, Luigi, *6 Symphonies, Opus 21*
  6 String Quartets, Opus 22
Bréval, Jean B., *2 Symphonies concertantes, Opus 4*
  6 Quatuors Concertants, Opus 1
Cannabich, Christian, *L'embarquement pour Cythère* (ballet)
Cimarosa, Domenico, *Il giorno felice* (cantata)
Dittersdorf, Carl von, *Lo sposo burlato* (opera)
  Il maniscalco (opera)
Furlanetto, Bonaventura, *Jerico* (oratorio)
  Melior fiducia vos ergo (cantata)
Galuppi, Baldassare, *Exitus Israelis de Aegypto* (oratorio)
  Venere al tempio (cantata)
Giardini, Felice de', *6 Violin Concertos, Opus 15*
  6 String Trios, Opus 17
Giordani, Giuseppe, *La fuga in Egitto* (oratorio)
Giordani, Tommaso, *3 Quartets for Flute, Violin and Cello with Cembalo*
  6 Chamber Concertos for German Flutes
Gossec, François, *Alexis et Daphné* (opera)
  Philémon et Baucis (pastorale)
Grétry, André, *La fausse magie* (opera)
Haydn, Franz J., *Symphony No 68 in B-flat Major*
  L'incontro improvviso (opera)
Mozart, Wolfgang A., *Serenade in D Major, K. 204*
  Violin Concertos No. 1-5
  Il rè pastore (opera)
  La finta giardiniera (opera)
  Missa Brevis in G Major, K. 220
  Missa Longa in C Major, K. 262
  Piano Sonata in D Major, K. 284
  Organ Sonata No. 6, K. 212
Mysliveček, Josef, *Ezio* (opera)
  Merope (opera)
Paisiello, Giovanni, *Il Demofoonte* (opera)
  Il grand Cid (opera)
Piccinni, Niccolò, *I vaggiatori* (opera)
  L'ignorante astuto (opera)
Reichardt, Johann, *Der Holzbauer* (opera)
Rousseau, Jean-Jacques, *Pygmalion* (opera)
Sacchini, Antonio, *Montezuma* (opera)
  Didone abbandonata (opera)
Saint-Georges, Joseph, *2 Violin Concertos, Opus 5*
Salieri, *La finta scema* (opera)
  Concerto for Organ and Orchestra

1776

World Events:
In the U.S., the Declaration of Independence is signed in August by the members of the Continental Congress; following the Battles of Trenton and Harlem, the colonial forces leave New York; the Stars and Stripes are first flown over Philadelphia; Nathan Hale is executed by the British as a spy; New Jersey becomes the first colony to grant women suffrage; the Phi Beta Kappa fraternity is founded at William and Mary College; Thomas Paine publishes his *Common Sense* and *The American Crisis*. Internationally, Russia and Denmark sign the Treaty of Copenhagen; Russia begins building a large-size Black Sea navy; Captain James Cook begins his third world voyage; reforms sought by the people in France are rejected by the King and the nobility.

Cultural Highlights:
The Albertini Art Collection is made public by the Archduke Albert of Sachsen-Teschen; the Johann Müller School of Engraving opens in Stuttgart; Jean Baptiste Regnault receives the Prix de Rome in Art; Gottfried von Swieten, appointed director of the Royal Library in Vienna, destroys many valuable manuscripts through lack of knowledge; William Tans'ur publishes his *The Beauty of Poetry*. Births in the literary field include British novelist Jane Porter, French novelist Marie Françoise Gay and Mexican novelist José Fernández de Lizardi; deaths include British author David Hume and French author Julie Jeanne de Lespinasse. Births in the art world include British artists Benjamin Barker and John Constable and German artist Gottlieb Schick; deaths include Russian artist Alexei Egorov, German artist George de Marsées and British artist Francis Hayman. Other highlights include:

Art: Antonio Canova, *Orpheus*; John Cozens, *Hannibal Crossing the Alps*; Gabriel Doyen, *La Peste des Ardents*; Jean-Honoré Fragonard, *The Washerwoman*; William Hodges, *Dusky Bay, New Zealand*; Jean-Baptiste Pigalle, *The Nude Voltaire*; Joshua Reynolds, *The Child Samuel* and *John the Baptiste*; Benjamin West, *Love in Three Elements*

Literature: Vittorio Alfieri, *Antigone*; George Campbell, *The Philosophy of Rhetoric*; William Combe, *The Diaboliad*; Hannah Cowley, *The Runaway*; Edward Gibbon, *The Decline and Fall of the Roman Empire I*; Johann von Goethe, *Proserpina*; Friedrich von Klinger, *Sturm und Drang*; Jakob Lenz, *Die Soldaten*; Johann M. Miller, *Siegwarts, eine Klostergeschichte*; Adam Smith, *The Wealth of Nations*;

MUSICAL EVENTS

A. Births:

Jan 24	E. T. A. Hoffmann (Ger-au-cm)	Mar 13	R. Ferreira da Costa (Por-the)
Feb 18	John Parry (Br-cd-cri)	Jun 1	J. George Schetky (Ger-cel-pub)
Feb 21	Vincenzo Lavigna (It-cm)	Aug 15	Ignaz X. Seyfried (Aus-cd-cm)
Mar 4	Robert Lindley (Br-cel)	Aug 16	Philipp Riotte (Ger-cd-cm)
Apr 8	Thaddeus Weigl (Aus-pub)	Oct 4	Charles Delezenne (Fr-acous)
May 1	Richard M. Bacon (Br-voc-au)	Nov 29	Ignaz Schuppanzigh (Aus-vn-cd)
May 5	Juan Bros y Bertomeu (Sp-cm)		Teresa Bertinotti (It-sop)
May 10	George T. Smart (Br-org)		

B. Deaths:

Apr 21	Filippo Finazzi (It-cas-cm)	Jun 27	Johann P. Stumm (Ger-org.m)
Apr 22	Johann A. Scheibe (Ger-cm)	Sep 20	Barbara Westenholz (It-sop)
Apr 24	Giuseppe Paolucci (It-cd)	Sep 26	Joseph Canavas (It-vn)
May 6	James Kent (Br-org)	Nov 22	Matthias Venta (It-cm-ed)
Jun 10	Leopold Widhalm (Ger-vn.m)		Giorgio Antoniotto (It-the)
Jun 12	Bartolomeo Felici (It-org)		Antonio Guerrero (Sp-gui)

C. Debuts:
> Other - Brigida Giorgi Banti (Paris), Marie Josephine Laguerre (Paris)

D. New Positions:
> Conductors: Joah Bates (Concerts of Ancient Music, London), Johann Gottlieb Naumann (kapellmeister, Dresden), Gaetano Pugnani (maestro di cappella, Turin), Joseph Schmittbauer (Karlsruhe)

> Others: Franz Vollrath Buttstett (organ, St. Jakob's, Rothenburg), Philip Hayes (organ, New College, Oxford), Thomas Norris (organ, Christ Church, Oxford), William Selby (Boston Trinity Church), Richard B. Sheridan (manager, Drury Lane Theater), Jean François Tapray (organ, École Royale Militaire), Daniel Gottlob Türk (organ, St. Ulrich, Halle)

E. Prizes and Honors:
> Honors: Johann Baptist Baumgartner (Swedish Academy), Francesco Bianchi (Accademia Filarmonia, Bologna), Georg "Padre" Martini (Roman Academy), Jean-Baptiste Rey (Court Musician to Louis XVI)

F. Biographical Highlights:
> Johann Christian Bach marries Cecilia Grassi; Charles Dibdin flees to France to avoid debtor's prison; Domenico Dragonetti, at age 13, becomes the principle bass player at the Venice Opera Bouffe; Louise Dugazon marries actor Jean Baptiste Dugazon for a short-lived marriage; Evstigney Fomin begins music study at the Academy of Fine Arts in St. Petersburg; Pietro Guglielmi settles in Naples; Franz Joseph Haydn loses more music in a second fire at the Esterházy estates; Francis Hopkinson resigns all his posts and becomes a member of the Continental Congress; Jean Baptiste Lebrun marries Marie Anne Vigée; Wolfgang Amadeus Mozart meets the Haffners and writes the *Serenade* for their daughter's wedding; Gasparo Pacchierotti, noted male soprano, leaves Naples for good; Giovanni Paisiello goes to St. Petersburg for an eight-year stay at the court of Catherine the Great; Niccolò Piccinni arrives in Paris and the controversy (the "War of the Buffoons") begins with the followers of Gluck's operatic reforms; Johann Friedrich Reichardt marries Juliane Benda; William Selby settles permanently in Boston and becomes an important musical influence in that city; Stephen Storace is sent to study violin at the Conservatorio di S. Onofrio in Naples.

G. Institutional Openings:
> Performing Groups: Bolshoi Opera Co. (Moscow); Concerts of Ancient Music (London); Concerts Spirituels (Leipzig); Opera Nova (Rio de Janeiro); Polish Opera Co. (Lvov)

> Other: Belfast Assembly Rooms; Bratislava Opera House; Societäts-Theater (Dresden); Teatro Coliseo (Havana); Théâtre de Rouen

H. Musical Literature:
> Azaïs, Hyacinthe, *Méthode de musique sur un nouveau plan*
> Bemetzrieder, Anton, *Traité de musique...*
> Burney, Charles, *General History of Music I*
> Hawkins, John, *A General History of the Science and Practice of Music*
> Hesse, Johann H., *Kurze doch hinlängliche anweisung zum General-Basse*
> Laporte/Chamfort, *Dictionnaire Dramatique...*
> Lolli, Antonio, *École du violon en quatuor*
> Mercadier, Jean B., *Nouveau système de musique théorique et pratique*
> Reichardt, Johann, *Über des Pflichten des Ripienviolinistens*
> Vogler, Georg, *Tonwissenschaft und Tonsetzkunst*

I. Musical Compositions:

André, Johann, *Der Barbier von Sevilien* (opera)
  Der alte Freyer (opera)
Anfossi, Pasquale, *Montezuma* (opera)
  La vera costanza (opera)
Arne, Thomas, *May Day* (operetta)
Bach, C. P. E., *4 Symphonies in 12 Voices*
Bach, Johann Christian, *Lucio Silla* (opera)
Bach, J. C. F., *Der Fremdling auf Golgotha* (oratorio)
Benda, George A., *Romeo und Julie* (singspiel)
Boccherini, Luigi, *6 String Sextets, Opus 23*
  Serenade in D Major
Bortniansky, Dmitri, *Creonte* (opera)
  Alcide (opera)
Cimarosa, Domenico, *I matrimoni in ballo* (opera)
  La frascatana nobile (opera)
Dittersdorf, Carl von, *La contadina fedele* (opera)
  Il barone di rocca antica (opera)
Furlanetto, Bonaventura, *David in Siceleg* (oratorio)
Galuppi, Baldassare, *Mundi salus* (oratorio)
  Moyses de Synai revertens (oratorio)
Gazzaniga, Giuseppe, *La fedeltà d'amore alla pruova* (opera)
Gossec, François, *Symphonie de Chasse (in D Major)*
  Les agre'ments d'*Hylas et Silvie* (opera)
Grétry, André, *Les mariages samnites* (opera)
Haydn, Franz J., *Symphony No. 61 in D Major*
  Symphonies No. 66 and 67
  La vera costanza (opera)
Holzbauer, Ignaz, *Günther von Schwarzburg* (opera)
Mozart, Wolfgang A., *Serenade in D Major, "Haeffner," K. 250*
  Serenade in D Major, "Notturna," K. 239
  2 Divertimentos, K. 247 and 251
  Piano Concertos No. 6 and 8, K. 238 and 246
  Concerto for 3 Pianos, K. 242
  Mass in C Major, K. 257, "Credo"
  2 Missa Brevis, K. 258 and 259
  Litany in E-flat Major, K. 243
Mysliveček, Josef, *Adriano in Siria* (opera)
  Isaaco Figura del Redentore (oratorio)
Naumann, Johann, *L'ipocondriaco* (opera)
Neefe, Christian, *6 Piano Sonatas III*
  Zemire und Azor (opera)
  Heinrich und Lyda (opera)
Paisiello, Giovanni, *La disfatta di Dario* (opera)
  Le due Contesse (intermezzo)
Piccinni, Niccolò, *La capricciosa* (opera)
Righini, Vincenzo, *Il convito di pietro* (opera)
Rutini, Giovanni, *Il finta amante* (opera)
Salieri, Antonio, *Daliso e Delmita* (opera)
  La Passione di Gésu Cristo
Sarti, Giuseppe, *Farnace* (opera)
  Le gelosie villane (opera)
Traetta, Tommaso, *La Merope* (opera)
  Germondo (opera)
  Symphony in D Major
Uttini, Francesco, *Aline Queen of Golconda* (opera)
Vachon, Pierre, *6 String Quartets, Opus 66*
Vanhal, Johann, *String Quartets, Opus 3*

1777

World Events:
In the U.S., the Stars and Stripes are officially adopted by the Continental Congress who flees when the British take over Philadelphia; General Washington spends a hard winter with his troops at Valley Forge; a colonial victory at Saratoga encourages the French to enter the conflict against the British; the Articles of Confederation are adopted by the Congress; the State Constitution makes Vermont the first state to outlaw slavery. Internationally, Spain and Portugal come to terms on their respective holdings in South America; James Cook explores Tasmania and vicinity; Joseph I of Portugal dies and is succeeded by Maria I and Pedro III; Lavoisier announces his discovery that air is basically nitrogen and oxygen.

Cultural Highlights:
Jean Antoine Houdon is taken into the French Academy; Friedrich Müller is appointed court painter at Mannheim; Gilbert Stuart becomes an apprentice to Benjamin West; Thomas Rowlandson settles in London and opens a studio. Births in the art field include German artist Philipp O. Runge, sculptor Christian Daniel Rauch and Italian sculptor Lorenzo Bartolini; deaths include French artist Charles J. Natoire and sculptor Guillaume Coustou II. Births in the field of literature include German poet Friedrich Heinrich de La Motte-Fouqué, poet and novelist Heinrich von Kleist and Scottish poet Thomas Campbell; deaths include German poet Friedrich Zachariä, French novelist Claude Crébillon and poet and dramatist Jean Baptiste Gresset, Russian dramatist Alexander Sumarokov, British actor and dramatist Samuel Foote and Swiss poet Albrecht von Haller. Other highlights include:

Art: Anonymous, *Mozart with the Golden Spur*; Thomas Gainsborough, *The Watering Place*; Francisco de Goya, *The Parasol*; Jean Baptiste Greuze, *La Cruche Cassee*; Francesco Guardi, *S. Giorgio Maggiore, Venice*; Jean Antoine Houdon, *Morpheus*; Joshua Reynolds, *Caroline Scott as "Winter"*; John Trumbull, *The Trumbull Family*; Benjamin West, *Saul and the Witch of Endor*

Literature: Vittorio Alfieri, *On Tyranny*; Antoine de Bertin, *Voyage de Bourgogne*; György Bessenyei, *The Philosopher*; James Cook, *A Voyage toward the South Pole and Round the World*; Henry Mackenzie, *Julia de Roubigné*; Hannah More, *Percy*; Clara Reeve, *The Champion of Virtue*; William Robertson, *History of America*; Richard B. Sheridan, *A School for Scandal*; Thomas Warton, *Poems*

MUSICAL EVENTS

A. Births:

Jan 6	Johannes Pressenda ((It-vn.m)
Jan 8	Filippo Traetta (It-cm)
Feb 9	Johann B. Logier (Ger-pn)
Feb 24	William Ayrton (Br-cm-cd)
Apr 18	Ludwig Berger (Ger-pn)
May 4	Charles Hanssens (Bel-cd)
May 28	Joseph H. Mees (Bel-cm-cd)
Jul 21	William Goodrich (Am-org.m)
Aug 28	Charles Hempel (Br-org)
Sep 20	R. Cuellar y Altarriba (Sp-org)
Oct 6	William Russell (Br-org)
Nov 5	Charles F. Kreube (Fr-vn-cd)
Nov 11	Johann Scheibler (Ger-acous)
Dec 16	János Fusz (Hun-cm)
	George Catlin (Am-inst.m)
	Stepan J. Davïdov (Rus-cm)

B. Deaths:

Jan 1	Emanuele Barbella (It-vn)
Jan 20	Simon Leduc (Fr-vn-pub)
Mar 1	George Wagenseil (Aus-cm)
Mar 26	Bernhardt Breitkopf (Ger-pub)
Apr 2	Maxim Berezovsky (Rus-cm)
Jul 27	William Hayes (Br-org-cd)
Aug 15	Pietro A. Gallo (It-cm)
Aug 17	Giuseppe Scarlatti (It-cm)
Aug 29	Andrea Basili (It-cm-the)
Sep 1	Johann E. Bach (Ger-law-cm)

Sep 25	Johann Lambert (Ger-the)	Nov 30	Jean Leclair, le cadet (Fr-vn)
Oct 13	Hatas Dismas (Cz-vn)	Dec 22	Anton Adlgasser (Ger-org)
Nov 22	Richard Woodward (Ir-cm)		Ernst Eichner (Ger-cm)

C. Debuts:
Other - Sarah Bates (London), Salomea Deszner (Warsaw), Paolo Mandini (Brescia), Antoinette Cécile Saint-Huberty (Paris)

D. New Positions:
Conductors: Antonio Boroni (maestro di cappella, St. Peter's, Rome), Franz Ignaz Kaa (kapellmeister, Cologne Cathedral), Pierre Lahoussaye (Concert Spirituel, Paris), Giacomo Rust (kapellmeister, Salzburg)

Educational: Philip Hayes (professor, Magdalen College)

Others: Olof Ahlström (organ, Marian Church, Stockholm), Charles Broche (organ, Rouen Cathedral), George Colman, Sr. (manager, Haymarket Theater), Laurent Desmazures (organ, St. Férréol, Marseilles), Michael Haydn (organ, Holy Trinity and St. Peter's, Salzburg), William Jackson (organ, Exeter Cathedral), Joseph Legros (manager, Concerts Spirituel, Paris), John Randell (organ, Trinity College)

E. Prizes and Honors:
Honors: Thomas Linley (Royal Society of Musicians)

F. Biographical Highlights:
Felice Alessandri, at the invitation of Joseph Legros, moves to a conducting job in Paris; Thomas Arne and his wife are reconciled only months before his death; Domenico Cimarosa marries Costanza Suffi, who dies only a year later; Franz Dusek meets the Mozart family and becomes a good friend of Wolfgang; Sébastien Erard manufactures the first known French-made piano; Christoph Willibald Gluck goes to Paris for the production of his opera *Armide*; Franziska Lebrun makes her London debut; Etienne Nicolas Méhul is sent to study with Wilhelm Hansen at the monastery in Lavaldieu; Pierre Alexandre Monsigny writes his last music and composes no more till his death; Wolfgang Amadeus Mozart, fired by the Archbishop of Salzburg, begins a tour with his mother and meets the Weber family in Mannheim; Johann Gottlieb Naumann, at the request of Gustavus II, reorganizes the Swedish Court music; Christian Friedrich Daniel Schubart, due to his political writings, is imprisoned by the Duke of Wurttemberg for ten years; Carl Stamitz leaves Paris for London as a traveling virtuoso.

G. Institutional Openings:
Festivals: Manchester Festivals (England)

Educational: Nobile Accademia di Musica

Other: Gesellschaft zur Beförderung des Guten un Gemeinnützen (Basel); Felix Meritis Society (Amsterdam); Norwich Pantheon

H. Musical Literature:
d'Alembert, Jean, *Reflexions sur le théorie de la musique*
Dressler, Ernst, *Theater-Schule für die Deutschen, das...Singe-Schauspiel betreffend*
Forkel, Johann N., *Über die Theorie de* musik...
Gerbert, Martin, *Monumenta veteris liturgiae alemannicae*
Heck, John C., *The Art of Playing Thorough Bass*
Jones, William, *Observations in a Journey to Paris*
Junker, Carl L., *Tonkunst*
Kraus, Joseph M., *Etwas von und über Musik fur Jahr 1777*
Marmontel, Jean F., *Essai sur les révolutions de la musique en France*
Wesley, Samuel, *Eight Lessons for Harpsichordists*

I. Musical Compositions:
André, Johann, *Die Bezauberten* (opera)
Anfossi, Pasquale, *Gengis-Kan* (opera)
    Il curioso indiscreto (opera)
Arne, Thomas, *Phoebe at Court* (opera)
Bach, Johann Christian, *6 Instrumental Quintets, Opus 11*
    6 Keyboard Concertos, Opus 13
Boccherini, Luigi, *6 String Quartets, Opus 24*
Cimarosa, Domenico, *Le tre Amanti* (opera)
    Il fanatico per gli antichi romani (opera)
    L'Armida immaginaria (opera)
Dezède, Nicolas, *Les trois fermiers* (opera)
Dittersdorf, Carl von, *L'Archifanfano, re de'matti* (opera)
    3 Viola Concertos
    Violin Concerto in D Major
Furlanetto, Bonaventura, *Israelis liberatio* (oratorio)
    Mors Adam (oratorio)
Giordani, Tommaso, *Aci e Galatea* (cantata)
Gluck, Christoph W., *Armide* (opera)
Grétry, André, *Matroco* (opera)
Haydn, Franz J., *Sinfonia in D Major*
    Il mondo della luna (opera)
Haydn, Michael, *Missa Sancte Hieronyni*
    Zaire (incidental music)
Homilius, Gottfried, *Die Freude der Hirten über die Geburt Jesu* (oratorio)
Insanguine, Giacomo, *Pulcinella* (opera)
    Le astuzie per amore (opera)
Manfredini, Vincenzo, *Olimpiade* (opera)
Monsigny, Pierre, *Félix, ou L'enfant trouvé* (opera)
Mozart, Wolfgang A., *Divertimento in B-flat Major, K. 287*
    Notturno in D Major, K. 28
    Concerto No. 9 in E-flat Major, K. 271, for Piano and Orchestra
    Quartet for Flute and Strings, K. 285
    Piano Sonata in C Major, K. 309
    Piano Sonata in D Major, K. 311
    Church Sonatas in C and G Major, K. 274 and 278
    Missa Brevis in B-flat Major, K. 275
    Motet, "Beatae Mariae Virgine", K. 273
    6 Contredanses, K. 462
Myslivecek, Josef, *Ezio* (opera)
    La Passione di Gésu Cristo (oratorio)
Neefe, Christian, *Die Zigeuner* (opera)
Paisiello, Giovanni, *Nitteti* (opera)
Piccinni, Niccolò, *Vittorina* (opera)
Raimondi, Ignazio, *Symphony: Les Aventures de Télémaque*
Sacchini, Antonio, *Esther* (oratorio)
Saint-Georges, Joseph, *Ernestine* (opera)
    2 Symphonie Concertante, Opus 9
    2 Symphonie Concertante, Opus 12
Salieri, Antonio, *La partenza inaspettata* (intermezzo)
    La passione de Gésu Cristo (oratorio)
Sarti, Giuseppe, *Medonte* (opera)
    Ifigenia (opera)
    Il militare bizarro (opera)
Toeschi, Carlo G., *6 Symphonies, Opus 12*
Traetta, Tommaso, *Telemacco* (opera)
    Il cavaliere errante (opera)

1778

World Events:

In the U.S., the Continental Congress signs a Treaty of Alliance with France who becomes the first country to recognize the new government; the British evacuate Philadelphia for fear of a French blockade; Savannah, Georgia, falls to the British; George Washington defeats the British at Monmouth and General Anthony Wayne occupies West Point; Philip Freneau publishes his *American Independence*. Internationally, France declares war on England and enters the conflict on the side of the American colonies; the War of the Bavarian Succession is fought between Prussia and Austria; Captain James Cook explores the western coast of North America after discovering the Sandwich Islands (Hawaii).

Cultural Highlights:

The Latour Free Art School is founded in Saint-Quentin; Giovanni Domenico Tiepolo becomes President of the Venetian Academy of Art; Henry Raeburn is able to devote full time to painting after marrying a rich widow; Thomas Warton publishes the second volume of his *History of English Poetry*. Births in the art world include American artist Rembrandt Peale, British artist John James Chalon and Scotch artist John Thomson; deaths include French sculptors Nicolas-Sébastien Adam and Jean Baptiste Lemoyne, British artist George Knapton, Belgian artist Laurent Delvaux and Italian architect Giambattista Piranesi. Births in the literary field include American poet and historian James Kirke Paulding, German poet Clemens Brentano and Italian poet and novelist Ugo Foscolo; dead is French philosopher Voltaire (François Marie Arouet). Other highlights include:

Art: Antonio Canova, *Daedalus and Icarus*; John Copley, *Watson and the Shark*; Henry Fuseli, *Oath on the Rütli*; Jean-Antoine Houdon, *Benjamin Franklin* (bust); Joseph Nollekens, *Venus Chiding Cupid*; Giovanni Battista Piranesi, *Vedute di Roma*; Giovanni Domenico Tiepolo, *Institution of the Eucharist*; John Trumbull, *Self-Portrait*; Benjamin West, *The Battle of La Hogue*

Literature: Fanny Burney, *Evelina*; Jonathan Carver, *Travels in the Interior Parts of America*; George Ellis, *Poetical Tales by Sir Gregory Gander*; Johann von Goethe, *Triumph der Empfindsamkeit*; Johann G. von Herder, *Stimmen der Völker in Lieder I*; Francis Hopkinson, *Battle of the Keys*; Ignacy Krasicki, *Mousiad* and *Monachomachia*; Friedrich Müller, *Fausts Leben I*; François Voltaire, *Irène*

MUSICAL EVENTS

A. Births:

Jan 5	Fortunato Santini (It-mus)	Jul 10	Sigismund Neukomm (Aus-cm)
Jan 13	Anton Fischer (Ger-ten-cm)	Jul 29	Carl Neuner (Ger-vn-cm)
Feb 14	Fernando Sor (Sp-gui)	Sep 3	Jean Auguste Kreutzer (Fr-vn)
Apr 6	Joseph Funk (Am-cm)	Sep 27	Karl Rungenhagen (Ger-cm)
Apr 10	William Hazlitt (Br-cri)	Nov 14	Johann N. Hummel (Ger-pn-cm)
May 8	Johann Gänsbacher (Aus-cm)	Dec 14	Nicolaus Kraft (Hun-cel-cm)
May 15	Benjamin Jacob (Br-org-cd)	Dec 29	Johann Hermstedt (Ger-cl)
Jun 14	Francesco Caffi (It-mus)		Domenico Barbaja (It-imp)
Jul	William F. Ayrton (Br-org)		Pauline Duchambge (Fr-pt-cm)
Jul 7	Antonio Pacini (It-cm-pub)		Joseph Kemp (Br-org)

B. Deaths:

Feb 15	Johann G. Görner (Ger-org)	Mar 27	Pasquale Pisari (It-bs-cm)
Mar	Lorenz C. Mizler (Ger-mus)	Apr 3	Francisco Corselli (It-cm)
Mar 5	Thomas Arne (Br-cm)	Apr 4	Georg A. Sorge (Ger-cm-the)
Mar 5	Giovanni Costanzi (It-cel)	Apr 7	Johann B. Kehl (Ger-cm)

Apr 29	Laurent Desmazures (Fr-org)	Oct 30	Davide Pérez (Sp-cm)
Jun	Johann H. Hesse (Ger-org)	Nov 26	Jean-Noël Hamal (Bel-cm)
Jun 1	Johann Gronemann (Ger-vn)	Dec 14	Giovanni Fioroni (It-cm)
Jun 26	Angelo A. Caroli (It-org)		Elisabeth Duparc (Fr-sop)
Aug 5	Thomas Linley, Jr. (Br-vn)		Georg Tzarth (Cz-vn-cm)
Oct 30	Quirino Gasparini (It-cm)		

C. Debuts:

Other - Ludwig van Beethoven (age 8), Wojciech Boguslawski (Warsaw), Jean Baptiste Bréval (Paris), Salomea Deszner (Warsaw), Elizabeth Mahon (London), Therese Teyber (Vienna)

D. New Positions:

Conductors: Giovanni Battista Borghi (maestro di cappella, Santa Casa, Loreto), Antonio Boroni (maestro di cappella, St. Peter's, Rome), Pietro Maria Crispi (maestro di cappella, Oratorio di S. Girolamo della Carità), Ignaz Fränzl (Mannheim Nationaltheater), Karl Hanke (kapellmeister, Brünn), Giuseppe Sarti (maestro di cappella, Milan Cathedral), Anton Schweitzer (kapellmeister, Gotha), Ignaz Umlauf (German Opera, Vienna)

Educational: Johann Nikolaus Forkel (music director, University of Göttingen)

Others: Leopold Kozeluch (music master, Archduchess Elisabeth, Vienna), Richard Langdon (organ, Bristol Cathedral), William Selby (organ, Stone Chapel, Boston)

E. Prizes and Honors:

Honors: Pehr Frigel (Swedish Royal Academy)

F. Biographical Highlights:

J. C. F. Bach visits London and leaves his son in Johann Christian's care; Ludwig van Beethoven's father, with the Mozart "wunderkind" in mind, lies about his son's age at his first recital appearance; George Benda resigns his court position in Gotha; Antonia Bernasconi makes her London debut; Salvatore Bertini becomes the maestro di cappella officially in Palermo after holding the post unofficially for thirty years; Christian Cannabich moves with the Court to Munich; Luigi Cherubini is given a grant by Duke Leopold II of Tuscany to study music with Sarti in Milan; Charles Dibdin, forced with all foreigners to leave France, returns to England; Christoph Willibald Gluck makes his last visit to Paris; Leopold Kozeluch gives up on law study and goes to Vienna where he becomes an important teacher and pianist; Franziska Lebrun makes her La Scala debut; Etienne Méhul is sent to Paris for further music study and while there meets Gluck; Wolfgang Amadeus Mozart loses his mother in Paris, but meets Johann Christian Bach in London.

G. Institutional Openings:

Performing Groups: Akademie-Konzerte (Mannheim); German National Singspiel Co.

Other: Astor and Co., Flute Manufacturers (London); Bonn Nationaltheater; La Scala Opera House (Milan)

H. Musical Literature:

Bemetzrieder, Anton, *Réflexions sur les leçons di musique*
Billings, William, *The Singing Master's Assistant*
Forkel, Johann N., *Musikalisch-kritischen Bibliothek I*
Hales, William, *Sonorum doctrina rationalis et experimentalis*
Junker, Carl L., *Betrachtungen über mahlerey, ton' und bildhauer kunst*s
Thomas, Christian G., *Praktische beiträge zur geschichte der Musik*
Trutovsky, Vasili, *Russian Folksongs II*
Vogler, Georg, *Churpfälzische Tonschule*

I. Musical Compositions:

Alessandri, Felice, *Calliroe* (opera)
André, Johann, *Der Alchymist* (opera)
Anfossi, Pasquale, *Ezio* (opera)
    La forza della donne (opera)
Bach, Johann Christian, *La clemenza di Scipione, Opus 14* (opera)
Benda, Georg A., *Der Holzhauer* (opera)
Boccherini, Luigi, *Cefalo et Procri* (ballet)
    6 String Quintets, Opus 25
    6 String Quintets, Opus 26
Cannabich, Christian, *Azakia* (opera)
    Das liebe des Cortes (ballet)
    6 Symphonies, Opus 10
Cimarosa, Domenico, *L'italiana in Londra* (opera)
    Il retorno di Don Caladrino (opera)
    Gli amanti comici (opera)
Giardini, Felice de', *Sappho* (incidental music)
Giordani, Tommaso, *Il re pastore* (opera)
    6 Keyboard Sonatas, Opus 15
Gluck, Christoph W., *Iphigénie en Tauride* (opera)
Gossec, François, *Annette et Lubin* (ballet)
    La fête de village (intermezzo)
    Symphonie Concertante No. 2 in F Major
Grétry, André, *Le jugement de Midas* (opera)
    Les trois âges de l'opéra (opera)
    L'amant jaloux (opera)
Haydn, Franz J., *Symphonies No. 66-69*
    Missa St. Johannis de Deo in B-flat Major
Haydn, Michael, *Abels Tod* (opera)
Hiller, Johann A., *Der Greis, Mann und Jüngling* (opera)
Insanguine, Giacomo, *Eumene* (opera)
Mozart, Wolfgang A., *Symphony No. 31, K. 297, "Paris"*
    Sinfonia Concertante in E-flat Major, K. 9
    7 Violin Concertos, K. 296, 301-306
    2 Flute Concertos, K. 313 and 314
    Concerto for Flute and Harp, K. 299
    2 Quartets for Flute and Strings, K. 285b, 298
    ·Piano Sonata in A Minor, K. 310
Mysliveček, Josef, *L'Olimpiade* (opera)
    La Calliroe (opera)
Naumann, Johann, *Mass in D Minor, "Pastoralmesse"*
    Amphion (opera-ballet)
Neefe, Christian, *Sophonisbe* (monodrama)
Paisiello, Giovanni, *Achille in Sciro* (opera)
    Lucinda e Armidoro (opera)
Piccinni, Niccolò, *Roland* (opera)
Sacchini, Antonio, *L'avaro deluso* (opera)
    L'amore soldato (opera)
Saint-Georges, Joseph, *Europa riconosciuta* (opera)
Salieri, Antonio, *Europa riconosciuta* (opera)
Sarti, Giuseppe, *Olimpiade* (opera)
    Scipione (opera)
    I Contrattempi (opera)
Shield, William, *The Flitch of Bacon* (operetta)
Smith, John S., *To Anacreon in Heaven* (tune, "Star-Spangled Banner")
Traetta, Tommaso, *Artenice* (opera)
    La disfatta di Dario (opera)
Winter, Peter, *Armida* (opera)

1779

World Events:
In the U.S., John Paul Jones, in the *Bonhomme Richard*, defeats the British frigate, *Serapis* off the coast of England, immortalizing Jones famous quote, "I have not yet begun to fight"; the British are defeated at Stony Point, New York by General Anthony Wayne; George Rogers Clark succeeds in taking over the Old Northwest Territory from the British; the University of Pennsylvania is founded and William and Mary College introduces student choice in classess. Internationally, the Treaty of Teschen ends the War of the Bavarian Succession; Spain joins France in warring against England; the British fight the Mahrattas in India; the first iron bridge is built over the river Severn in England; Samuel Crompton patents the Spinning Mule.

Cultural Highlights:
Marie Anne Elisabeth Vigée-Lebrun is appointed Court Painter to the Queen in Paris; John Singleton Copley is taken into the Royal Academy in London; Philip Morin Freneau begins a sea career as a privateer; Lorenzo da Ponte is banned from Venice for adultery. Births in the field of literature include Danish dramatist Adam Gottlob Oehlenschläger and Spanish author Serafin Estébanez Calderón; dead is British poet John Langhorne. Births in the field of art include American artist and poet Washington Allston, artist Thomas Birch and British artist Augustus Callcott; deaths include British artists Thomas Chippendale and Thomas Hudson, German artist Anton Raphael Mengs and French artist Jean Baptiste Chardin. Other highlights include:

Art: John Bacon, *Chatham Monument* (Westminster Abbey); Antonio Canova, *Daedalus and Icarus*; John Singleton Copley, *The Copley Family*; Jacques-Louis David, *St. Jerôme*; Ralph Earl, *William Carpenter*; Jean-Antoine Houdon, *Molière*; Pietro Longhi, *The Alchemists* and *Girl Spinning*; Francis Wheatley, *Lord Spencer Hamilton*; Joseph Wright, *Grotto in the Kingdom of Naples*

Literature: Johannes Ewald, *The Fishers*; Robert Fergusson, *Poems II*; Edward Gibbon, *Vindication*; David Hume, *Dialogues on Natural Religion*; Tomás de Iriarte y Oropesa, *La Música*; Ignacy Krasicki, *Fables and Tales*; Gotthold E. Lessing, *Nathan, the Wise*; Vincenzo Monti, *Saggio di Poesie*; Hannah More, *Fatal Falsehood*; Richard Sheridan, *The Critic*; Christian zu Stolberg, *Gedichte*

MUSICAL EVENTS

A. Births:

Jan 22	Stefano Pavesi (It-cm)	Jun 23	Johann Schiedermayer (Ger-cm)
Feb 5	François van Campenhout (Bel-vn)	Jul 21	Gottlob Wiedeban (Ger-org)
		Aug 17	Franz de Paula Rosa (Aus-cm)
Feb 17	Friedrich W. Riem (Ger-org)	Sep 8	Johann P. Schmidt (Ger-cm)
Feb 23	Johann Aiblinger (Ger-cm-cd)	Oct 15	August Haeser (Ger-cm)
Mar 1	Gottfried Weber (Ger-cm-the)	Oct 22	Jean Ancot, père (Bel-vn)
Mar 21	Alexis de Garaudé (Fr-voc)	Nov 20	Peter Turtchaninov (Rus-cm)
Mar 28	Angelo M. Benincori (It-vn)	Dec 19	Mariano Rodriguez de Ledesma (Sp-cm)
Mar 30	Carl F. Peters (Ger-pub)		
Apr 11	Louise Reichardt (Ger-sop)		George Bridgetower (Br-vn)
Apr 21	William Knyvett (Br-c.ten)		Auguste Leduc (Fr-pub)
May 28	Thomas Moore (Ir-pt-cm)		

B. Deaths:

Feb 2	Ignace Dobrzyński, Sr. (Pol-cm)	Feb 12	Hinrich P. Johnson (Ger-org.m)
Feb 2	Georg P. Kress (Ger-vn)	Feb 25	Johann G. Sulzer (Ger-mus)
Feb 7	William Boyce (Br-cm)	Apr 6	Ernst C. Dressler (Ger-ten)

Apr 6   Tommaso Traetta (It-cm)
Apr 18 François Granier (Fr-cel-cm)
Sep 9   Edmund Broderip (Br-org)
Nov 13 Johann Adam (Ger-cm)

Nov 25 F. Bédos de Celles (Fr-org.m)
Dec 15 M. Romero de Avila (Sp-cm)
Dec 19 Joseph de Laporte (Fr-mus)
        Domenico Annibali (It-cas)

C. Debuts:
Other - Gaetano Andreozzi (Rome) Luigi Bassi (age 13, Pesaro), Friedrich Ludwig Dulon (Berlin) Jan Ladislav Dussek (Mechelen), Anne-Marie Krumpholtz (Paris), François Lays (Paris), Aloysia Weber (Vienna)

D. New Positions:
Conductors: Bernardo Bittoni (maestro di cappella, Rieti Cathedral), Dmitri Bortniansky (Russian Imperial Church Choir), Luigi Braccini (maestro di cappella, S. Annunziata Monastery, Florence), Pierre Lahoussaye (Concerts Spirituel, Paris), Christian Gottlob Neefe (Grossmann-Hellmuth Co., Bonn), Vasili Pashkevich (St. Petersburg Theater), Giuseppe Sarti (maestro di cappella, Milan Cathedral), Jan Stefani (Warsaw Court Opera)

Educational: Daniel Gottlob Türk (music director, University of Halle)

Others: Thomas Dupuis (organ, Chapel Royal), Jan Ladislav Dussek (organ, Malines, The Netherlands), Johann Baptist Rauch (organ, Strasbourg Cathedral)

E. Prizes and Honors:
Honors: Friedrich H. Graf (Swedish Royal Academy), John Stanley (Master of the King's Music, London)

F. Biographical Highlights:
Joseph Beer begins touring the continent as a clarinet virtuoso; Ludwig van Beethoven begins futher piano lessons with Tobias Pfeiffer in Bonn; Dmitri Bortniansky leaves Italy after ten years to return to Russia and begin his career in choral conducting at the imperial court; William Crotch, age four, plays at Buckingham Palace for the King and Queen; Johann Ernst Dauer makes his Vienna debut; Brigida Giorgi goes to London for the season where she meets her future husband, dancer Zaccaria Banti; Christoph Willibald Gluck, suffering a severe stroke that leaves him partially paralyzed, retires from the music scene and returns to Vienna; Charles Incledon joins the British Navy; Antonio Lolli leaves Russia for a wasteful life of gambling in which he loses the fortune he gained in Russia; Gertrud Elisabeth Mara succeeds in escaping royal service in the Berlin Opera; Wolfgang Amadeus Mozart leaves Paris and returns to Salzburg.

G. Institutional Openings:
Performing Groups: Mannheim National Opera Co.; Russian Imperial Chapel Choir

Other: Erard Piano and Harp Manufacturers (Paris); James Harrison, Music Publisher (London); Mannheim National Theater; Teatro del Fondo (Naples); Teatro della Cannobiana (Milan)

H. Musical Literature:
Alcock, John, *An Instructive and Entertaining Companion*
Amiot, Jean Joseph, *Mémoire sur la musique des Chinois*
Bemetzreider, Anton, *Le Tolérantisme musical*
Billings, William, *Music in Miniature*
Chabanon, Michel de, *Observations sur la musique...*
Cowper/Newton, *Olney Hymns*
Kirnberger, Johann, *Die Kunst der reinen Satzes in der Musik...II*
Law, Andrew, *Select Harmony*
Smith, John, *Collection of English Songs, c. 1500*
Solano, Francisco, *Novo tratado de Musica metrica e rythmica*

Vallotti, Francesco, *Della scienza teorica e pratica della moderne musica*
Wesley, John,   *The Power of Music*

I. Musical Compositions:
Anfossi, Pasquale, *Cleopatra* (opera)
   Il matrimonio per inganno (opera)
Bach, Johann Christian,   *14 Sonatas for Violin and Harpsichord, Opus 15-17*
   Amadis de Gaule (opera)
Bach, William F., *Lausus und Lydie* (unfinished opera)
Benda, Friedrich, *Pygmalion* (opera)
Benda, Georg A., *Philon und Theone* (opera)
Boccherini, Luigi, *6 String Quintets, Opus 27*
   6 String Quintets, Opus 28
   6 String Quintets, Opus 29
Bortniansky, Dmitri, *Quinto Fabio* (opera)
Cimarosa, Domenico, *L'infedeltà fedele* (opera)
   L'Italiana in Londra (opera)
Fomin, Evstigney, *Melnik* (opera)
Giardini, Felice de', *6 String Trios, Opus 20*
Giordani, Giuseppe, *Epponina* (opera)
Gluck, Christoph W., *Echo et Narcisse* (opera)
Gossec, François, *Mirza* (ballet)
   Les scythes enchainés (ballet)
Grétry, André, *Aucassin et Nicolette* (opera)
   Les événemens imprévus (opera)
Hasse, Johann A., *Mass in E-flat Major*
Haydn, Franz J., *Symphony No. 70 in D Major*
   L'isola disabitata (opera)
   La vera costanza (opera)
Hiller, Johann A., *Das Grab des Mufti* (singspiel)
Holzbauer, Ignaz, *La morte di Didone* (opera)
Insanguine, Giacomo, *Medonte* (opera)
Martín y Soler, Vicente, *Ifigenia in Aulide* (opera)
Mozart, Wolfgang A., *Symphonies No. 32 and 33, K. 318 and 319*
   Serenade in D Major, K. 320, "Posthorn"
   Sinfonia Concertante in E-flat Major, K. 364
   Concerto in E-flat Major, K. 365, for Two Pianos and Orchestra
   "Coronation" Mass in C Major, K. 317
   Vesper Service in C Major, K. 321
   Regina Coeli in C Major, K. 276
   2 Church Sonatas, K. 328 and 329
   Zaïde, K. 344 (singspiel)
Mysliveček, Josef, *Armida* (opera)
   Il Demetrio (opera)
Neefe, Christian, *Macbeth* (opera)
Paisiello, Giovanni, *Lo sposo burlato* (opera)
Piccinni, Niccolò, *Il vago disprezzato* (opera)
Reichardt, Johann, *Ino* (opera)
   Der Hufschmied (opera)
Sacchini, Antonio, *Enea e Lavinia* (opera)
Saint-Georges, Joseph, *2 Symphonies, Opus 11*
   2 Symphonies Concertantes, Opus 10
Salieri, Antonio, *La partenza inaspettata* (intermezzo)
Sarti, Giuseppe, *Siroe* (opera)
   Adrianno in Sciro (opera)
Shield, William, *The Cobbler of Casterbury* (operetta)
Traetta, Tommaso, *The Passion According to St. John*

1780

World Events:
In the U.S., the estimated colonial population is 2,781,000; the colonial forces suffer a defeat at the Battle of Camden but win a victory at King's Mountain; Major John André is hanged as a spy when plans are discovered showing Benedict Arnold's plot to surrender West Point to the British; Nashville, Tennessee, is founded as a fort; Benjamin Franklin invents the bifocal glasses; the Great Dark Day takes place in New England on May 19. Internationally, Holland and Great Britain declare war on one another; the Second Mysore War takes place in India; Bohemia and Hungary both abolish serfdom in their territories; Maria Theresa dies and Joseph II becomes sole ruler of the Austrian Empire; the natives of Peru rebel against the rule of the Spanish government.

Cultural Highlights:
The American Academy of Arts and Sciences is incorporated in Boston; Johan Henrik Kellgren becomes librarian to Gustavus III of Sweden; Francisco José de Goya is taken into the Royal Academy of Fine Arts in San Fernando; Philippe Jacques de Loutherbourg is taken into the Royal Academy in London; Friedrich Maximilian von Klinger is ennobled in Russia; Richard Brinsley Sheridan becomes a member of the British Parliament. Births in the art world include American artist Edward Hicks, British artist Alfred Edward Chalon, German artist Ferdinand Jagemann and French artist Jean-Auguste Ingres; deaths include British artist Joseph Highmore, Italian artist Bernardo Bellotto (Canaletto) and French architect Jacques Germain Soufflot. Births in the literary field include American lawyer and poet Francis Scott Key, minister and author William Ellery Channing, French poet Pierre Jean de Beranger and British novelist Anna Maria Porter; deaths include French author and critic Charles Batteux, poet Nicolas Joseph Gilbert, philosopher Étienne Bonnot de Condillac and Spanish poet and dramatist Nicolás Fernández de Moratín. Other highlights include:

Art: William Blake, *Glad Day*; John Copley, *The Death of the Earl of Chatham*; Thomas Gainsborough, *Miss Haverfield*; Jean-Antoine Houdon, *Diana* (marble); George Morland, *The Angler's Repast*; Charles W. Peale, *George Washington*; Joshua Reynolds, *Mary Robinson as Perdita*; Élisabeth Vigée-Lebrun, *Marie Camargo*; Johann Zoffany, *Tribuna of the Uffizi Gallery*

Literature: William Beckford, *Biographical Memoirs of Extraordinary Painters*; Antoine de Bertin, *The Loves*; Matthias Claudius, *Lieder für das Volk*; Hannah Cowley, *The Belle's Stratagems*; George Crabbe, *The Candidate*; Frederick the Great, *On German Literature*; Friedrich Klopstock, *Fragments Concerning Language and Literature*; William Mason, *The English Garden*; Christoph M. Wieland, *Oberon*

MUSICAL EVENTS

A. Births:

Jan 14	François J. Dizi (Bel-hp)	Jun 5	Auguste Bertini (Fr-pn)
Jan 27	Giuseppe Siboni (It-ten)	Jun 18	Michael Henkel (Ger-cm)
Feb 19	F. Heinrich von der Hagen (Ger-mus)	Jun 19	Johann Heinroth (Ger-cm)
		Jul 25	Christian Weinlig (Ger-org)
Feb 20	Charles S. Richault (Fr-pub)	Aug 4	Louis Nourrit (Fr-ten)
May 10	Angelica Catalani (It-sop)	Nov 3	Victor C. Dourlen (Fr-cm)
May 10	Peter Lichtenthal (Hun-mus)	Nov 17	Franz Clement (Aus-vn-cd)
May 16	Friedrich Berner (Ger-org)	Nov 22	Konradin Kreutzer (Ger-cm)
May 22	Johann Doležálek (Boh-cm)	Dec 10	Friedrich von Drieberg (Ger-mus)
May 28	Joseph Fröhlich (Ger-cm)		Uri Hill (Am-cm-ed)

B. Deaths:

Jan 1	Johann L. Krebs (Ger-org)	Sep	M. Tollis de la Roca (Mex-cm)
Jan 10	Francesco Vallotti (It-cm)		Benedetta E. Agricola (It-sop)
May 14	Pierre M. Berton (Fr-cm-cd)		Domenico Ferrari (It-vn)

C. Debuts:
Other - Pietro Angiolini (Venice), Matteo Babbini (Italy), Antonio Bartolomeo Bruni (Paris), Louis Chardiny (Paris), Celeste Cotellini (Milan), Rodolphe Kreutzer (Paris)

D. New Positions:
Conductors: Eleutério Leal (mestre de capela, Lisbon Cathedral), Antonio Lolli (kapellmeister, St. Petersburg), Johann Abraham Schulz (kapellmeister, Rheinsberg), Anton Schweitzer (kapellmeister, Gotha), Carlo Giuseppe Toeschi (kapellmeister, Munich),

Educational: Giacomo Tritto (subteacher, Naples Conservatory)

Others: Friedrich Ludwig Benda (director, Hamburg Opera), Robert Broderip (organ, Mayor's Chapel, Bristol), Philip Cosgan (organ, St. Patrick's Cathedral, Dublin)

E. Prizes and Honors:
Honors: Franz Joseph Haydn (Modena Philharmonic Society), Joseph Martin Kraus (Swedish Royal Academy)

F. Biographical Highlights:
Lucrezia Aguiari marries Giuseppe Colla and retires from the stage; Maria Theresia Ahlefeldt marries Count Ferdinand Ahlefeldt; Elizabeth Anspach separates from her husband, William Craven; Bonifazio Asioli studies music with Angelo Morigi in Parma; Joah Bates marries singer Sarah Harrop; Muzio Clementi begins a concert tour of the main cities of Europe and engages in a friendly keyboard "duel" with Mozart in Vienna; Antoine Dauvergne becomes a director of the Paris Opera for the third time; Sébastien Erard builds what is believed to be the first "modern" piano; François Joseph Gossec becomes second conductor at the Paris Opera; William Herschel joins the Bath Literary and Philosophical Society; Antonio Lolli, broke from gambling, returns to Russia and regains his position as kapellmeister and soloist in the court of Catherine the Great in St. Petersburg; Wolfgang Amadeus Mozart moves to Munich for the production of his *Idomeneo*; Johann Peter Salomon, on the disbandment of the orchestra in Rheinsburg, leaves Germany, visits Paris and finally settles in London; Giovanni Battista Viotti joins Gaetano Pugnani in a concert tour of Germany, Poland and Russia.

G. Institutional Openings:
Performing Groups: Dramatiske Selskab (Oslo)

Other: John Betts, Violin Maker (London); Bordeaux Grand Theater; Johannes Köhler, Wind Instrument Maker (London); Leipzig Gewandhaus; Petrovsky Theater (Moscow)

H. Musical Literature:
Engel, Johann J., *Über die musikalische Malerei*
Forkel, Johann N., *Genauere Bestimmung einiger musikalischer Begriffe*
Frick, Philipp J., *The Art of Musical Modulation*
Hiller, Johann A., *Anweisung zum musikalisch-zierlichen Gesang*
La Borde, Jean de, *Essai sur la musique ancienne et moderne*
Lefébure, Louis F., *Nouveau Solfège*
Nares, James, *Treatise on Singing*
Sacchi, Giovenale,   *Delle quinte successive nel contrappunto e delle regolo degli accompagnamenti*
Solano, Francisco, *Dissertação sobre o caracter do musica*

Vogler, Georg, *Entwurf einer neuen Wörtersbuch für die Tonschule*

I. Musical Compositions:

Alessandri, Felice, *Erifile* (opera)
    Attalo re di Bitinia (opera)
Anfossi, Pasquale, *Tito nelle Gallie* (opera)
    La finta cingara per amore (opera)
Bach, C. P. E., *4 Hamburg Symphonies, Wg. 183*
Benda, Georg, *Das tartarische Gesetz* (opera)
Boccherini, Luigi, *6 String Quartets, Opus 30*
    6 String Quartets, Opus 31
    6 String Quartets, Opus 32
Cannabich, Christian, *La descente d'Hercule* (ballet)
Cherubini, Luigi, *Il Quinto Fabio* (opera)
Cimarosa, Domenico, *Caio Mario* (opera)
    Li sposi per accidente (opera)
    Le donne rivali (opera)
    Il falegname (opera)
Clementi, Muzio, *5 Piano Sonatas, Opus 1*
    3 Four-Hand Duets, Opus 3
    3 Keyboard Sonatas, Opus 5
    6 Piano Sonatas, Opus 4
Danzi, Franz, *Azakia* (opera)
    Cleopatra (opera)
Dauvergne, Antoine, *Le sicilien* (opera-ballet)
Dittersdorf, Carl von, *Job* (oratorio)
Galuppi, Baldassare, *L'Anfione* (cantata)
Giardini, Felice de', *6 Trios, Opus 18, for Guitar, Violin and Piano*
    6 Harpsichord Quartettos, Opus 21
Giordani, Tommaso, *6 Flute Concertos, Opus 19*
Grétry, André, *Andromaque* (opera)
Haydn, Franz J., *Symphonies No. 71, 74 and 75*
    Piano Sonatas No. 31-36
    La fedeltà premiata (opera)
Insanguine, Giacomo, *Montezuma* (opera)
Martín y Soler, Vicente, *Ipermestra* (opera)
    Andromaca (opera)
    La bella Arsene (ballet)
Mozart, Wolfgang A., *Symphony No. 34 in C Major, K. 338*
    Divertimento in D Major, K. 334
    Church Sonata in C Major, K. 336
    Solemn Mass in C Major, K. 337
    Vespers in C Major, K. 339
Mysliveček, Josef, *Antigono* (opera)
    Medonte (opera)
    6 String Quartets, Opus 1
Neefe, Christian, *Adelheit von Veltheim* (opera)
Piccinni, Niccolò, *Atys* (opera)
Reichardt, Johann, *Liebe nur beglückt* (opera)
    Oden und Lieder II
Reinagle, Alexander, *48 Short and Easy Pieces for Piano, Opus 1 and 2*
Saint-Georges, Joseph, *L'amant anonyme* (opera)
Schweitzer, Anton, *Rosamunde* (opera)
Shield, William, *The Deaf Lover* (operetta)
    The Siege of Gibraltar (operetta)
Vanhal, Johann B., *6 String Quartets, Opus 4*
Zumsteeg, Johann, *Das tartarische Gesetz* (singspiel)

1781

World Events:

In the U.S., the British forces under General Cornwallis surrender at Yorktown after the French Navy blockades Chesapeake Bay; the Articles of Confederation are ratified by Maryland, the last colony to do so; the Bank of North America is established by the Continental Congress; the Massachusetts Medical Society is founded. Internationally, Emperor Joseph II abolishes serfdom in the Austrian territories and grants religious tolerance and freedom of the press; the British seize all the Dutch holdings in the East Indies and in the West Indies; William Herschel discovers the planet Uranus.

Cultural Highlights:

John Trumbull enters law practice in Hartford, Connecticut; Johann von Schiller goes AWOL in order to attend the premiere of his first play, *Die Räuber*; Jean Paul Richter begins studying theology at Leipzig; Piat Joseph Sauvage is taken into the French Academy; Thomas Warton publishes Volume III of his *History of English Poetry*; Samuel Johnson publishes Volumes V-X of his *Lives of the English Poets*; Clarendon Press is founded at Oxford. Births in the world of art include American architect Robert Mills and British sculptor Francis Chantrey. Births in the literary world include German poet Achim von Arnim, author Adelbert von Chamisso, Austrian poet and librettist Ignaz Franz Castelli and British poet Ebenezer Elliott; deaths include German poet and critic Gotthold Lessing, poet Samuel Gotthold Lange and Danish poet and dramatist Johannes Ewald. Other highlights include:

Art: Thomas Banks, *Cupid Catching a Butterfly*; Jacques-Louis David, *Belisarius*; Jean-Antoine Houdon, *Marquis de Lafayette*; Johann Mansfield, *Franz Joseph Haydn*; Johann Nepomuk, *Mozart Family*; Joshua Reynolds, *Charles Burney*; Hubert Robert, *Fire at the Opera*; Piat Joseph Sauvage, *The Triumph of the Infant Bacchus*; Élisabeth Vigée-Lebrun, *Young Woman with a Rose*; Joseph Wright, *Sir Brooke Boothby*

Literature: George Crabbe, *The Library*; Philip Freneau, *The British Prison-Ship*; William Hayley, *The Triumphs of Temper*; Thomas Holcroft, *Duplicity*; Immanuel Kant, *Critique of Pure Reason*; Charles Macklin, *The Man of the World*; Johann H. Pestalozzi, *Lienhard und Gertrud*; Jean Jacques Rousseau, *Confessions*; Johann F. von Schiller, *The Robbers*; Thomas Thorild, *Passionerna*

MUSICAL EVENTS

A. Births:

Jan 22	François Habeneck (Fr-cm-cd)	Aug 9	Michael Umlauf (Aus-vn)
Jan 28	Giovanni Velluti (It-cas)	Sep 6	Anton Diabelli (Aus-cm)
Mar 11	Anthony Heinrich (Cz-vn-cm)	Sep 6	Vincent Novello (Br-pub)
Mar 18	Gustav Vogt (Fr-ob-cm)	Nov 7	John C. Clifton (Br-cd)
Apr 22	Christian Uber (Ger-cm)	Nov 18	Felice Blangini (It-ten)
May 3	Dorothea von Ertmann (Ger-pn)	Dec 1	Charles Lafont (Fr-vn)
May 6	Karl C. F. Krause (Ger-mus)	Dec 18	Louis Pradher (Fr-pn)
Jun 10	Giovanni Polledro (It-vn-cm)	Dec 18	Guillaume Wilhem (Fr-m.ed)
Jul 27	Mauro Giuliani (It-gui)		François Nadermann (Fr-hp)

B. Deaths:

Jan 22	Johann Siebenkäs (Ger-org)	Jul 11	Adolf Kunzen (Ger-hps-org)
Feb 4	Josef Mysliveček (Boh-cm)	Sep 4	Antonio Aurisicchio (It-cm)
Mar 16	Jean-Esprit Isnard (Fr-org.m)	Oct 16	Anton Zimmerman (Aus-cm)
Apr	John Barker (Br-org)	Nov 4	Faustina Bordoni (It-mez)
Apr	Giuseppe Bustelli (It-imp)	Nov 17	Jean de Béthizy (Fr-the)
May 16	Giacomo Puccini (It-org-cm)	Dec 15	Anna F. Hatasova (Boh-sop)
May 22	Garrett Mornington (Ir-cm)	Dec 16	Georg S. Löhlein (Ger-cm)

C. Debuts:
Other -Martin Joseph Adriens (Paris), Johann Baptiste Cramer (London), Heinrich Domnich (Paris), Samuel Harrison (Gloucester, as tenor), Jean Lebrun (Paris)

D. New Positions:
Conductors: Domenico Corri (Edinburgh Opera), Giacomo Antonio Insanguine (maestro di cappella, San Gennaro), Joseph Martin Kraus (Stockholm Theater), Pierre Lahoussaye (Comédie-Italienne, Paris), Jean François Lesueur (maître de chapelle, Dijon Cathedral), Giovanni Antonio Perotti (maestro di cappella, Vercelli Cathedral)

Others: Henry Delamain (organ, St. Finn Barre's Cathedral, Cork), Thomas Greatorex (organ, Carlisle Cathedral), Karl Hanke (music director, Warsaw)

E. Prizes and Honors:
Honors: Giovanni Gaiani (Accademia Filarmonica, Bologna)

F. Biographical Highlights:
Maddalena Allegranti makes her London debut; Josefa Barbara Auernhammer begins the study of piano with Mozart; Cristoforo Bartolomeo Babbi goes to Dresden as concertmaster of the Kapelle; Ludwig van Beethoven quits schools and begins studying music with Neefe, Koch and Rovantini; Christoph Willibald Gluck suffers a second stroke; Johannes Simon Mayr begins the study of theology at the University of Ingolstadt; Wolfgang Amadeus Mozart cuts his ties with Salzburg and moves permanently to Vienna where he meets Franz Joseph Haydn with whom he becomes fast friends; Alessio Prati moves to St. Petersburg; Antonio Maria Sacchini goes to Paris on the invitation of Marie Antoinette; Antoinette Saint-Huberty makes her Paris Opera debut; Georg Joseph "Abbe" Vogler goes to Paris for the production of his *La Kermesse*.

G. Institutional Openings:
Performing Groups: Leipzig Gewandhaus Orchestra

Educational: Collège Dramatique et Lyrique (Amsterdam); Università de' Filarmonici (Piacenza)

Other: Heinrich Bossler Music Publishing Co. (Speyer--to Darmstadt in 1792); Broadwood Grand Piano (first known); Esterházy Opera House II; William Forster Publishing Co. (London); Friedrich Meyer, Music Publisher (St. Petersburg); Nuovo Teatro Civico del Verzaro (Perugia); Ständetheater (Prague)

H. Musical Literature:
Bertezen, Salvatore, *Principi della musica teorico-prattica*
Billings, William, *Psalm Singer's Amusement*
Hiller, Johann A., *Über die Musik und deren werkungen*
Kirnberger, Johann P., *Grundsätze des Generalbasses, als erste Linien zur Composition*
Löhlein, Georg S., *Clavier-Schule II*
Martini, Giovanni, *Storia della Musica III*
Maxwell, John, *An Essay upon Tune*
Parry, John, *Cambrian Harmony: A Collection of Ancient Welsh Airs*
Tiraboschi, Girolamo, *Biblioteca Modenese I*
Wolf, Georg F., *Kurzer aber deutlicher Unterricht in Klavierspielen*

I. Musical Compositions:
Alessandri, Felice, *Betulia liberata* (oratorio)
    Arbace (opera)
André, Johann, *Die Entführung aus dem Serail* (opera)
Anfossi, Pasquale, *Il trionfo d'Arianna* (opera)
    Lo sposo per equivoco (intermezzo)
Bach, Johann Christian, *6 Grand Overtures, Opus 18*

Bertoni, Ferdinando, *Ezio* (opera)
Boccherini, Luigi, *6 String Quartets, Opus 33*
    6 String Trios, Opus 34
Cannabich, Christian, *Electra* (opera)
Cimarosa, Domenico, *Alessandro nell'Indie* (opera)
    Il convito di pietra (opera)
    Giannina e Bernardone (opera)
    Artaserse (opera)
Clementi, Muzio, *3 Keyboard Sonatas, Opus 5*
    2 Keyboard Sonatas, Opus 6, No. 2 and 3
    Keyboard Duet, Opus 6, No. 1
Dalayrac, Nicolas, *Le petit souper* (opera)
    Le chevalier à la mode (opera)
    6 String Quartets
Danzi, Franz, *Laura Rosetti* (incidental music)
Dittersdorf, Carl von, *6 Symphonies, Opus 13*
Furlanetto, Bonaventura, *Dies extrema mundi* (oratorio)
    David Goliath triumphator (oratorio)
Gatti, Luigi, *Antigono* (opera)
Gazzaniga, Giuseppe, *La stravagante* (opera)
    I profeti al Calvario (oratorio)
Giordani, Giuseppe, *Elpinice* (opera)
Giroust, François, *Rosemonde* (opera)
Gossec, François, *La fête de Mirza* (ballet)
Grétry, André, *Emilie* (opera)
Haydn, Franz J., *Symphony No. 72 in D Major*
    Symphony No. 73, "La Chasse"
    6 String Quartets, Opus 33, "Russian"
    12 Songs, Sets I and II
Hopkinson, Francis, *The Temple of Minerva* (dramatic cantata)
Martín y Soler, Vicente, *Astartea* (opera)
    La regina di Golconda (ballet)
Mozart, Wolfgang A., *Serenades, K. 361 and 375, for Winds*
    Concerto Rondo, K. 371, for Horn and Orchestra
    Rondo in C Major, K. 373, for Violin and Orchestra
    Quartet in F Major, K. 370, for Oboe and Strings
    5 Violin Sonatas, K. 376-380
    Piano Sonata in D Major, K. 448, for 2 Pianos
    Variations in G Major, K. 359, for Violin and Piano
    Variations in G Minor, K. 360, for Violin and Piano
    Kyrie in D Minor, K. 341
    Idomeneo, K. 366 (opera)
Mysliveček, Josef, *6 String Quartets, Opus 2*
Naumann, Johann G., *Elisa* (opera)
    Osiride (opera)
Neefe, Christian, *Lessings Totenfeier-Overture*
Paisiello, Giovanni, *La serva padrona* (opera)
Piccinni, Niccolò, *Iphigénie en Tauride* (opera)
    Adèle de Ponthieu (opera)
Reichardt, Johann, *Oden und Lieder III*
Sacchini, Antonio, *Mitridate* (opera)
    Il don Caladrino (opera)
Sarti, Giuseppe, *Giulio Sabino* (opera)
Shield, William, *Robinson Crusoe* (operetta)
Vogel, Johann, *Jephté* (oratorio)
Vogler, Georg, *Albert III von Baiern* (opera)
Zingarelli, Nicola, *Montezuma* (opera)

1782

World Events:
In the U.S., a Treaty of Peace is negotiated with the British; the Great Seal of the United States is adopted by the Continental Congress; the Bald Eagle is chosen as the official national bird; George Washington establishes the Order of the Purple Heart for those soldiers wounded in battle; Harvard Medical School opens its doors; American statesman Daniel Webster and future President Martin Van Buren are born. Internationally, the British sign a peace treaty with the Mahrattas in India; the Spanish fail in their attempt to take Gibraltar away from the British; James Watt builds the first rotary steam engine; Roma I becomes the first ruler of the new Chakkri Dynasty in Thailand.

Cultural Highlights:
Charles Horace Vernet receives the Prix de Rome in Art; Jacques Louis David is taken into the French Academy; Ekaterina Dashkova becomes director of the Academy of Arts and Sciences in St. Petersburg; James Barry becomes a professor in the Royal Academy of Art in London; Johann von Schiller escapes from Württemberg and begins his "wanderjahre"; Richard Sheridan is made an Undersecretary of State for foreign affairs. Births in the field of art include British artist John S. Cotman, Scotch artist William Allan and Dutch artist Johannes de Troostwijck; deaths include British artist Richard Wilson and French architect Jacques A. Gabriel. Births in the literary world include Canadian poet Michel Bibaud, French author Félicité de Lamennais, Scotch novelist Susan E. Ferrier, Danish poet Steen S. Blicher, Swedish poet Esaias Tegnér and Italian poet Giovanni Niccolini; Spanish author José de Cadalso y Vázquez dies. Other highlights include:

Art: Antonio Canova, *Theseus and the Minotaur*; Étienne Falconet, *Peter the Great* (equestrian statue); Henry Fuseli, *The Nightmare*; Francisco de Goya, *Cornelis van der Goten*; Francesco Guardi, *Fêtes for the Archduke Paul*; Angelica Kauffmann, *Poetry Embracing Painting*; Joseph Lange, *Constanze Weber*; John Opie, *Samuel Johnson*; George Romney, *Lady Hamilton as Circe*; Gilbert Stuart, *Gentlemen Skating*

Literature: Vittorio Alfieri, *Saul*; William Beckford, *Vathek*; Fanny Burney, *Cecilia*; George Colman, *The Female Dramatist*; Michel de Crèvecoeur, *Letters from an American Farmer*; Denis I. Fonvizin, *The Minor*; Johann von Herder, *The Spirit of Hebrew Poetry*; Tomás de Iriarte y Oropesa, *Fábulas Literarias*; Hannah More, *Sacred Dramas*; Jean Jacques Rousseau, *Rêveries du Promeneur Solitaire*

MUSICAL EVENTS

A. Births:

Jan 11	Thaddäus Amadé (Hun-pn-cm)	Sep 23	Jacques Mazas (Fr-vn)
Jan 24	Friedrich Hofmeister (Ger-pub)	Oct 27	Niccolò Paganini (It-vn)
Jan 29	Daniel F. Auber (Fr-cm)	Nov 1	Joseph von Blumenthal (Bel-vn)
Feb 17	François Foignet (Fr-ten)	Nov 17	Conrad Graf (Aus-pn.m)
Apr 14	Carlo Coccia (It-cm)	Dec 10	Friedrich Griepenkerl (Ger-mus)
May 26	Josef Drechsler (Aus-org)	Dec 21	T. Benoît-Berbiguier (Fr-fl)
Jul 26	John Field (Br-pn-cm)		Thomas S. Cooke (Br-ten)

B. Deaths:

Jan 1	Johann C. Bach (Ger-cm)	May 20	Christoph Schröter (Ger-org)
Feb 28	Johann N. Ritter (Ger-org.m)	May 20	Carlo G. Testori (It-the)
Mar 17	Daniel Bernoulli (Swi-acous)	Jun 17	Kane O'Hara (Ir-cm)
Mar 19	Louis H. Paisible (Fr-vn)	Jun 24	Johann C. Monn (Aus-pn-cm)
Apr 12	Pietro Metastasio (It-pt-lib)	Jul 13	Samuel Howard ((Br-org)
May	Cecilia Grassi (It-sop)	Jul 15	Farinelli (It-cas)
May 18	Johann Baumgartner (Ger-cel)	Jul 15	Robert Wainwright (Br-org)

Aug   Jean B. Forqueray (Fr-cm)
Aug 27 Catherine Hamilton (Br-hps)
Sep 3   John Burton (Br-pn)
Oct 7   John Parry (Br-hp)

Oct 23 Joseph Riepel (Aus-vn)
        Pedro A. Avondano (Por-cm)
        Giovanni Plantanida (It-vn)

C. Debuts:

Other - Amélie Julie Candeille (Paris), Francois Devienne (Paris), Charles H. Florio (London), Thomas Lowe (London), Giovanni Battista Viotti (Paris)

D. New Positions:

Conductors: Joachim Albertini (kapellmeister, Warsaw), Jean Baptiste Rey (Concerts Spirituel, Paris), Alessandro Rolla (Parma SO), Candido Ruano (maestro de capilla, Avila Cathedral),

Others: Carl Christian Agthe (organ, Ballenstedt Court), Benjamin Cooke (organ, St. Martin-in-the-Fields), Giovanni Battista Grazioli (organ, St. Mark's, Venice), Ignaz Anton Ladurner (organ, Benediktbeuren), Richard Langdon (organ, Armagh Cathedral), Christian Gottlob Neefe (organ, Bonn Court), William Selby (organ, Stone Chapel, Boston), William Shrubsole (organ, Barger Cathedral), Richard Wainwright (organ, St. Peter's, Liverpool)

F. Biographical Highlights:

Ludwig Abeille joins the violin section of the Württemberg orchestra; Carl Friedrich Abel visits Germany and begins performing and composing for the Russian Court at St. Petersburg; Pasquale Anfossi achieves his first London success at the King's Theatre; François Bainville retires from his Angers post as organist and returns to Chartres; Ludwig van Beethoven begins substituting for Neefe at the organ in the Bonn court chapel; Domenico Cimarosa becomes the music master at a girl's school in Venice; Jan Ladislav Dussek begins a successful career as a virtuoso and composer; William Herschel makes his last public appearance as a musician and turns permanently to astronomy; Wolfgang Amadeus Mozart marries Constanze Weber and moves to Vienna; Daniel Read opens a singing school in North River, Massachusetts; Joseph Weigl begins the study of music with Johann Georg Albrechtsberger.

G. Institutional Openings:

Educational: Royal Irish Academy of Music (Dublin)

Other: Alexander Brothers, Instrument Makers (Mainz); F. Ernst Leuckart Publishing Co. (Breslau); *Musikalisches Kunstmagazin*; Riga City Theater; William Southwell, Piano Maker (Dublin); Stockholm Opera House; Teatro degli Armeni (Livorno)

H. Musical Literature:

Christmann, Johann F., *Elementarbuch der Tonkunst*
Graf, Christian E., *Thoroughbass Method*
Junker, Carl L., *Einige der vornehmsten pflichten eines Kapellmeister oder Musikdirector*
Kirnberger, Johann P., *Anleitung zur Singcomposition...*
Koch, Heinrich, *Versuch einer Anleitung zur Composition*
Law, Andrew, *Collection of Hymns for Social Worship*
Roussier, Pierre, *Mémoire sur la nouvelle Harpe...*
Schröter, Christoph G., *Letzte beschäftigung mit musikalischen dingen*
Vogler, Georg, *Essai de diriger le goût des amateurs de musique*
Wolf, Ernst W., *Kleine musikalische Reise*

I. Musical Compositions:

Alessandri, Felice, *La finta principessa* (opera)
André, Johann, *Elmine* (opera)
    Die Werbung aus Liebe (opera)
Anfossi, Pasquale, *Zemira* (opera)

Il trionfo della costanza (opera)
Azaïs, Hyacinthe, *6 Symphonies*
Boccherini, Luigi, *6 Symphonies, Opus 35*
Cherubini, Luigi, *Il Messenzio* (opera)
　　　Adriano in Siria (opera)
　　　Armida abbandonata (opera)
Cimarosa, Domenico, *L'eroe cinese* (opera)
　　　L'amor constante (opera)
　　　La ballerina amante (opera)
Clementi, Muzio, *3 Keyboard Sonatas, Opus 7*
Dalayrac, Nicolas, *L'éclipse totale* (opera)
Dittersdorf, Carl von, *6 String Quintets*
Galuppi, Baldassare, *Il ritorno di Tobia* (oratorio)
Gazzaniga, Giuseppe, *Amor per oro* (opera)
Giordani, Giuseppe, *Ritorno d'Ulisse* (opera)
Giordani, Tommaso, *Il bacio* (opera)
Gluck, Christoph W., *De Profundis*
Gossec, François, *Thésée* (opera)
　　　Electre (incidental music)
Grétry, André, *La double épreuve* (opera)
　　　L'embarras des richesses (opera)
Haydn, Franz J., *Symphonies No. 76-78*
　　　Orlando paladino (opera)
　　　Missa Cellensis in C Major (Mariazeller-Messe)
Haydn, Michael, *Missa Sancte Ruperti*
　　　Sanctificatio Julilaei (cantata)
Insanguine, Giacomo, *Calipso* (opera)
Martín y Soler, Vicente, *Partenope* (opera)
　　　L'amore geloso (opera)
Méhul, Etienne, *Ode Sacrée*
Mozart, Wolfgang A., *Symphony No. 35, "Haffner"*
　　　Serenade in C Minor, K. 388, for Winds
　　　Concerto in A Major, K. 414, for Piano and Orchestra
　　　Rondo in A Major, K. 386, for Piano and Orchestra
　　　Concerto No. 1 in D Major, K. 412, for Horn and Orchestra
　　　Quintet in E-flat Major, K. 407, for Horn and Strings
　　　String Quartet in G Major, K. 387
　　　2 Violin Sonatas, K. 402 and 404
　　　Variations on "Ah vous dirai-je, maman," K. 265
　　　3 Marches, K. 408
　　　The Abduction from the Seraglio (opera)
Nardini, Pietro, *6 String Quartets*
Neefe, Christian, *Concerto for Piano and Orchestra*
Paisiello, Giovanni, *Il barbiere di Siviglia* (opera)
Righini, Vincenzo, *Armida* (opera)
Saint-Georges, Joseph, *2 Violin Concertos, Opus 7*
Salieri, Antonio, *Semiramide* (opera)
Sarti, Giuseppe, *Fra i due litiganti il terzo gode* (opera)
　　　Attalo, Re di Bitinia (opera)
　　　Alessandro e Timoteo (opera)
Schwanenberg, Johann, *L'Olimpiade* (opera)
Shield, William, *Lord Mayor's Day* (operetta)
　　　Friar Bacon (operetta)
Vachon, Pierre, *6 Quartets Concertant, Opus 11*
Viotti, Giovanni, *Concerto No. 1, for Violin and Orchestra*
Vogel, Johann, *Concerto for Violin and Orchestra*
Winter, Peter, *Bellerophon* (opera)

1783

World Events:
In the U.S., the Treaty of Paris formally ends the warfare and Great Britain and most of the other European countries recognize the United States; the Continental Army is disbanded, but the officers form the Society of Cincinnati with George Washington as the first President-General; slavery is abolished in both Massachusetts and Maryland; Charleston, South Carolina, is incorporated. Internationally, William Pitt becomes Prime Minister of Great Britain; Russia proceeds to annex the Crimea region, provoking further warfare with Turkey; the Montgolfier brothers make the first ascent in a hot-air balloon; the parachute is invented by L. Lenormand of France; future South-American liberator Simón Bolivar is born.

Cultural Highlights:
Samuel Johnson forms the Essex Head Club in London; Marie Anne Vigée-Lebrun is taken into the French Academy; Jean François Marmontel is made secretary of the French Academy; Richard Sheridan is appointed British Secretary of the Treasury; Étienne Maurice Falconet suffers a stroke. Births in the art field include American artist Samuel Lovett Waldo, British artists David Cox and Thomas Sully, Danish artist Kristoffer Eckersberg and German artist Peter von Cornelius; French artist Jean Baptiste Perroneau dies. Births in the literary field include American author Washington Irving, French novelists Victor Henri Ducange and (Marie Henri) Stendhal, Italian poet Giovanni Berchet and Russian poet Vasili Zhukovski; deaths include Irish novelist Henry Brooke, French author Louise Florence Épinay and Swiss historian and critic Johann Jakob Bodmer. Other highlights include:

Art: James Barry, *Progress of Human Culture*; John Copley, *Death of Major Pierson*; Jacques Louis David, *The Grief of Andromache*; Thomas Gainsborough, *Ladies in the Mall*; Francisco de Goya, *The Family of Don Luis*; Jean Antoine Houdon, *Girl Shivering*; Joseph Lange, *Wolfgang Amadeus Mozart*; John Opie, *The Peasant's Family*; Jean Baptiste Regnault, *The Education of Achilles*; George Stubbs, *The Reapers*

Literature: William Beckford, *Dreams, Waking Thoughts and Incidents*; Hugh Blair, *Lectures on Rhetoric*; William Blake, *Poetical Sketches*; Hannah Cowley, *A Bold Stroke for a Husband*; George Crabbe, *The Village*; Thomas Day, *History of Sandford and Merton*; Denis Fonvizin, *Nedorosl*; William Herschel, *Motion of the Solar System...*; Moses Mendelssohn, *Jerusalem*; Friedrich von Schiller, *Fiesco*

MUSICAL EVENTS

A. Births:

Jan 27	August A. Klengel (Ger-cm)	Jun 20	Friedrich Dotzauer (Ger-cel)
Feb 15	Johann N. Poiszl (Ger-cm)	Aug 21	Nathan Adams (Am-br.m)
Mar 7	Gottfried Fink (Ger-cri)	Aug 28	Joseph A. Roeckel (Ger-ten)
Mar 26	Johann B. Weigl (Ger-org)	Dec 23	Heinrich Praeger (Hol-vn-cd)
Apr 21	Reginald Heber (Br-hymn)	Dec 28	Wenzel Gullenberg (Aus-cm)
May 10	Nicola Benvenuti (It-cm)		Filippo Galli (It-bs)
Jun 8	Joseph Lincke (Ger-cel)		George Hogarth (Scot-cri)

B. Deaths:

Jan 20	Daniel Dow (Scot-gui)	Apr 8	Franz Habermann (Boh-cm-cd)
Jan 20	Antonio Uberti (Ger-cas)	May 4	Franz A. Holly (Boh-org)
Feb 10	James Nares (Br-org)	May 18	Lucrezia Aguiari (It-sop)
Feb 11	Johann Silbermann (Ger-org.m)	Jul 26	Johann Kirnberger (Ger-cm)
Feb 14	M. Joséphine Laguerre (Fr-sop)	Sep 3	Leonhardt Fuler (Swi-the)
Mar 1	Thomas Lowe (Br-ten)	Oct 7	William Tans'ur (Br-the)
Mar 23	Gaspard Fritz (Swi-vn)	Oct 29	Jean d'Alembert (Fr-the)
Apr 7	Ignaz Holzbauer (Ger-cm)	Nov 8	Buono Chiodi (It-cm)

Nov 30   Caffarelli (It-cas)   Dec 20   Antonio Soler (Sp-org)
Dec 16   Johann A. Hasse (Ger-cm)   Thomas Pinto (Br-vn)

C. Debuts:
U.S. -- William Brown (N.Y.)

Other - Elizabeth Billington (Dublin), Elisabeth Böhm (Berlin), Girolamo Crescentini (Rome), Jean Xavier Lefèvre (Paris), Maria Mandini (Vienna)

D. New Positions:
Conductors: Wojciech Boguslawski (Polish National Theater), Arthur Thomas Corfe (choir, Westminster Cathedral), Federigo Fiorillo (kapellmeister, Riga), Luigi Maria Gatti (kapellmeister, Salzburg Cathedral), Wenzel Müller (Brno Theater), Christian Gottlob Neefe (kapellmeister, Bonn), Ignace Joseph Pleyel (kapellmeister, Strasbourg Cathedral), Giacomo Rust (maestro de capilla, Barcelona Cathedral)

Others: Samuel Arnold (organ, Royal Chapel, London), William Billings (editor, *Boston Magazine*), John Ross (organ, St. Paul's Chapel, Aberdeen), Nicolas Séjan (organ, St. Sulpice, Paris)

E. Prizes and Honors:
Honors: William Jones (knighted), Marcos de Portugal (Lisbon St. Cecilia Society), Jean Baptiste Regnault (French Academy)

F. Biographical Highlights:
Maddalena Allegranti joins the Dresden Court Opera; Thomas Attwood, on a royal grant, begins two years of music study in Italy; Ludwig van Beethoven is made court cembalist in Bonn with no salary; Francesco Benucci makes his Viennese debut; Amélie Julie Candeille gives up opera and goes into acting; Christoph Willibald Gluck is hit with a third stroke; Charles Incledon leaves the British Navy and returns to London; Antonio Lolli is finally relieved of his duties in St. Petersburg and is replaced by Paisiello; Alessio Prati leaves Russia to return to Vienna; Giovanni Battista Viotti gives up public performances but continues to perform privately for small occasions; Georg Joseph "Abbe" Vogler travels to England seeking approval of his new musical system; Elizabeth Weichsel marries musician James Billington and begins her Dublin career; Joseph Wölfl becomes chorister at Salzburg Cathedral; Johann Zoffany visits in India.

G. Institutional Openings:
Performing Groups: Casino- und Musikgesellschaft (Worms); Concerts Spirituels (Berlin)

Educational: Caracas Academy of Music (Venezuela); Pro Istituto Filarmonico (Milan)

Other: Joseph Dale, Music Publisher (London); Hermitage Theater (St. Petersburg); Franz Anton Hoffmeister, Music Publisher (Vienna); Jean Imbault, Music Publisher (Paris); *Magazin der Musik* (Hamburg); *The New Musical Magazine* (London); Rellstab Music Lending Library (Berlin); Soren Sonnichsen, Music Publisher (Denmark); Teatro de la Ranchería (Buenos Aires); Tyl Theater (Prague)

H. Musical Literature:
Arteaga, Esteban de, *Le rivoluzioni del teatro musicale italiano...I*
Eberhard, Johann A., *Théorie der schönen Wissenschaften*
Gruber, Johann S., *Literatur der Musik*
Junker, Carl L., *Musikalischer Almanach, 1783*
Kellner, Johann C., *Grundriss des Generalbasses*
Klein, Johann J., *Lehrbuch der praktischen Musik*
Law, Andrew, *The Rudiments of Music*
Miller, Edward, *Institutes of Music*

Moreau, Henri, *L'harmonie mise en pratique*
Wolf, Georg F., *Kurzer aber deutlicher unterricht im Klavierspielen*

I. Musical Compositions:

Abel, Carl F., *6 Overtures, Opus 17*
    Sinfonia Concertante, K.8
Alessandri, Felice, *La virtù rivali* (cantata)
    I puntigli gelosi (opera)
André, Johann, *Der Barbier von Bagdad* (opera)
Anfossi, Pasquale, *I vecchi burlati* (opera)
    Le gelosie fortunate (opera)
Beethoven, Ludwig van, *Rondo in A Major, WoO49, for Piano*
Boccherini, Luigi, *4 Villancios for Voices and Orchestra*
    Cello Sonata in C Major
Cherubini, Luigi, *Lo sposo di tre* (opera)
Cimarosa, Domenico, *Oreste* (opera)
    Nina e Martuffo (opera)
    La villana riconosciuta (opera)
Clementi, Muzio, *3 Keyboard Sonatas, Opus 8*
    3 Keyboard Sonatas, Opus 9
    3 Keyboard Sonatas, Opus 10
Dalayrac, Nicolas, *Le Corsaire* (opera)
    Les deux soupers (opera)
Giordani, Giuseppe, *Erifile* (opera)
Gluck, Christoph W., *Ode an der Tod* (chorus)
Grétry, André, *La caravane du Caire* (opera)
Haydn, Franz J., *Armida* (opera)
    Concerto No. 2 in D Major for Cello and Orchestra
Haydn, Michael, *Symphony in G Major* (old Mozart No. 37)
Holzbauer, Ignaz, *Tancredi (opera)*
Martín y Soler, Vicente, *Vologeso* (opera)
Méhul, Etienne, *3 Piano Sonatas, Set I*
Mozart, Wolfgang A., *Symphony No. 36, K. 425, "Linz"*
    Concerto No. 2 in E-flat Major for Horn and Orchestra
    Concertos No. 11 and 13, K. 413 and 415, for Piano and Orchestra
    2 String Quartets, K. 421 and 428
    5 Divertimentos, K. 439b, for Woodwinds
    Piano Trio in D Minor, K. 442
    3 Piano Sonatas, K. 330-332
    3 Minuets, K. 363
    Lo sposo deluso (opera)
    L'oca del Cairo (opera)
Naumann, Johann, *Zeit und Ewigkeit* (cantata)
Paisiello, Giovanni, *Il mondo della luna* (opera)
    La passione di Gesù Cristo (oratorio)
Piccinni, Niccolò, *Didon* (opera)
    Le Faux lord (opera)
    Le Dormeur éveillé (opera)
Reichardt, Johann, *La Passione di Gesú Cristo* (oratorio)
Reinagle, Alexander, *6 Sonatas with Violin Accompaniment*
Sarti, Giuseppe, *Olimpiade* (opera)
    Il trionfo della pace (opera)
    Idalide (opera)
Shield, William, *Rosina* (operetta)
Tarchi, Angelo, *Ademira* (opera)
Vogler, Georg, *La kermesse* (opera)
Weigl, Joseph, *Mass in E-flat Major*

1784

World Events:
In the U.S., trade routes are opened to China by the voyage of the *Empress of China* to the port of Canton; the Mason-Dixon Line is extended westward into the new territories; the Potomac Company is formed to provide canal transportation for all the colonies; Connecticut and Rhode Island abolish slavery in their states; a major depression falls over the American scene until 1788; the first law school opens in Litchfield, Connecticut; future President Zachary Taylor is born. Internationally, the British India Act, passed by the Parliament, strengthens the British hold on India; the British make peace with the ruler of Mysore; the Hungarian Constitution is abrogated by Joseph II; Denmark abolishes all serfdom in its borders; China puts down a Muslim uprising in its provinces.

Cultural Highlights:
Pierre Paul Prud'hon wins the Prix de Rome in Art; Joshua Reynolds becomes Painter to the King in London; Francesco Guardi is taken into the Venetian Academy; William Cowper begins his translation of Homer; Thomas Astle publishes his *Origin and Progress of Writing*. Births in the world of literature include British actor and dramatist James Sheridan Knowles, poet Leigh Hunt, Scotch poet Allan Cunningham and German poet and dramatist Ernst Benjamin Raupach; deaths include Brazilian poet José de Durão, French lawyer and poet Jean Jacques Pompignan, philosopher Denis Diderot and British poet and critic Samuel Johnson. Births in the art world include Belgian sculptor Matthieu Kessels, German sculptor Johann B. Straub and French sculptor François Rude; deaths include Irish artists George Barret and Nathaniel Hone, Scotch artist Allan Ramsay, French artist Nicolas Bernard Lepicié and Italian artist Giuseppe Zais. Other highlights include:

Art: Thomas Banks, *Achilles Enraged*; Jacques Louis David, *Oath of the Horatii*; Francisco de Goya, *Don Manuel de Zunigo*; John Opie, *Children of the Duke of Argyll*; Charles W. Peale, *Washington at Yorktown*; Henry Raeburn, *Reverend Walker Skating*; Joshua Reynolds, *Mrs Siddons as the Tragic Muse*; Hubert Robert, *Mouth of the Cave*; Andreas Stöttrup, *C. P. E. Bach and the Artist*; Joseph Wright, *The Maid of Corinth*

Literature: Pierre de Beaumarchais, *The Marriage of Figaro*; Gottfried A. Bürger, *Die Kuh*; Benjamin Franklin, *The Savages of North America;* Johann von Goethe, *Scherz, List und Rache*; Thomas Jefferson, *Notes on Virginia*; Friedrich Klopstock, *Hermann und die Fürsten*; Ignacy Krasicki, *Epistles*; William J. Mickle, *Cumnor Hall*; Friedrich von Schiller, *Kabale und Liebe*; Charlotte Smith, *Elegiac Sonnets and Other Essays*

MUSICAL EVENTS

A. Births:

Jan 1	William Beale (Br-org)		May 3	Henri M. Berton (Fr-cm)
Jan 22	Edward Taylor (Br-m.ed)		Jun 14	Francesco Morlacchi (It-cm)
Jan 27	Martin Mengal (Bel-cd)		Jul 2	Teresa Belloc-Giorgi (It-alto)
Jan 28	Karl Winterfeld (Ger-mus)		Jul 27	Georges Onslow (Br-cm)
Jan 31	Carl W. Henning (Ger-cm-cd)		Aug 15	Pierre Blondeau (Fr-cm)
Feb 14	Heinrich Bäermann (Ger-cl)		Oct 15	Thomas Hastings (Am-hymn)
Mar 25	François J. Fetis (Bel-the)		Nov 29	Ferdinand Ries (Ger-pn-cm)
Mar 28	Charles Neate (Br-pn)		Dec 1	François H. Blaze (Fr-mus)
Apr 5	Louis Spohr (Ger-cm)			Franz X. Gebauer (Ger-org)
Apr 8	Dionysio Aguado y García (Sp-gui)			Karl Leibl (Ger-org-cd)
				Giuseppe Pilotti (It-cm)

B. Deaths:

Jan 5	Friedrich W. Riedt (Ger-fl)		Jan 29	Andrea Bernasconi (It-cm-cd)
Jan 11	Ferdinand Lobkowitz (Cz-pat)		Feb 24	Anton Laube (Boh-cm-cd)

Jun 3	Girolamo Tiraboschi (It-mus)	Sep 14	Nicolas Capron (Fr-vn)
Jun 7	Jean B. Canavas (It-cel)	Sep 15	Benedetto Micheli (It-pt-cm)
Jul 1	Wilhelm F. Bach (Ger-cm)	Oct 4	G. "Padre" Martini (It-the)
Sep	John Bennett (Br-org)	Nov 6	Giuseppe Arena (It-org)
Sep 12	Manuel Blasco de Nebra	Dec	Jean B. Lefèvre (Fr-org.m)
	(Sp-org)	Dec 5	Phillis Wheatley (Afr-pt)

C. Debuts:

Other - Joseph Ambrosch (Bayreuth), Luigi Bassi (Prague, adult debut), Charles Dignum (London), Anton Eberl (Vienna), Friedrich Hurka (Leipzig), Charles Incledon (Southampton), Luisa Laschi (Vienna), Halifax Lowe (London)

D. New Positions:

Conductors: Ferdinando Bertoni (maestro di cappella, St. Mark's, Venice), Paul Grua (kapellmeister, Munich), Melchor López Jiménez (maestro de capilla, Santiago Cathedral), Johann A. Kozeluch (kapellmeister, St. Vitus Cathedral, Prague), Jean François Lesueur (maître de chapelle, Tours), Giovanni Paisiello (maestro di cappella, Naples), Brizio Petrucci (maestro di cappella, Ferrara Cathedral), Giuseppe Sarti (kapellmeister, St. Petersburg), Georg "Abbe" Vogler (kapellmeister, Munich)

Educational: François Joseph Gossec (director, École Royal du Chant), Honoré François Langlé (voice, Ecole Royal de Chant, Paris), Niccolò Piccinni (voice, Ecole Royal, Paris), Jean Joseph Rodolphe (composition, Paris Conservatory)

E. Prizes and Honors:

Honors: Edmund Ayrton (honorary doctorate, Cambridge), Franz Joseph Haydn (Gold Medal of Prince Henry of Prussia), Pietro Terziani (Accademia Filarmonica, Bologna)

F. Biographical Highlights:

Gennaro Astarita becomes director of the Petrovsky Theater in Moscow; Ludwig van Beethoven is appointed second court organist at Bonn, this time with a salary; Anne Catley retires and marries General F. Lascelles; Luigi Cherubini is invited to London for the production of his operas; Muzio Clementi fails in an attempt to elope to the New World with Victoire Imbert; Charles Dibdin spends some time in a debtor's prison; Jan Ladislav Dussek enjoys a very successful German concert tour; Gertrud Mara makes her London debut; Wolfgang Amadeus Mozart, settled in Vienna, meets Sarti and Paisiello and joins the Masonic Order; Georg Gottfried Müller, Moravian violinist, settles in Lititz, Pennsylvania, as minister, composer and violinist; Giuseppe Sarti leaves for St. Petersburg and the Court of Catherine the Great; Daniel Steibelt deserts the Prussian Army and flees the country; Franz X. Süssmayr begins the study of law and philosophy; Samuel Wesley joins the Catholic Church.

G. Institutional Openings:

Performing Groups: Brotherhood of St. Cecilia (Brazil)

Educational: Armonici Uniti (Bologna); École Royale du Chant et de Déclamation (Paris, founded by François Gossec)

Other: Bland and Weller, Publishers and Instrument Makers (London); Institution for the Encouragement of Church Music (Uranian Society in 1787, Philadelphia); Italian Opera House (Prague); Kozeluch Music Publishing Co. (Vienna); New Swedish Theater (Stockholm); *Review of New Music Publications*; Royal Bohemian Academy of Sciences; Teatro della Società (Casale Monferrato); Teatro Eretenio (Vicenza)

H. Musical Literature:

Gehot, Joseph, *The Theory and Practice of Music*
Gerbert, Martin, *Scriptores ecclesiastici de musica sacra potissimum*
Gregor, Christian F., *Choralbuch* (Moravian)
Hiller, Johann A., *Lebensbeschreibungen berühmter Musikgelehrten und Tonkunstler*

Jones, Edward, *Musical and Poetical Relicks of the Welsh Bards*
Jones, William, *Treatise on the Art of Music*
Keeble, John, *The Theory of Harmonics*
Schubart, Daniel, *Ideen zu einer aesthetik der Tonkunst*
Thiéme, Frédéric, *Éléments de musique pratique*

I. Musical Compositions:

Bréval, Jean B., *Cello Concerto No. 1 and 2, Opus 14 and 17*
Calegari, Antonio, *Le Sorelle rivali* (opera)
Cannabich, Christian, *Perseé et Andromède* (ballet)
　　　Corésus et Callihoé (opera)
Cherubini, Luigi, *L'Idalide* (opera)
　　　Alessandro nell'Indie (opera)
Cimarosa, Domenico, *L'Olimpiade* (opera)
　　　Artaserse (opera)
　　　La bella greca (opera)
Clementi, Muzio, *Piano Sonata in E-flat Major, Opus 11*
　　　4 Piano Sonatas, Opus 12
　　　6 Piano Sonatas, Opus 13
Dalayrac, Nicolas, *Les deux tuteurs* (opera)
Fioravanti, Valentino, *Le avventure di Bertoldino* (opera)
Giordani, Giuseppe, *Tito Manlio* (opera)
　　　Pizarro nell'Indie (opera)
Giordani, Tommaso, *Gibraltar* (opera)
　　　The Haunted Castle (opera)
Grétry, André, *Théodore et Paulin* (opera)
　　　Richard Coeur-de-Lion (opera)
　　　L' preuve villageoise (opera)
Haydn, Franz J., *Symphonies No. 79-81*
　　　Concerto No. 4 for Piano and Orchestra
　　　Piano Trios No. 1 and 2
　　　Piano Sonatas No. 39-42
Kozeluch, Leopold, *Concerto No. 7 for Piano and Orchestra*
Mozart, Wolfgang A., *Piano Concertos No. 14-19*
　　　String Quartet in B-flat Major, K. 458, "The Hunt"
　　　Quintet in E-flat, K. 452, for Piano and Winds
　　　Piano Sonata in C Minor, K. 457
　　　Violin Sonata in B-flat Major, K. 454
　　　10 Variations on a Theme of Gluck, K. 455, for Piano
　　　8 Variations on a Theme of Sarti, K. 460, for Piano
　　　6 Contradances, K. 462
Paisiello, Giovanni, *Antigono* (opera)
　　　Il re Teodoro in Venezia (opera)
Piccinni, Niccolò, *Lucette* (opera)
　　　Diane et Endymion (opera)
Pugnani, Gaetano, *Adone e Venere* (opera)
Sacchini, Antonio, *Dardanus* (opera)
Salieri, Antonio, *Les Danaïdes* (opera)
　　　Il ricco d'un giorno (opera)
Sarti, Giuseppe, *Didone abbandonata* (opera)
　　　Gli amanti consolati (opera)
Shield, William, *Robin Hood* (operetta)
　　　The Noble Peasant (operetta)
Toeschi, Carlo, *Florine* (ballet)
　　　Die Amerikaner (ballet)
Vogler, Georg, *Castor e Polluce* (opera)
Weigl, Joseph, *Mass in F Major*
Winter, Peter, *Scherz, List und Rache* (opera)

1785

World Events:
In the U.S., the American Bald Eagle is added to the Great Seal; Thomas Jefferson is appointed Minister to France and John Adams Minister to Great Britain; the U.S. and Spain begin arguments over navigation rights on the Mississippi River; stage coach service begins between the major east-coast cities; New York makes slavery illegal; future President James Monroe is born. Internationally, the Russian charter puts an end to the ongoing peasant reforms and gives the nobility full right to property and ownership of serfs; Russia begins the settlement of the Aleutian Islands of Alaska; the London *Times* begins life as the *Universal Register*; the first balloon crossing of the English Channel takes place; French naturalist John J. Audubon is born.

Cultural Highlights:
The Beefsteak Society is formed in London; the magazine *Allgemeine Litteratur-Zeitung* begins publication; Thomas Warton becomes the British Poet Laureate; Johan H. Kellgren becomes the private secretary to Gustavus III of Sweden; Jean Antoine Houdon is commissioned to do a statue of George Washington; William Paley publishes his *Principles of Moral and Political Philosophy*. Births in the art world include German artist Georg F. Kersting and Scottish artist David Wilkie; deaths include Italian artists Giovanni Cipriani and Pietro Longhi, Scottish artist Alexander Runciman and French sculptor Jean Baptiste Pigalle. Births in the literary field include British critic Thomas de Quincy, poet Thomas L. Peacock and novelist Caroline Lamb, Scotch poet and critic John Wilson, German authors Bettina Brentano von Arnim and Jacob Grimm, French poet and dramatist Pierre A. Lebrun and Italian poet Alessandro Manzoni; deaths include British poets Richard Glover and William Whitehead and Swedish poet Gustav P. Creutz. Other highlights include:

Art: John Copley, *The Children of George IV*; Jean-Honoré Fragonard, *The Fountain of Love*; Thomas Gainsborough, *The Morning Walk* and *The Cottage Girl*; Francisco de Goya, *Annunciation*; Pierre Guérin, *Franz X. Richter*; Thomas Jefferson, *Virginia State Capitol*; Henry Raeburn, *Mrs. Campbell of Baltimore*; Joshua Reynolds, *The Infant Hercules*; George Romney, *Lady Hamilton as a Bacchante*

Literature: Jens Baggesen, *Comical Tales*; James Boswell, *Journal of a Tour to the Hebrides*; Gottfried A. Bürger, *Der Wilde Jäger*; William Cowper, *The Task and Other Poems*; Timothy Dwight, *The Conquest of Canaan*; Francis Hopkinson, *A Letter from a Gentleman in America*; Rudolph Raspe, *Baron Munchausen's Narrative of His Marvellous Travels and Campaigns*; Clara Reeve, *The Progress of Romance*

MUSICAL EVENTS

A. Births:

Feb 2	Isabella Colbran (Sp-sop)	Nov 2	Johann L. Fuchs (Ger-pn)
Mar 6	Karol Kurpinski (Pol-cm)	Nov 8	Frédéric Kalkbrenner (Fr-pn)
Mar 19	Pierre Zimmerman (Fr-pn)	Dec 13	Pauline Milder-Hauptmann
Apr 19	Alexandre Boëly (Fr-org)		(Ger-sop)
May 2	John Meacham, Jr. (Am-pn.m)	Dec 22	John Abbey (Br-org.m)
Jun 21	William Hawes (Br-cd)	Dec 26	Thomas Appleton (Am-org.m)
Aug 18	Friedrich Wieck (Ger-pn)		Violante Camporese (It-sop)
Sep 5	Thomas Adams (Br-org)		Alberico Curioni (It-ten)
Oct 14	Henri Valentino (Fr-cd)		James A. Hamilton (Br-the)
			Giovanni Ricordi (It-pub)

B. Deaths:

Jan 3	Baldassare Galuppi (It-cm)	Jun 6	Johann M. Demmler (Ger-org)
Apr 26	Karl von Seckendorff (Ger-cm)	Jun 2	Gottfried Homilius (Ger-org)
May 10	Étienne Floquet (Fr-cm)	Jun 22	M. van den Gheyn (Bel-org)

Jun 25	Pierre Talon (Fr-cel)	Oct 11	Paolo Alberghi (It-vn)
Jul 29	Carlo Cotumacci (It-org)	Nov 19	Bernard de Bury (Fr-cm)
Aug 2	Robert Burton (Br-hps-org)	Dec 6	Catherine Clive (Br-sop)
Aug 24	Gabriel L. Besson (Fr-vn)	Dec 8	Antonio Mazzoni (It-cm)
Sep 28	Johann Snetzler (Br-org.m)	Dec 29	Johann H. Rolle (Ger-cm)

C. Debuts:
Other - Vincenzo Calvesi (Venice), Giacomo Davide (Paris), Franz Xavier Gerl (Erlangen), Anna de Santi (Venice), Sarah Mahon Secord (London)

D. New Positions:
Conductors: Ferdinando Gioseffo Bertoni (maestro di cappella, St. Mark's, Venice), Francesco Antonio Rosetti (kapellmeister to Prince Öttingen-Wallenstein), Johann Gottfried Schicht (Leipzig Gewandhaus), Christian Theodor Weinlig (cantor, Kreuzkirche, Dresden), Georg F. Wolf (kapellmeister, Stolberg)

Educational: Giacomo Insanguine (director, Conservatorio di San Onofrio, Naples)

Others: Giovanni Grazioli (organ, St. Mark's, Venice), Jérôme Joseph de Momigny (organ, St. Pierre, Lyons), Gaetano Valeri (organ, Padua Cathedral)

E. Prizes and Honors:
Honors: Bernard de Bury (ennobled by Louis XVI), Joseph Farington (Royal Academy), Evstigney Fomin (Accademia Filarmonica, Bologna)

F. Biographical Highlights:
Martin Joseph Adrien makes his opera debut in Paris; Giuseppe Aprile retires from the stage and gains success as a voice teacher; Bonifazio Asioli has his first compositional success in Correggio; Thomas Attwood goes to Vienna where he takes lessons from Mozart; Ludwig van Beethoven studies violin with Ries; Charlotte Brent gives her final performance at Covent Garden; Domenico Cimarosa becomes the second organist at the Neapolitan Chapel; Muzio Clementi, following a short concert season in Paris, returns to London for a long stay; Celeste Coutinelli makes her Vienna debut; Jan Ladislav Dussek spends a year on the estate of Prince Radziwill; Giuseppe Farinelli enters the Naple Conservatory; Adriana Ferraresi begins a three-year stay in London; Friedrich Heinrich Himmel begins the study of theology at Halle University; Rodolphe Kreutzer becomes first violinist in the Chapelle du Roi; Antonio Lolli, leaving Russia, visits in London, Paris and Naples before settling in Palermo; Johann Gottlieb Naumann is given the task of reforming the Danish Hofkapelle in Copenhagen; Anton Reicha becomes flutist in the Bonn Orchestra; Johann Reichardt visits London with great success as a performer.

G. Institutional Openings:
Performing Groups: London Caecilian Society; Musical Society of Boston

Educational: Adgate Free School (Uranian Academy, Philadelphia)

Other: Pascal Boyle Publishing Co. (Paris); Krämert and Bossler, Darmstadt Branch; *Les Lunes*; Redoutensale Theater (Brno); William Rolfe and Co., Piano Maker and Publisher (London); Teatro do Salitre (Lisbon); Robert Woffington, Organ and Piano Maker (Dublin)

H. Musical Literature:
Adgate, Andrew, *Lessons for the Uranian Society*
Burney, Charles, *Account of the Musical Performances in Westminster Abbey...*
Chabanon, Michel de, *De la musique...*
Despréaux, Louis F., *Cours d'éducation de Clavecin ou Pianoforte*
Gruber, Johann S., *Beyträge zur literature der musik I*
Hook, James, *Guida de Musica I*

Knecht, Justin H., *Erklärung einiger missverstandenen Grundsätze aus der Vogler'schen Theorie*
Lacépède, Bernard, *Poétique de la Musique*
Lirou, Jean F., *Explication su système de l'harmonie*
Read, Daniel, *The American Singing Book*

I. Musical Compositions:

Bach, J. C. F., *Singet dem Herrn ein neues Lied* (cantata)
  Die Hirten bei der Krippe Jesu (oratorio)
Cherubini, Luigi, *La finta principessa* (opera)
Cimarosa, Domenico, *Il marito disperato* (opera)
Clementi, Muzio, *3 Four Hand Duets, Opus 14*
  3 Piano Sonatas, Opus 15
Dalayrac, Nicolas, *La Dot* (opera)
  L'amant-statue (opera)
Danzi, Franz, *Der Sylphe* (opera)
Dittersdorf, Carl von, *3 Symphonies on Ovid's "Metamorphoses"*
Giordani, Giuseppe, *Osmano* (opera)
Giordani, Tommaso, *Calypso* (opera)
  Gretna Green (opera)
  The Hypochondriac (opera)
  6 String Quartets, Opus 18
  12 Harpsichord Sonatas, Opus 25 and 28
Gossec, François, *Athalie* (incidental music)
Grétry, André, *Panurge dans l'île des lanternes* (opera)
Haydn, Franz J., *Symphony No. 83 in G Minor, "La Poule"*
  Symphony No. 85 in B-flat Major
  Symphony No. 87 in A Major
  String Quartet in D Minor, Opus 42
  Piano Trios No. 3-7
Méhul, Etienne, *Alonzo et Cora* (opera)
Mozart, Wolfgang A., *Masonic Funeral Music, K. 477*
  Piano Concertos No. 20-22, K. 466, 467 and 482
  2 String Quartets, K. 464 and 465
  Piano Quartet in G Minor, K. 478
  Violin Sonata in E-flat Major, K. 481
  Piano Fantasy in C Minor, K. 475
  Die Mauerfreude Cantate, K. 471
Naumann, Johann, *Tutto per amore* (opera)
  Il ritorno del figliolo prodigo (oratorio)
Paisiello, Giovanni, *La grotta di Trofonio* (opera)
Philidor, François, *L'amitié au village* (opera)
Piccini, Niccolò, *Pénélope* (opera)
Pugnani, Gaetano, *Achille in Sciro* (opera)
Raimondi, Ignazio, *Symphony, The Battle*
Reichardt, Johann, *Auferstehungs* (oratorio)
Salieri, Antonio, *La grotta di Trofonio* (opera)
Sarti, Giuseppe, *I finti eredi (opera)*
Shield, William, *The Choleric Fathers* (operetta)
  Frederick in Prussia (operetta)
Süssmayr, Franz X., *Karl Stuart* (opera)
Vanhal, Johann B., *6 String Quartets, Opus 33*
Viotti, Giovanni, *Concerto No. 11 for Violin and Orchestra*
Winter, Peter, *Der Bettelstudent* (opera)
Zingarelli, Nicola, *Alsinda* (opera)
  Ricimero (opera)
Zumsteeg, Johann R., *Armide* (opera)

1786

World Events:
In the U.S., Shays' Rebellion takes place in Massachusetts and is put down by state militia; the Annapolis Convention sets the stage for the first Constitutional Congress; Virginia gives up its Illinois Territory; the first Indian reservation west of the Mississippi is created; John Fitch sails the first steamboat in the New World; New Jersey bans slavery within its borders. Internationally, Lord Cornwallis becomes the Governor-General of India and seeks to bring about reforms in the governing of that country; Frederick Wilhelm II begins his reign in Prussia; Pedro III of Portugal dies and is succeeded by Maria I as sole ruler.

Cultural Highlights:
The Peale Exhibition Gallery, first in the New World, is opened in Philadelphia; the Shakespeare Gallery opens in the Pall Mall section of London; Michel Jean Sedaine is taken into the French Academy; inventor Robert Fulton spends time studying art with West in London. Births in the literary field include German authors Ludwig Börne and Wilhelm Grimm, poet Andreas Kerner, Hungarian poet and novelist Andras Fáy and French poet Marceline Desbordes-Valmore; deaths include Italian author Gasparo Gozzi, Dutch poet Jacobus Bellamy and German philosopher and grandfather of Felix, Moses Mendelssohn. Births in the world of art include British artist Benjamin Robert Haydon and German artist Franz Riepenhausen; British artist Alexander Cozens is dead. Other highlights include:

Art: François Beaucourt, *Negro Slave Girl*; Jacques Louis David, *Death of Ugolino*; Thomas Gainsborough, *Rural Scene*; Francisco de Goya, *The Seasons*; John Hoppner, *A Lady*; John Opie, *Assassination of James I*; Joshua Reynolds, *Duchess of Devonshire*; George Romney, *Sir Christopher and Lady Sykes*; Salvatore Tonci, *Giuseppe Sarti*; John Trumbull, *The Death of Montgomery at Quebec* and *Battle of Bunker Hill*

Literature: Vittorio Alfieri, *The Prince and Literature*; Gottfried A. Bürger, *Gedichte*; John Burgoyne, *The Heiress*; Robert Burns, *Poems, Chiefly in the Scottish Dialect*; Jean F. Collin d'Harleville, *L'Inconstant*; Philip Freneau, *Poems*; David Humphreys, *Poem of the Happiness of America*; Harriet Lee, *Errors of Innocence*; Johann K. Musäus, *Volkmärchen der Deutschen*; John Horne Tooke, *The Diversions of Purley I*

MUSICAL EVENTS

A. Births:

Jan 3	Friedrich Schneider (Ger-org)	Sep 12	Jean L. Tulou (Fr-fl)
Feb 2	Karel F. Pitsch (Boh-org)	Sep 27	José Elízaga (Mex-cm)
Feb 26	Marie P. Hamel (Fr-org.m)	Nov 10	Karl Eberwein (Ger-vn-cd)
Mar 4	M. Bigot de Morogues (Fr-pn)	Nov 16	Francisco Andrevi (Sp-cm)
Mar 9	John F. Danneley (Br-the)	Nov 18	Henry R. Bishop (Br-cd-cm)
Jun 21	Charles E. Horn (Br-cm-cd)	Nov 18	Carl Maria von Weber (Ger-cm)
Jul 7	John Crosse (Br-mus)	Dec 3	Iwan Müller (Ger-cl)
Jul 20	Johanna Kollmann (Br-sop)	Dec 16	Conrad Kocher (Ger-cm)
Jul 25	Giacomo Cordella (It-cm)	Dec 20	Pietro Raimondi (It-cm)
Sep 4	Tommaso Barsotti (It-cm)		Karl L. Blum (Ger-cm)
Sep 11	Friedrich Kuhlau (Ger-pn-cm)		

B. Deaths:

Jan 6	Frederica Weichsell (Br-sop)	Mar 7	Franz Benda (Cz-cm)
Jan 14	Michael Arne (Br-cm)	Apr 16	Johann Quallenberg (Ger-cl)
Feb 16	Johann Schürer (Boh-cm)	May 19	John Stanley (Br-org)
Feb 20	Johann Kleinknecht (Ger-vn)	Jul 29	Franz Asplmayr (Aus-cm)
Feb 23	Johanna Döbricht (Ger-sop)	Aug 7	Friedrich Schwindl (Hol-vn)

Aug 16 Henri de Croes (Bel-vn)   Sep 18 Giovanni Guadagnini (It-vn.m)
Aug 17 Frederick the Great (Ger-cm)   Oct 6   Antonio M. Sacchini (It-cm)
Sep 6   Carlo d'Ordonez (Aus-vn)   Dec 24 John Keeble (Br-org)

C. Debuts:
Other - Maria Theresa Bland (London), Alexander-Jean Boucher (Paris), Dorothea Bussani (Vienna), Francesca Gabrielli (London), Nicola Mestino (Paris), Jeanne Saint-Aubin (Paris), Anna de Santi (Venice), Benedikt Schack (Salzburg)

D. New Positions:
Conductors: Jean François Lesueur (maître de chapel, Notre Dame, Paris), Raimondo Lorenzini (maestro di cappella, S. Maria Maggiore, Rome), Juan Morata (maestro de capilla, Segorbe Cathedral), Wenzel Müller (kapellmeister, Leopoldstadt-Theater, Vienna), Ignaz Vitzthumb (maître de musique, Brussels Royal Chapel), Georg Joseph "Abbe" Vogler (kapellmeister, Stockholm)

Others: Olaf Ahlström (organ, Jacobskyrka, Stockholm), Luigi Boccherini (chamber composer to Friedrich Wilhelm II)

E. Prizes and Honors:
Honors: Andrew Law (honorary doctorate, Yale), William Parsons (Master of the King's Music, London)

F. Biographical Highlights:
Josepha Auernhammer marries Johann Bessenig but retains her maiden name for her concert career; bass Francesco Bussani marries soprano Dorothea Bussani; Luigi Cherubini leaves London and his position as Composer to the King and begins a year's stay in Paris; Jan Ladislav Dussek begins three years of concertizing and teaching in Paris; Thomas Greatorex goes to Italy to study singing; Franz Joseph Haydn writes his "Paris Symphonies" for the Concerts de la Loge Olympique in Paris; Friedrich Heinrich Himmel decides to devote full time to music and drops his theology study; Charles Incledon makes his London debut; Gertrud Mara makes her London stage debut at the King's Theater; Luigi Marchesi debuts in the court of Catherine the Great; Alexander Reinagle travels to New York, but finally settles in Philadelphia; Johann Peter Salomon introduces the symphonies of Haydn and Mozart in London; Georg "Abbe" Vogler resigns his Munich post in order to become kapellmeister at the Stockholm Court.

G. Institutional Openings:
Performing Groups: Salomon Concert Series (London); Stoughton Musical Society (Massachusetts)

Other: *American Musical Magazine*; J. J. Astor Music Shop (N.Y.); Besançon Opera House (France); *Columbian Magazine*; George Goulding and Co., Music Publishers (London); Liverpool Concert Hall; Nationaltheater (Old French Theater, Berlin); Pierre Jean Porro, Music Publisher (Paris)

H. Musical Literature:
Arnold/Busby, *Dictionary of Music*
Billings, William, *The Suffolk Harmony*
Frick, Philipp S., *Treatise on Thorough-Bass*
Gruber, Johann S., *Biographien einiger Tonkünstler*
Hiller, Johann A., *Über Metastasio und seine Werke*
Junker, Carl L., *Über den werth der Tonkunst*
Nares, James, *A Concise...Treatise on Singing...*(posthumous publication)
Schubart, Daniel, *Musikalisches Rhapsodien*
Tromlitz, Johann G., *Kurze abhandlung vom flötenspiel*
Walker, Joseph C., *Historical Memoirs of the Irish Bards*

I. Musical Compositions:

Anfossi, Pasquale, *L'inglese in Italia* (opera)
Bach, J. C. F., *Pygmalion* (secular cantata)
Boccherini, Luigi, *6 String Quintets, Opus 36*
 2 Symphonies, Opus 37, No. 1 and 2
Bortniansky, Dmitri, *Le faucon* (opera)
Calegari, Antonio, *L'amor soldato* (opera)
Cherubini, Luigi, *Il Giulio Sabino* (opera)
Cimarosa, Domenico, *Il credulo* (opera)
 Il sacrificio d'Abramo (oratorio)
Clementi, Muzio, *Capriccio in B-flat Major, Opus 17*
Dalayrac, Nicolas, *Nina* (opera)
 Azémia (opera)
Dittersdorf, Carl von, *Doktor und Apotheker* (opera)
 Giobbe (oratorio)
Fomin, Evstigney, *Novgorod Hero Vassily Boyeslavich* (opera)
Giordani, Giuseppe, *La vestale* (opera)
 Ifigenia in Aulide (opera)
 La morte de Abelle (oratorio)
Gossec, François, *Rosine* (opera)
Grétry, André, *Amphitryon* (opera)
 Le comte d'Albert (opera)
Guglielmi, Pietro, *Enea e Lavinia* (opera)
 L'inganno amoroso (opera)
Haydn, Franz J., *Symphony No. 82 in C Major, "L'ours"*
 Symphony No. 84 in E-flat, Major
 Symphony No. 86 in D Major
Martín y Soler, Vicente, *Una cosa rara* (opera)
 Il burbero di buon cuore (opera)
Mozart, Wolfgang A., *Symphony No. 38, K. 504, "Prague"*
 Concerto in E-flat Major, K. 495, for Horn and Orchestra
 Piano Concertos No. 23-25, K. 488, 491 and 503
 String Quartet in D Major, K. 499
 Piano Quartet in E-flat Major, K. 493
 Piano Trios No. 5-7, K. 496, 498 and 502
 Die Schauspieldirektor, K. 486 (opera)
 The Marriage of Figaro, K. 492 (opera)
Naumann, Johann, *Gustaf Wasa* (opera)
 Orpheus og Eurydike (opera)
 6 Quartets, Opus 1, for Flute, Violin, Bass and Piano
Paisiello, Giovanni, *Olimpiade II* (opera)
 Le gare generose (opera)
Philidor, François, *Thémistocle* (opera)
Reichardt, Johann, *Panthee* (opera)
 Tamerlan (opera)
Sacchini, Antonio, *Oedipe à Colone* (opera)
Salieri, Antonio, *Les Horaces (opera)*
 Amore e matrimonio (opera)
 Armida e Rinaldo (opera)
Sarti, Giuseppe, *Amore e Matrimonio* (opera)
 Armida e Rinaldo (opera)
Shield, William, *Richard Coeur de Lion* (operetta)
 The Enchanted Castle (operetta)
Süssmayr, Franz X., *Die Drillinge* (opera)
Vogel, Johann, *La toison d'or* (opera)
Zingarelli, Nicola, *Armida* (opera)
 Antigono (opera)

1787

World Events:

In the U.S., the Constitutional Convention drafts the Constitution and sends it to the States for ratification; Delaware, Pennsylvania and New Jersey become the first to ratify; the Northwest Ordinance provides for the territory north of the Ohio River and east of the Mississippi River; the Pennsylvania Society for the Encouragement of Manufactures and Useful Acts is organized; the first cotton factory is opened in Massachusetts. Internationally, the Hapsburgs claim the Austrian Netherlands; Turkey goes to war again with the Russians; the British Anti-Slavery Committee is formed; the settlement of Freetown is founded in Sierra Leone in Africa; the Edict of Versailles gives French Protestants religious freedom.

Cultural Highlights:

The Paris Museum opens; John Opie is taken into the Royal Academy of Art in London; Christian Friedrich Schubart is appointed Court Poet at Stuttgart; William Cowper suffers a temporary period of insanity; André Marie de Chénier takes an embassy post in London; Gilbert Stuart, fleeing his London creditors, goes to Dublin. Births in the field of literature include British author Mary Russell Mitford, poet Bryan Waller Procter, German poet Johann Ludwig Uhland and Russian poet Konstantin Batyushkov; deaths include German author Johann Karl Albert Musäus and British author Stephen Paxton. In the world of art, American architect William Strickland is born; dead are Italian artist Pompeo Girolamo Batoni and British artist Arthur W. Devis. Other highlights include:

Art: Antonio Canova, *Monument to Pope Clement XIV*; Jacques Louis David, *The Death of Socrates*; Thomas Gainsborough, *The Wood-Gatherers*; Charles W. Peale, *Benjamin Franklin*; Joshua Reynolds, *Angel's Heads*; Hubert Robert, *Maison Carrée*; George Stubbs, *Phaeton and Pair*; Johann H. Tischbein, *Goethe in the Roman Campagna*; Francis Wheatley, *Mr. Howard Relieving Prisoners*; Joseph Wright, The Dead Soldier

Literature: François G. Andrieux, *The Scatterbrained*; Anonymous, *Select Poems on Various Occasions, Chiefly American*; Joel Barlow, *The Vision of Columbus*; Thomas Day, *History of Sandford and Merton II*; Johann von Goethe, *Iphigenie auf Tauris*; Wilhelm Heinse, *Ardinghello und die Glückseligen Inseln*; Friedrich Klopstock, *Hermanns Tod*; Friedrich von Schiller, *Don Carlos*

MUSICAL EVENTS

A. Births:

Jan 8	Ludwig Böhner (Ger-pn)	Oct 30	Karl Guhr (Ger-cd-cm)
Feb 15	Hieronymus Payer (Aus-org-cd)	Nov 17	Michele Carafa (It-cm)
Feb 24	Christian F. Barth (Den-ob)	Nov 25	Franz Gruber (Ger-hymn)
Mar 1	Tobias Haslinger (Aus-pub)	Nov 27	Christian Rummel (Ger-cd)
Mar 13	Joseph Sellner (Ger-ob)	Dec 3	Edward Lannoy (Aus-cd)
Apr 23	John F. Burrowes (Br-org)	Dec 23	Pierre I. Begrez (Fr-ten)
Aug 5	Charles Gand, père (Fr-vn.m)		Franz X. Gebel (Ger-cm)
Aug 15	Alexander Alyabyev (Rus-cm)		Eliza Salmon (Br-sop)

B. Deaths:

Feb 8	Johann F. Gräfe (Ger-pt-cm)	May 20	Giovan Brunetti (It-cm)
Feb 21	A. Rodriguez de Hita (Sp-cm)	May 28	Leopold Mozart (Ger-vn-cm)
Mar	Matthias Hawdon (Br-org)	Jun	Ignazio Fiorillo (It-cm)
Apr 5	Adelheid Eichner (Ger-sop)	Jun 13	Josef Bárta (Cz-cm)
Apr 8	Gottfried Beck (Boh-org)	Jun 20	Karl F. Abel (Ger-vla)
Apr 22	Joseph Starzer (Aus-vn)	Aug 5	François Francoeur (Fr-vn)
		Sep 30	Anna Amalia (Ger-cm)

Oct 25   Pasquale Cafaro (It-ped)
Nov 15   Christoph W. Gluck (Ger-cm)
Nov 23   Anton Schweitzer (Ger-cm)

Charles Alexandre (Fr-vn)
Paul C. Gibert (Fr-ped)
Carlo Graziani (It-cel)

C. Debuts:

Other - John Braham (London's Covent Garden, as boy soprano), Margarethe Danzi (Munich), Johann Nepomuk Hummel (Vienna), Feliks Janiewicz (Paris), Louis Sébastien Lebrun (Paris)

D. New Positions:

Conductors: Ignazio Alberghi (kapellmeister, Warsaw), Johann Adam Hiller (Breslau), Antonio Moreira (mestre de capela, Royal Chapel, Lisbon), Vincenzo Orgitano (maestro di cappella, Naples), Vincenzo Righini (kapellmeister, Mainz), Johann Abraham Peter Schulz (kapellmeister, Copenhagen), Franz Seydelmann (kapellmeister, Dresden Italian Opera), Antonio da Silva Leite (mestre de capela, Oporto Cathedral)

Educational: Charles Simon Catel (Ecole Royale du Chant, Paris)

Others: José Lidón (organ, Chapel Royal, Madrid), Josef Preindl (organ, St. Michael's, Vienna), Joseph Supries (organ, St. Sauveur Cathedral), Daniel Gottlob Türk (organ, Liebfrauenkirche, Halle)

F. Biographical Highlights:

John Aitken brings out the first compilation of Catholic music in the New World; Ludwig van Beethoven meets Mozart while in Vienna but returns to Bonn without taking any lessons with him when he receives the news of his mother's death; Domenico Cimarosa is invited to the Russian Court in St. Petersburg by Catherine the Great and while en route, is given a hero's welcome at Vienna, Warsaw and St. Petersburg as he travels northward; Oliver Holden leaves the U.S. Navy and settles in Charleston, South Carolina; Johannes Simon Mayr is sent by a patron of music to Italy to study music with Carlo Lenzi and Ferdinando Bertoni; Wolfgang Amadeus Mozart visits Prague where he learns of the death of his father; Giuseppe Sarti loses his Russian position due to the intrigues of soprano Luiza Todi and is hired by Prince Potemkin; Johann George Schetky emigrates to the U.S. and begins teaching music in Philadelphia; Samuel Wesley suffers severe skull damage in a fall causing him considerable difficulty in future concert work.

G. Institutional Openings:

Performing Groups: Bonn Lesegesellschaft; Bordeaux Lycée; Konzerte für Kenner und Liebhaber; London Glee Club; Opéra de Marseilles

Other: Casino dei Nobili (Bologna); *Harrison's New German Flute Magazine* (London); Irish Music Fund (Dublin); Lille Opera House

H. Musical Literature:

Bernoulli, Daniel, *Essai théorique sur les vibrations des plaques vibrantes*
Chladni, Ernst, *Entdeckungen über der Theorie des Klanges*
Dalberg, Johann F., *Blicke eines Tonkünstlers in die Musik der Geister*
Hiller, Johann A., *Über alt und neu in der Musik*
Johnson, James, *The Scot's Musical Museum*
Jones, William, *The Nature and Excellence of Music*
Lesueur, Jean F., *Essai de musique sacrée ou musique motivée et méthodique...*
Miller, Edward, *Elements of Thorough Bass and Composition*
Read, Daniel, *American Singing Book Supplement*
Türk, Daniel G., *Von den wichtigsten Pflichten eines Organisten...*
Wolf, Georg F., *Kurzegefasstes musikalisches Lexikon*

I. Musical Compositions:
   Anfossi, Pasquale, *Creso* (opera)
      L'orfanella americana (opera)
   Arne, Thomas, *6 Favorite Concertos for Keyboard*
   Attwood, Thomas, *3 Piano Trios, Opus 1*
   Bach,. C. P. E., *The Resurrection and Ascension of Jesus* (oratorio)
   Bach, J. C. F., *Gott wird deinen Fuss nicht gleiten lassen* (cantata)
   Boccherini, Luigi, *2 Symphonies, Opus 37, No. 3 and 4*
      5 Sextets, Opus 38
      3 String Quintets, Opus 39
   Bortniansky, Dmitri, *Le fils rival* (opera)
   Cherubini, Luigi, *Amphion* (Freemason cantata)
   Cimarosa, Domenico, *Il fanatico burlato* (opera)
      Vôlodimirö (opera)
      Requiem pro defunctis in G Minor
   Clementi, Muzio, *Piano Sonata in C Major, Opus 20*
      6 Piano or Harpsichord Sonatas, Opus 21 and 22
   Dezède, Nicolas, *Alcindor* (opera)
   Dittersdorf, Carl von, *Orpheus der zweite* (operetta)
      Die Liebe im Narrenhause (opera)
      Hieronimus Knicker (operetta)
   Fomin, Evstigney, *The Coachmen* (opera)
   Furlanetto, Bonaventura, *Judith triumphans* (oratorio)
   Gatti, Luigi, *Demofoonte* (opera)
   Gazzaniga, Giuseppe, *Don Giovanni Tenorio* (opera)
      La Didone (opera)
      L'amor costante (opera)
   Giordani, Giuseppe, *Alciade e Telesia* (opera)
   Gossec, François, *Le pied de boeuf* (ballet)
   Grétry, André, *Le prisonnier anglais* (opera)
   Haydn, Franz J., *Symphonies No. 88 and 89*
      6 String Quartets, Opus 50, "Russian"
      The Seven Last Words (instrumental)
   Haydn, Michael, *Jubelfeier* (cantata)
      Andromeda e Perseo (opera)
   Martín y Soler, Vicente, *L'arbore di Diana* (opera)
   Méhul, Etienne, *Hypsipile* (opera)
   Mozart, Wolfgang A., *Serenade, K. 525, "Eine kleine Nachtmusik"*
      Don Giovanni (opera)
      Concerto in E-flat, K. 447, for Horn and Orchestra
      A Musical Joke, K. 522
      2 String Quintets, K. 515 and 516
      Violin Sonata in A Major, K. 526
      Piano Sonata, Four Hands, K. 521
      6 German Dances, K. 509
      9 Contradances, K. 510
   Naumann, Johann, *La reggia d'Imeneo* (opera)
      La passione di Gesù Christo II (oratorio)
   Philidor, François, *La belle esclave* (opera)
   Reichardt, Johann, *Andromeda* (opera)
      Macbeth (incidental Music)
   Saint-Georges, Joseph, *La Fille Garçon* (opera)
   Salieri, Antonio, *Tarare* (opera)
   Sarti, Giuseppe, *Alessandro nell'Indie* (opera)
   Shield, William, *Marian* (vaudeville)
      The Farmer (operetta)
   Zingarelli, Nicola, *Ifigenia in Aulide* (opera)
   Zumsteeg, Johann, *Zalaor* (opera)

1788

World Events:

In the U.S., all of the states ratify the new Constitution except for Rhode Island and North Carolina who eventually are coerced into joining the Union; Virginia and Maryland donate territory for the proposed District of Columbia. Internationally, the presentation of a List of Grievances from the people causes Louis XVI to call for a meeting of the French Estates-General; the first convicts are settle in Sydney, Australia; the Russo-Swedish War begins; George II suffers another bout of temporary insanity.

Cultural Highlights:

Francesco José de Goya is appointed as Painter to the King in Spain; Johann Gottfried Schadow is made Court Sculptor in Berlin; Anne Louis Girodet-Trioson receives the Prix de Rome in Art; John Lemprière publishes his *Classical Dictionary*. Births in the literary field include German poets Joseph von Eichendorff and Friedrich Rückert, philosopher Arthur Schopenhauer, Hungarian poet and dramatist Károly Kisfaludy and British poet George Gordon Byron; deaths include British authors Thomas Amory and Mary Delany, poet Evan Evans and Scotch poet John Logan. Births in the art world include British artist William Collins, sculptor Edward Hodges Baily, French sculptor Pierre David d'Angers and Norwegian artist Johan Christian Dahl; deaths include Dutch sculptor Pierre Antoine Tassaert, British artist Thomas Gainsborough, artist and architect James Stuart, Italian artist Francesco Zuccarelli, Swiss poet and artist Salomon Gessner and French artist Maurice-Quentin de La Tour. Other highlights include:

Art: James Barry, *King Lear Weeping over Cordelia*; Jacques-Louis David, *Paris and Helen* and *Lavoisier and His Wife*; Thomas Gainsborough, *The Haymaker and the Sleeping Girl* and *The Woodman*; Francisco de Goya, *Life of St. Francis Borgia*; John Trumbull, *Thomas Jefferson*; Benjamin West, *Edward the Black Prince and King John of France*

Literature: Francois Andrieux, *Les Étourdis*; Jean Jacques Barthélemy, *Travels of Anacharsis the Younger in Greece*; Jacques Bernadin de Saint-Pierre, *Paul et Virginie*; Vicente García de la Huerta y Muñoz, *La Raquel*; Johann von Goethe, *Egmont*; Immanuel Kant, *The Critique of Practical Reason*; Susanna Rowson, *The Inquisitor*; Charlotte Smith, *Emmeline*

MUSICAL EVENTS

A. Births:

Jan 5	Kaspar Ett (Ger-cm)	Aug 20	José B. Alcido (Peru-cm)
Jan 8	Erik Drake (Swe-cm)	Aug 26	Aloys Schmitt (Ger-pn)
Jan 23	Joseph Damse (Pol-cl-cm)	Sep 22	Johann Mosewius (Ger-mus)
Jan 31	Felice Romani (It-lib)	Oct 11	Simon Sechter (Boh-org-the)
Feb 10	Johann P. Pixis (Ger-pn)	Dec 18	Camille Pleyel (Fr-pn-cm)
Feb 25	Mateo Ferrer (Sp-org-cd)	Dec 27	Prosper Simon (Fr-org)
Mar 25	François Chanot (Fr-vn.m)		

B. Deaths:

Jan 5	Johann Schneider (Ger-org)	Apr 12	Carlo A. Campioni (It-cm)
Jan 15	Gaetano Latilla (It-cm)	Apr 12	Carlo G. Toeschi (It-vn-cm)
Jan 17	Johann G. Müthel (Ger-org)	Apr 15	Giuseppe Bonno (It-cm-cd)
Jan 17	Alessio Prati (It-cm)	Apr 30	Jean B. Cupis (Fr-vn)
Jan 31	Francesco Zannetti (It-cm)	Jun 26	Johann C. Vogel (Ger-cm)
Mar 1	Orazio Mei (It-org-cm)	Aug 23	Johann H. Stumm (Ger-org.m)
Mar 29	Charles Wesley, Sr. (Br-cm)	Sep 14	Théodore Tarade (Fr-vn)

Sep 26	Francois Bainville (Fr-org)	Dec 12	Joseph Gibbs (Br-org)
Oct 18	Jean Baptiste Cardon (Fr-vn)	Dec 14	C. P. E. Bach (Ger-cm)

C. Debuts:
Other - Francesco Albertarelli (Vienna), Dorothea Wendling (Munich)

D. New Positions:
Conductors: Gaetano Brunetti (Royal Chamber Orchestra, Madrid), Franz Götz (kapellmeister, Archbishop of Olomouc), Joseph Martin Kraus (kapellmeister, Stockholm), Johann Christoph Kühnau (cantor, Trinity Church, Berlin), Vicente Martín y Soler (kapellmeister, St. Petersburg), Antonio Salieri (kapellmeister, Vienna), Carl Bernhard Wessely (Berlin Royal Theater), Peter Winter (kapellmeister, Munich)

Educational: Ignaz Anton Ladurner (organ, Paris Conservatory)

Others: Charles Louis André (organ, St. Rombout, Mechelen), Theodore Aylward (organ, St. George's, Windsor), Nicolas Etienne Framery (editor, *Calendrier Musical Universal*)

E. Prizes and Honors:
Honors: Jean Baptiste Cordonne (Master of the King's Music, Paris)

F. Biographical Highlights:
Olof Ahlström is given a monopoly on all music printing done in Sweden; Ludwig van Beethoven, back in Bonn following the death of his mother, meets Count Waldstein and the von Breuning family; Francesco Benucci makes his London debut; Luigi Cherubini returns to Italy for one last time before moving permanently to Paris; Friedrich Johann Eck becomes concert-master of the Munich Court Orchestra; Adriana Ferraresi del Bene begins a three-year stay at the Vienna Opera; Pierre Gaviniès is given an annuity by a wealthy patron; Johann Gottlieb Graupner is discharged from the army band and goes to London where he begins playing in local orchestras; Thomas Greatorex returns to London and soon becomes a popular singing teacher; Johann Nepomuk Hummel begins a four-year concert tour throughout Europe; Jean François Lesueur retires from active conducting and moves to the country in order to be able to compose in peace; Franz Xaver Süssmayr moves to Vienna; Francesco Antonio Uttini retires from the active musical life of the Swedish Court; Georg Joseph "Abbe" Vogler visits the Court in St. Petersburg.

G. Institutional Openings:
Performing Groups: Gentlemen's Private Concerts (Glasgow); New York Musical Society

Other: Chromatic (sic) Trumpet and French Horn (by C. Clogget); *The Gentleman's Musical Magazine* (London); Nathaniel Gow Music Shop and Publisher (Edinburgh); *Journal de Guitare* (by P. J. Porro); *The Lady's Musical Magazine* (London); Mainz Nationaltheater; *Musikalische Realzeitung*; Valentine Metzler Music Shop (London--publishing by 1814); Teatro Communale (Faenza)

H. Musical Literature:
Adgate, Andrew, *Rudiments of Music*
Arteaga, Esteban de, *Rivoluzioni del teatro musicale italiano IV*
Bellermann, Johann F., *Bemerkungen über Russland*
Busby, Thomas, *The Divine Harmonist*
Dibdin, Charles, *The Musical Tour of Mr. Dibdin*
Forkel, Johann N., *Allgemeine geschichte der musik I*
Manfredini, Vincenzo, *Difesa della moderna musica*
Walder, Johann J., *Anleitung zur Singkunst*
Wolf, Ernst W., *Musikalischer unterricht für Liebhaber...*

I. Musical Compositions:

Anfossi, Pasquale, *Artaserse* (opera)
 La maga Circe (opera)
Arnold, Samuel, *The Gnome* (opera)
Boccherini, Luigi, *6 String Quintets, Opus 40*
 2 String Quartets, Opus 41
 Symphony in C Minor, Opus 41
Cannabich, Christian, *Le Croisée* (opera)
Cherubini, Luigi, *Demofoonte* (opera)
 Ifigenia in Aulide (opera)
Cimarosa, Domenico, *La vergine del sole* (opera)
 La felicità inaspettata (cantata)
Clementi, Muzio, *Piano Sonata in F Major, Opus 21*
 3 Keyboard Sonatas, Opus 22
 6 Piano Sonatas, Opus 25
Dalayrac, Nicolas, *Sargines* (opera)
 Fanchette (opera)
 Les deux sérénades (opera)
Danzi, Franz, *Die Mitternachtsstunde* (opera)
Dittersdorf, Carl von, *5 Symphonies*
 6 String Quartets
 Das rote Käppchen (opera)
Furlanetto, Bonaventura, *De solemni nuptiae in domum Lebani* (oratorio)
Giordani, Giuseppe, *Scipione* (opera)
 Il Corrivo (opera)
 Caio Ostilio (opera)
 Scipione (opera)
Giordani, Tommaso, *3 Violin Sonatas, Opus 34*
Grétry, André, *Le Rival confident* (opera)
Haydn, Franz J., *Symphonies No. 90 and 91*
 3 String Quartets, Opus 54
 3 String Quartets, Opus 55
 Piano Sonata No. 47 in D Major
Kotzwara, Franz, *The Battle of Prague* (piano)
Méhul, Etienne, *3 Piano Sonatas II*
Mozart, Wolfgang A., *Symphonies No. 39-41*
 Piano Concerto No. 26, K. 537, "Coronation"
 3 Piano Trios No. 8-10, K.542, 548 and 564
 Violin Sonata in F Major, K. 547
 Piano Sonata No. 15 in C Major, K. 545
 Adagio and Fugue in C Minor, K. 546 for String Quartet
 String Trio in E-flat Major, K. 563
 12 German Dances, K. 536 and 567
Naumann, Johann, *Medea* (opera)
Paisiello, Giovanni, *Fedra* (opera)
 L'amor contrastato (opera)
Pugnani, Gaetano, *Demofoönte* (opera)
Reichardt, Johann, *Brenno* (opera)
Saint-Georges, Joseph, *Le Marchand de Marrons* (opera)
Salieri, Antonio, *La princesse de Babylone* (opera)
 Le jugement dernier (oratorio)
 Il Talismano (opera)
Sarti, Giuseppe, *Cleomene* (opera)
Shield, William, *Alladin* (operetta)
Vogel, Johann C., *Démophon* (opera)
Zumsteeg, Johann, *Concerto No. 1 for Cello and Orchestra*
 Tamira (opera)

1789

World Events:
In the U.S., the new Constitution becomes effective; the first Congressional Session opens in April; George Washington is unanimously chosen as first President; Thomas Jefferson becomes the first Secretary of State, Henry Knox the first Secretary of War, Alexander Hamilton the first Secretary of the Treasury and John Jay is the first Supreme Court Justice; the Federalist Party is formally founded; the Federal Judiciary Act is passed; New York City becomes the first capitol; Georgetown University is opened; Thanksgiving Day is first celebrated. Internationally, the French Estates-General declares itself to be the National Assembly and passes the Declaration of the Rights of Man; the Parisian Bastille is stormed on July 14 and becomes the French Independence Day; the Brabant Revolution takes place in the Low Countries; the mutiny on the *H. M. S. Bounty* takes place and the mutineers settle on the remote island of Pitcairn in the South Pacific.

Cultural Highlights:
The magazine *Moniteur* begins publication in Paris; Anne Louis Girodet-Trioson receives the Prix de Rome in Art; Francisco José de Goya becomes Painter to the King in Spain; Nikolai Abildgaard becomes director of the Copenhagen Academy of Art; Johann Heinrich Wilhelm Tischbein becomes director of the Naples Academy of Art. Births in the art field include French artists Jules R. Auguste and Horace Vernet, German artist Johannes Riepenhausen and British artist John "Mad" Martin; deaths include German artist Johann Heinrich Tischbein, Swiss artist Jean Étienne Liotard and French artist Claude-Joseph Vernet. Births in the literary field include American novelist James Fenimore Cooper, British author Marguerite Blessington, Scotch poet Thomas Pringle, German author Friedrich von Heyden, Danish poet and novelist Bernhard Ingemann and Italian author Silvio Pellico; deaths include British novelist John Cleland and author Thomas Day. Other highlights include:

Art: Jacques Louis David, *Brutus Receiving His Son's Body*; Ralph Earl, *Daniel Boardman*; François Gérard, *Joseph and His Brothers*; Jean-Antoine Houdon, *Thomas Jefferson* (bust); Jean Baptiste Regnault, *The Descent from the Cross*; Hubert Robert, *Pulling Down of the Bastille*; Johann G. Schadow, *Tomb of Count von der Marck*; John Trumbull, *Sortie, Garrison of Gibraltar*

Literature: Vittorio Alfieri, *Brutus the Second*; William Blake, *Songs of Innocence*; William Bowles, *14 Sonnets*; Robert Burns, *Auld Lang Syne*; Francisco Clavijero, *Storia della California*; Thomas Day, *History of Sandford and Merton III*; William Dunlap, *The Father of an Only Child*; Johann von Goethe, *Torquato Tasso*; Friedrich Schiller, *Die Künstler*; Thomas Thorild, *Sermon of Sermons*

MUSICAL EVENTS

A. Births:

Jan 12	Davidde Banderali (It-ten)	Aug 15	Alexander Alyabyev (Rus-cm)
Jan 23	Giulio Bordogni (It-ten)	Sep 17	Christian Fischer (Ger-bs)
Jan 30	George A. Kollmann (Br-pn)	Oct 1	John Firth (Am-pn.m)
Feb 1	Hippolyté Chélard (Fr-vn)	Oct 13	Josephine Fodor-Mainvielle
Feb 8	Ludwig W. Maurer (Ger-vn)		(Fr-sop)
Feb 15	Friedrich E. Fesca (Ger-vn)	Oct 18	Giovanni Tadolini (It-cm)
May 16	Johann Schelble (Ger-ten-cd)	Oct 24	Ramón Carnicer (Sp-cm)
Jun 27	Friedrich Silcher (Ger-cm)	Oct 26	Joseph Mayseder (Aus-vn)
Jul 19	Horace Maecham (Am-pn.m)	Oct 28	Johann G. Schneider (Ger-org)
Jul 21	Joseph M. Wolfram (Boh-cm)	Dec 8	John Fawcett (Br-cm)
Jul 28	Pierre Hédouin (Fr-mus)	Dec 14	Maria Szymanowska (Pol-pn)
Aug 9	Nicholas C. Bochsa (Fr-hp)		György Adler (Hun-cm)

B. Deaths:

Jan 1	Christlieb Binder (Ger-cm)	Jul 15	Jacques Duphly (Fr-hps)
Jan 24	Karl Westenholz (Ger-cm)	Sep 12	Franz X. Richter (Ger-cm)
Feb 2	Armand L. Couperin (Fr-hps)	Sep 27	Giovanale Sacchi (It-mus)
Apr 1	Johann Hartknoch (Ger-pub)	Oct 6	Cecilia Young (Arno)(Br-sop)
May 5	Giuseppe Baretti (It-cri)	Oct 10	Pierre L. Couperin (Fr-org)
May 12	Robert Bremner (Br-pub)	Oct 14	Anne Catley (Br-sop)
May 21	John Hawkins (Br-mus)	Oct 24	Joaquín de Oxinaga (Sp-org)
Jun 14	Johann W. Hertel (Ger-vn)	Oct 31	Pasquale Bondini (It-bs-imp)
Jul	Nicola Mestrino (It-vn)		Johann G. Wagner (Ger-pn.m)

C. Debuts:

Other - George Bridgetower (age 9, Paris), Pierre Gaveaux (Paris), Josephina Grassini (Parma), Jean-Blaise Martin (Paris), Giuseppe Naldi (Milan)

D. New Positions:

Conductors: João Baldi (mestre de capela, Guarda Cathedral), Ferdinand Fränzl (Munich Court Orchestra), Stanislao Mattei (maestro di cappella, S. Petronio, Bologna), Ignace Pleyel (kapellmeister, Strasbourg Cathedral), Francesco A. Rosetti (kapellmeister, Duke of Mecklenburg-Schwerin)

Educational: Johann Ada, Hiller (cantor, Leipzig Thomasschule), Ambrogio Minoja (director, Milan Conservatory)

Others: Cayetano Carreño (organ, Caracas Cathedral), George Colman, Jr. (manager, Haymarket Theater), Gervais-François Couperin (organ, St. Gervais, Paris), August Müller (organ, St. Ulrich, Magdeburg), Nicolas Séjan (organ, Royal Chapel, Paris)

E. Prizes and Honors:

Honors: Pierre-Louis Couperin (Organist to the King, Paris)

F. Biographical Highlights:

Felice Alessandri returns to Berlin where he becomes assistant director at the Court Opera; Vincenzo Calvesi makes his Vienna debut; Charles Dibdin begins his "Table Entertainments" in London which become extremely popular; Jan Ladislav Dussek flees the French Revolution to London where he settles for an 11-year stay; William Herschel finishes building his 40-foot telescope; Samuel Holyoke graduates from Harvard and begins teaching music; Nicolas Isouard, forced to leave France during the Revolution, goes to Italy; Konradin Kreutzer is sent to the Monastery of Zweifalten to study with Rieger; Johannes Simon Mayr studies with Lenzi in Bergamo and Ferdinando Bertoni in Venice; Wolfgang Amadeus Mozart visits Berlin, Leipzig and Dresden with Prince Lichnowsky; Johann Friedrich Peter writes what is believed to be the oldest preserved chamber music written in the New World; Louis Spohr, age five, begins taking violin lessons; Nicola Zingarelli moves to Paris.

G. Institutional Openings:

Performing Groups: Hamburger Harmonic Gesellschaft

Educational: French Conservatory of Music (Paris)

Other: Charles Albrecht, Piano Maker (Philadelphia); Bacon Piano Co. (N.Y.); Saitenharmonika (by Johann Andreas Stein); Théâtre de Monsieur (Paris); Théâtre de Société (Montreal)

H. Musical Literature:

Adgate, Andrew, *Philadelphia Harmony*
Arteaga, Esteban de, *Investigaciones filósoficas sobre la belleza ideal...*
Bayly, Anselm, *The Alliance of Musick, Poetry and Oratory*
Forkel, Johann N., *Geschichte der italianischen Oper...*

French, Jacob, *New American Melody*
Furlanetto, Bonaventura, *Lezioni de contrappunto*
Grétry, André, *Mémoires*
Gunn, John, *Theory and Practice of Fingering the Violoncello*
Hiller, Johann A., *Wer ist wahre Kirchenmusik?*
Sabbatini, Luigi, *Elementi teorici della musica...*
Türk, Daniel G., *Clavierschule*

I. Musical Compositions:

Beethoven, Ludwig van, *2 Preludes, Opus 39, for Piano or Organ*
Boccherini, Luigi, *Symphony in D Major, Opus 42*
    6 String Quartets, Opus 42
    Octet in E-flat Major, Opus 42
Cimarosa, Domenico, *Cleopatra* (opera)
Clementi, Muzio, *2 Piano Sonatas, Opus 24*
Dalayrac, Nicolas, *Raoul, sire de Créqui* (opera)
    Les deux petits Savoyards (opera)
Danzi, Franz, *Der Triumph der Treue* (opera)
    Der Quasimann (opera)
Dittersdorf, Carl von, *Hieronymus Knicker* (opera)
    Der Schiffspatron (opera)
    6 String Quintets
Furlanetto, Bonaventura, *Triumphus Jephte* (oratorio)
Giordani, Tommaso, *Perseverance* (opera)
Grétry, André, *Aspasie* (opera)
    Raoul Barbe-bleue (opera)
Haydn, Franz J., *Symphony No. 92 in G Major, "Oxford"*
    Piano Sonatas No. 43 and 44
    Arianna a Naxos (solo cantata)
    Fantasie in C Major for Piano
    Piano Trios No. 8-10
Martín y Soler, Vicente, *Mock Hero Kosometovich* (opera)
Mozart, Wolfgang A., *String Quartet in D Major, "King of Prussia I"*
    Clarinet Quintet in A Major, K. 581
    Piano Sonata No. 17, K. 576
    6 German Dances, K. 571
    12 German Dances, K. 586
    12 Minuets, K. 585
Paisiello, Giovanni, *Nina* (opera)
    Catone in Utica (opera)
    I Zingari in fiera (opera)
    Requiem in C Minor for Double Choir
Peter, Johann, *6 String Quintets*
Pugnani, Gaetano, *Demetrio a Rodi* (opera)
Reichardt, Johann, *Jery und Bätely* (opera)
    Claudine von Villa Bella (opera)
Rosetti, Francesco, *Das Winterfest der Hirten* (opera)
Salieri, Antonio, *La Cifra* (opera)
    Il pastor fido (opera)
Sarti, Giuseppe, *Te Deum*
Schuster, Josef, *Rübezahl* (opera)
Storace, Stephen, *The Haunted Tower* (opera)
Süssmayr, Franz X., *Die väterliche Rache* (opera)
    Die liebe auf dem Lande (opera)
Weinlig, Christian T., *Die Feier des Todes Jesu* (oratorio)
Wranitzky, Paul, *Oberon, König der Elfen* (opera)
Zingarelli, Nicola, *Antigone* (opera)
    Artaserse (opera)

1790

World Events:

In the U.S., the Census shows a population of 3,929,214 within 13 states; Philadelphia, the largest colonial city, becomes the temporary new capitol of the country; the U.S. Patent Office is created and the first copyright act is passed; the U.S. Coast Guard is formed; publication begins on *Dobson's Encyclopedia*; the Treaty of Greenville with the Indians settles the Ohio problem; Benjamin Franklin dies and future President John Tyler is born. Internationally, the French National Assembly draws up a constitution forming a limited monarchy; Austria crushes the Brabant Revolution in Belgium; the Third Mysore War is fought in India; Joseph II of Austria dies and is succeeded by Leopold II; the manufacture of wristwatches and sewing machines begins; Edmund Burke publishes his *Reflections on the French Revolution*.

Cultural Highlights:

George Ellis publishes his *Early English Poets*; Henry James Pye is made British Poet Laureate; Henry Fuseli is taken into the Royal Academy in London; Asmus Jakob Carstens becomes a professor at the Berlin Academy of Art; Edmund Malone publishes his own edition of Shakespeare. British sculptor John Gibson is born; deaths in the art world include British sculptor John Bacon and French artist Charles Cochin. Births in the field of literature include American poet Fitz-Greene Halleck, French poet Alphonse de Lamartine, British novelist Anna Eliza Bray, Swedish poet Per Daniel Atterbom, Austrian poet and dramatist Joseph von Zedlitz and Italian poet Tommaso Grossi; deaths include British poet Thomas Warton, French poet Antoine de Bertin and Scottish economist and philosopher Adam Smith. Other highlights include:

Art: Henry Fuseli, *Titania and Bottom*;   Francisco de Goya, *The Plain of Isidro*; Francesco Guardi, *Island in the Lagoon*;   Jean-Antoine Houdon, *Apollo* (bronze); Thomas Lawrence, *The Countess of Denby*;   George Morland, *Inside the Stable*; Alexander Roslin, *Self-Portrait*; Johann Zoffany, *Charles Towneley among His Marbles*

Literature: Archibald Alison, *Essays on the Nature and Principles of Taste*;   Joanna Baillie, *Fugitive Verses*;   Karl Bellmann, *Fredmans Epistlar*;   William Blake, *Marriage of Heaven and Hell*; William Bligh, *Mutiny on Board the Bounty*; James Bruce, *Travels to Discover the Source of the Nile*;   Robert Burns, *Tam O'Shanter*;   Immanuel Kant, *Critique of Judgment*;   Ann Radcliffe, *A Sicilian Romance*

MUSICAL EVENTS

A. Births:

Feb 1	Franz J. Antony (Ger-mus)	Jun 21	Wilhelm Speyer (Ger-vn)
Feb 2	Domenico Donzelli (It-ten)	Jul 3	Christian Pohlenz (Ger-org)
Feb 11	Ignaz Assmayr (Aus-org)	Jul 13	Albrecht W.J. Agthe (Ger-pn)
Feb 16	Chretien Urhan (Fr-vn)	Oct 8	Waldemar Thrane (Nor-cd)
Mar 15	Nicola Vaccai (It-cm)	Oct 15	Giovanni Davide (It-ten)
Mar 17	Luiz Lambertini (It-pn.m)	Oct 30	Karl Lipinski (Pol-vn)
May 14	William L. Viner (Br-hymn)	Nov 7	Luigi Legnani (It-gui)
Jun 8	Anton Forti (Aus-bar)		Isaac Nathan (Br-cm)

B. Deaths:

Jan 16	Johann Küchler (Ger-cm)	Feb 21	Johann F. Klöffler (Ger-cd)
Jan 25	Giusto Tenducci (It-cas)	Apr 2	Carlo Ferrari (It-cel)
Feb 12	Wilhelm Enderle (Ger-vn)	Apr 13	C. H. Eisenbrandt (Ger-inst.m)
Feb 14	Capel Bond (Br-org)	May 24	François Clicquot (Fr-org.m)
Feb 19	Johann Krumpholtz (Boh-hp)	Jun 8	Charles van Helmont (Bel-cm)

Aug 24 John Worgan (Br-org)   Dec 16 Ludwig A. Lebrun (Ger-ob)
Sep 3 Thomas Morris (Br-ten-org)   Angiola Calori (It-sop)
Sep 28 Nicholas Esterházy (Hun-pat)

C. Debuts:
U.S. -- John Christopher Moller (N.Y.)

Other - Antonio Peregrino Benelli (Naples), Jean Elleviou (Paris), Jacques-Pierre Rode (Paris), Elizaveta Sandunova (St. Petersburg)

D. New Positions:
Conductors: Mathieu Frederic Blasius (Comédie-Italienne, Paris), Antonio Brunetti (maestro di cappella, Chieti Cathedral), Luigi Caruso (maestro di cappella, Cingoli) Ignaz Fränzl (Mannheim Orchestra), Franz Xaver Glöggl (kapellmeister, Linz Cathedral), Johann Baptist Henneberg (Theater an der Wien), Pierre Lahoussaye (Théâtre de Monsieur, Paris), Antonio Moreira (Italian Opera Theater, Lisbon), Philippe Jacques Pfeffinger (maître de musique, Strasbourg)

Educational: Philip Hayes (organ, St. John's College), Christian Ruppe (kapellmeister, University of Leiden)

Others: William Crotch (organ, Christ Church, Oxford), Johann Christian Rinck (municipal organ, Giessen), Bishop Simms (organ, Birmingham Cathedral)

E. Prizes and Honors:
Honors: Anton Walter (Royal Court Chamber Organ and Instrument Maker)

F. Biographical Highlights:
Inácio António de Almeida becomes acting mestre de capela at Nossa Senhora de Oliviera in Guimaraes; Johann Anton André is ordained a priest; Pasquale Anfossi gives up composing and enters the service of the church; Ludwig van Beethoven meets Haydn; Muzio Clementi makes his last public appearance; Domenico Corri moves to London; Franz Danzi marries singer Marguerite Marchand; Jan Ladislav Dussek, settled in London, quickly becomes a favorite of the public; Josephina Grassini makes her La Scala debut; Franz Joseph Haydn is retired with a pension; Johann Nepomuk Hummel begins a two-year stay in London; Charles Incledon debuts at Covent Garden; Wolfgang Amadeus Mozart misses the kapellmeister position in Vienna; Sigismund Neukomm enters the Benedictine school in Salzburg; Johann Reichardt is given a three-year leave of absence with pay; Antoinette Saint-Huberty marries the Comte d'Entraigues and retires from the stage; Daniel Steibelt takes up permanent residence in Paris; Václav Jan Tomášek enters Prague University to study law; Joseph Weigl becomes assistant to Salieri at the Vienna Court; Joseph Wölfl goes to Vienna to study with Mozart; Paul Wranitzky becomes concertmaster of the Vienna Opera.

G. Institutional Openings:
Performing Groups: Abo Musical Society (Finland)

Educational: Perugia Musical Institute; Society of Musical Graduates (London)

Other: Maurice Hime, Music Publisher (Liverpool); Oliver Holden Music Store (Charleston, South Carolina); James Johnson Music Shop (Lawnmarket); *Journal de Modinhas*; Theobald Monzani Flute Co. (London); Tannenberg Organ, Zion Lutheran Church (Philadelphia); Théâtre Royal (Nice); George Walker, Music Publisher (London)

H. Musical Literature:
Albrechtsberger, Johann, *Gründliche Anweisung zur Composition*
Böcklin, Franz F., *Beiträge zur Geschichte der Musik...*
Gatayes, Guillaume, *Guitar Method*

Gehot, Joseph, *The Art of Bowing the Violin*
Gerber, Ernest L., *Historisch-biographisches Lexikon der Tonkünstler I*
Kauer, Ferdinand, *Singschule nach dem neuesten System der Tonkunst*
Marpurg, Friedrich, *Neue Methode, allerley Arten von Temperaturen dem Claviere auf bequemste Mitzutheilen*
Schulz, Johann A., *Gedanken über den Einfluss der Musik auf die Bildung eines Volks*
Solano, Francisco, *Exame instructivo sobre a Musica multiforme, metrica e rythmica*

I. Musical Compositions:

Alessandri, Felice, *L'ouverture du grand opéra italien à Nankin* (opera)
Arnold, Samuel, *New Spain* (opera)
Beethoven, Ludwig van, *Cantata on the Death of Joseph II*
Boccherini, Luigi, *3 String Quintets, Opus 43*
    Symphony in D Major, Opus 43
    2 String Quartets, Opus 43
Clementi, Muzio, *3 Piano Sonatas, Opus 23*
    6 Piano Sonatas, Opus 25
Dalayrac, Nicolas, *La Soirée orageuse* (opera)
    Le Chêne patriotique (opera)
    Vert-Vert (opera)
Dittersdorf, Carl von, *Hokus-Pokus* (opera)
    Der Teufel ein Hydraulikus (opera)
Giardini, Felice de', *6 String Trios, Opus 26*
    6 String Quartets, Opus 29
    6 Piano Trios, Opus 30
    2 Keyboard Sonatas, Opus 31
Giordani, Giuseppe, *Caio Mario* (opera)
Giordani, Tommaso, *6 Keyboard Sonatas, Opus 34*
    6 Keyboard Sonatas, Opus 35
Gossec, François, *Te Deum* (male voices)
Grétry, André, *Pierre le Grand* (opera)
Guglielmi, Pietro, *La serva innamorata* (opera)
Haydn, Franz J., *6 String Quartets, Opus 64*
    Piano Trios No. 11-14
Haydn, Michael, *Quintet in E-flat Major*
Holyoke, Samuel, *Washington* (song)
Kashin, Daniil, *Concerto for Piano and Orchestra*
Kozeluch, Leopold, *Didone abbandonata* (opera)
Kreutzer, Rodolphe, *Jeanne d'Arc a Orleans* (opera)
Martín y Soler, Vicente, *La melomania* (opera)
Méhul, Etienne, *Euphrosine et Coradin* (opera)
Mozart, Wolfgang A., *Cosi fan tutti, K. 588* (opera)
    String Quartets No. 22 and 23, K. 589 and 590
    String Quintet in D Major, K. 593
    Adagio and Allegro, K. 594, for Mechanical Organ
    3 Contradances, K. 106
Naumann, Johann, *La morte d'Abel* (oratorio)
Paisiello, Giovanni, *Zenobia in Palmira* (opera)
    Le vane gelosie (opera)
Reichardt, Johann, *L'Olimpiade* (opera)
    Faust I (incidental music)
Righini, Vincenzo, *Alcide al Birio* (opera)
Salieri, Antonio, *Catilina* (opera)
    Sappho (opera)
Shield, William, *The Czar Peter* (operetta)
Winter, Peter, *Jery und Bäteli* (opera)
Zingarelli, Nicola, *La morte de Cesare* (opera)

1791

World Events:
In the U.S., the Bill of Rights is ratified and goes into effect; Vermont becomes State No. 14, the first to enter following the original thirteen states; the Bank of the United States is the first to be chartered by the Congress; the Lancaster Pike is opened between Philadelphia and Lancaster in Pennsylvania; Congress passes a tax on distilled spirits, the first internal revenue law; future President James Buchanan is born. Internationally, Louis XVI and his family try to slip out of France, but are caught and put under house arrest in Paris; the Canada Act divides that country into Ontario and Quebec, the English and French sectors; the International Copyright Agreement is passed by several European countries.

Cultural Highlights:
The magazine *Journal de Débats* begins publication in Paris; Peter François Bourgeois is given the Polish Order of Merit; Philip Morin Freneau becomes editor of the Philadelphia *National Gazette*; Johann Wolfgang von Goethe becomes director of the Weimar Court Theater; William Cowper completes his translation of Homer; Lorenzo da Ponte is dismissed from the Viennese Court and goes to London; Isaac Disraeli publishes his *Curiosities of Literatures, Volume I*. Births in the world of art include American sculptor Hezekiah Augur and French artist Jean Louis Théodore Géricault; French sculptor Étienne Maurice Falconet dies. Births in the literary field include Austrian poet and dramatist Franz Grillparzer, French poet Émile Deschamps, dramatist and librettist Augustin Eugène Scribe, German poet Karl Theodor Körner, Russian novelist Sergei Aksakov, Irish dramatist Richard Lalor Sheil and Polish poet Kazimierz Brodzinski. Other highlights include:

Art: Charles Bulfinch, *Beacon Hill Monument*; John Copley, *The Siege of Gibraltar*; Jacques-Louis David, *The Tennis-Court Oath*; Ralph Earl, Mrs. Moseley and Son; Francesco Guardi, *Gondola*; Jean-Antoine Houdon, *George Washington* (Virginia); Carl G. Langhans, *Brandenburg Gate* (Berlin); Augustin Pajou, *Psyché Abandoned*; John Trumbull, *Eliza Rutledge*; Elisabeth Vigée-Lebrun, *Self-Portrait*

Literature: Jens Baggesen, *Labyrinthen*; Karl Bellmann, *Fredmans Sänger*; William Blake, *French Revolution*; Manuel Bocage, *Rimas I*; James Boswell, *Life of Samuel Johnson*; Marie Chénier, *Henry VIII*; Benjamin Franklin, *Autobiography*; Elizabeth Inchbald, *A Simple Story*; Friedrich Klinger, *Fausts Leben, Toten und Höllenfahrt*; Ann Radcliffe, *Romance of the Forest*; Susanna Rowson, *Charlotte Temple*

MUSICAL EVENTS

A. Births:

Jan 6	José H. Gomis (Sp-cm)	May 29	Pietro Romani (It-cm)
Jan 28	Ferdinand Hérold (Fr-cm)	Jun 30	Félix Savant (Fr-acous)
Feb 20	Karl Czerny (Aus-pn-cm)	Sep 5	Giacomo Meyerbeer (Ger-cm)
Mar 9	Nicholas Levasseur (Fr-bs)	Oct 7	Friedrich Grund (Ger-cm)
Apr	Henri L. Blanchard (Fr-vn)	Nov 28	Gottfried Fischer (Ger-voc)
Apr 11	Désiré Beaulieu (Fr-cm-au)	Dec 4	Johann G. Töpfer (Ger-org)
May 11	Jan Václav Voríšek (Boh-cm)	Dec 9	Peter von Lindpainter (Ger-cd)
May 27	Johann Gabrielski (Ger-fl)	Dec 9	John Sinclair (Scot-ten)

B. Deaths:

Jan 22	Guillaume Boutmy (Bel-org)	May 14	Franziska Lebrun (Ger-sop)
Feb 5	John Beard (Br-ten)	Aug 25	Pietro D. Paradies (It-cm)
Mar 2	John Wesley (Br-hymn)	Sep 2	Franz Kotzwara (Cz-vn)
Mar 27	John Alcock, Jr. (Br-org)	Sep 25	Giovanni Ferrandini (It-cm)
May 9	Francis Hopkinson (Am-mus)	Oct 10	Christian Schubart (Ger-cm)

Nov 1 Carl Türrschmidt (Ger-hn)   Luigi Braccini (It-cm)
Dec 5 Wolfgang A. Mozart (Aus-cm)   Marie Anne Quinault (Fr-sop)
                                          Isabella Young (Br-alto)

C. Debuts:
Other - Sophia Giustina Corri (London), Margarete Luise Schick (Mainz), Luigi Zamboni (Ravenna)

D. New Positions:
Conductors: Pasquale Anfossi (maestro di cappella), Domenico Cimarosa (kapellmeister, Vienna), Giuseppe Gazzaniga (maestro di cappella, Crema Cathedral), Giuseppe Giordani (maestro di cappella, Fermo Cathedral), Jan Kucharz (Prague Opera), José Mauricio (mestre de capela, Coimbra Cathedral), Johann Rudolf Zumsteeg (Stuttgart Opera)

Others: François Boieldieu (organ, St. Andre, Rouen), George Thomas Smart (organ, St. James Chapel, London)

E. Prizes and Honors:
Honors: Antonio Calegari (Accademico Filarmonica, Bologna), Franz Joseph Haydn (honorary doctorate, Oxford)

F. Biographical Highlights:
Maria Theresia Ahlefeldt moves with her husband to Copenhagen where she experiences some success as a composer; Johann Georg Albrechtsberger becomes the assistant kapellmeister at St. Stephen's in Vienna; Joseph Karl Ambrosch is appointed first tenor of the Berlin Royal Theater; Elizabeth Anspach marries her second husband, the Margrave Christian Frederick; Theodore Aylward receives his doctorate in music from Oxford; Isidore Bertheaume flees the French Revolution and goes to Germany; Domenico Cimarosa leaves Russia and returns to Vienna; Józef Elsner becomes concert master of the Brünn Opera orchestra; Adrianna Ferraresi leaves Vienna for Trieste with Lorenzo da Ponte who is dismissed from service at the Court; Margarete Luise Hamel marries violinist Ernst Schick; Franz Joseph Haydn visits London for the first time when his symphonies are performed at Salomon's concerts; Jozef Kozlowski moves to Russia; Wolfgang Amadeus Mozart receives a visit from the "mysterious stranger" who commissions him to write a *Requiem*; Niccolò Piccini leaves Paris for Naples; Ignace Joseph Pleyel begins a year's stay in London conducting the Professional Concerts; Daniel Steibelt goes to Paris and wins a keyboard competition with Pleyel; Carl Friedrich Zelter begins music study with Fasch.

G. Institutional Openings:
Performing Groups: Berliner Singakademie; Noblemen's Subscription Concerts (London); Philo-Harmonic Society (Boston); St. Cecilia Society of New York

Other: Her Majesty's Theater II (London); Hug and Co., Music House and Publishers (Zürich); *Musikalisches Magazin auf der Höhe* (Brunswick); *Musikalisches Wochenblatt*; Orchestrion (by Thomas Anton Kunz); Teatro Riccardi (Bergamo); Théâtre de St. Pierre (New Orleans); Théâtre Français de la Rue Richelieu (Paris)

H. Musical Literature:
Aprile, Giuseppe, *Vocal Method*
Campagnoli, Bartolomeo, *Nouvelle méthode de la mécanique progressive du jeu de violon*
Dalberg, Johann F., *Vom Erfinden und Bilden*
Galeazzi, Francesco, *Elementi teorico-pratici di Musica I*
Holyoke, Samuel, *Harmonia Americana*
Jackson, William, *Observations on the Present State of Music in London*
Sarti, Giuseppe, *Trattato del basso generale*

Schubart, Daniel, *Leben und gesinnungen*
Tromlitz, Johann G., *Ausführlicher und gründlicher unterricht die Flöte zu spielen*
Türk, Daniel G., *Kurze anweisung zum generalbassspielen*
Zinck, Harnack, *Kompositionen für den Gesang I*

I. Musical Compositions:
Alessandri, Felice, *Dario* (opera)
Arnold, Samuel, *The Surrender of Calais* (opera)
Attwood, Thomas, *3 Piano Sonatas, Opus 2, with Cello*
Cherubini, Luigi, *Lodoïska* (opera)
Clementi, Muzio, *Sonata in F Major for Piano, Opus 26*
    3 Piano Sonatas, Opus 27, with Violin and Cello
Dalayrac, Nicolas, *Camille* (opera)
    Philippe et Georgette (opera)
    Agnès et Olivier (opera)
Fomin, Evstigney, *Magician, Fortune-Teller and Match-maker* (opera)
Gazzaniga, Giuseppe, *La disfatta dei Mori* (opera)
Giordani, Giuseppe, *Don Mitrillo contrastato* (opera)
    Medonte (opera)
Giordani, Tommaso, *The Distressed Knight* (opera)
Gossec, François, *Le chant du 14 juillet*
Grétry, André, *Guillaume Tell* (opera)
Haydn, Franz J., *Symphony No. 93 in D Major*
    Symphony No. 94 in G Major, "Surprise"
    Symphony No. 95 in C Minor
    Symphony No. 96 in D Major, "Miracle"
    L'anima del filosofo (opera)
Haydn, Michael, *Der fröhliche wiederschein* (cantata)
Kreutzer, Rodolphe, *Paul et Virginie* (opera)
    Lodoiska (opera)
Martín y Soler, Vicente, *Fedul and His Children* (opera)
    Il castello d'Atlante (opera)
Méhul, Etienne, *Cora* (opera)
Mozart, Wolfgang A., *The Magic Flute, K. 620* (opera)
    La clemenza di Tito, K. 621 (opera)
    Concerto No. 27, K. 595, for Piano and Orchestra
    Concerto in A Major, K. 622, for Clarinet and Orchestra
    Motet, "Ave verum corpus", K. 618
    Eine Kleine Freimauer-Cantata, K. 623
    Requiem Mass, K. 626 (finished by Süssmayr)
    String Quintet in E-flat Major, K. 614
    Adagio and Rondo in C Major, K. 617
    6 Variations on a Theme by Schack, K. 613
    12 Minuets, K. 599, 601 and 604
    20 German Dances, K. 600, 602, 605, 606 and 611
Naumann, Johann, *La dama soldato* (opera)
    Mass in A Major
Paër, Ferdinando, *Circe* (opera)
Paisiello, Giovanni, *Ipermestra* (opera)
    Te Deum
Reichardt, Johann, *Erwin und Elmire* (opera)
    Egmont (incidental music)
Sarti, Giuseppe, *Il trionfo d'Atalanta* (opera)
Schenk, Johann, *Der Erntekranz* (opera)
Shield, William, *The Woodman* (operetta)
Süssmayr, Franz X., *Der rauschige Hans* (opera)
Zingarelli, Nicola, *Pirro, Ré d'Epiro* (opera)

1792

World Events:
In the U.S., George Washington is re-elected as President; the Republican Party, or Democratic-Republican Party is formed in opposition to the Federalists with Thomas Jefferson as party head; Congress passes a Coinage Act establishing the first mint at Philadelphia and providing for a decimal system of of money; the motto "E Pluribus Unum" is first used; Kentucky becomes State No. 15; Columbus Day is created; the New York Stock Exchange is organized in New York; *The Farmer's Almanac* begins publication. Internationally, Poland suffers invasion by both Russia and Prussia; the Russo-Turkish War ends; the War of the First Coalition begins with France declaring war on Austria and Prussia; Denmark abolishes the slave trade; Leopold II of Austria dies and is succeeded by Francis II.

Cultural Highlights:
Benjamin West becomes President of the Royal Academy of Art in London; Thomas Lawrence is appointed Painter to the King in London; Wilhelm von Kobell is appointed painter to the Munich Court; William Thornton wins the design competition for the National Gallery in Washington, D.C. Births in the art world include American artist Chester Harding, British artists George Cruikshank and George Hayter and French sculptor James Pradier; deaths include American artist John Greenwood, French sculptor Jean Jacques Caffieri, British artists William Hoare and Joshua Reynolds and architect Robert Adam. Births in the literary field include British novelist Frederick Marryat and poet John Keble; deaths include Russian dramatist Denis Ivanovich Fonvizin and German poet and dramatist Jakob Reinhold Lenz. Other highlights include:

Art: Charles Bulfinch, *Hartford State House*; Jacques-Louis David, *Devienne*; Ralph Earl, *Justice Ellsworth and His Wife*; John Flaxman, *The Fury of Athamas*; Henry Fuseli, *Falstaff in the Buck Basket*; Thomas Hardy, *Franz Joseph Haydn*; George Morland, *Ale House Door*; George Romney, *Lady Hamilton as Cassandra*; Jacques Soufflot, *Pantheon of Ste. Geneviève*; George Stubbs, *Hound and Bitch in Landscape*

Literature: Thomas Holcroft, *The Road to Ruin*; Gabriel Legouvé, *La Mort d'Abel*; Jakob Lenz, *Pandaemonium Germanicum*; Hannah More, *Village Politics*; Thomas Paine, *The Rights of Man*; Charles Pigault-Lebrun, *L'Enfant du Carneval*; Jean Paul Richter, *Die Unsichtbare Loge*; Samuel Rogers, *The Pleasures of Memory*; Susanna Rowson, *Rebecca*; Charlotte Smith, *Celestina*

MUSICAL EVENTS

A. Births:

Jan 8	Lowell Mason (Am-m.ed)		Aug 31	Emanuel Langbecker (Ger-mus)
Feb 26	Anton Fürstenau (Ger-fl)		Oct 2	Marie Pachler-Koschak (Aus-pn)
Feb 29	Gioacchino Rossini (It-cm)		Oct 3	Philip C. Potter (Br-pn)
Apr 5	Sylvanus B. Pond (Am-pub)		Oct 13	Moritz Hauptmann (Ger-cm)
Apr 30	Johann F. Schwenke (Ger-org)		Nov 8	Phillippe Musard (Fr-cm)
Jul 22	Guillaume C. Gand (Fr-vn.m)			Louis Drouet (Fr-fl)
Aug 13	Peter J. Simrock (Ger-pub)			Giovanni Puzzi (It-hn)

B. Deaths:

Jan 10	Jean L. Laruette (Fr-cm)		Jun 30	Francesco Rosetti (Boh-cm)
Feb 29	Ernst J. Haas (Ger-inst.m)		Jul 6	Giovanni Casali (It-cd-cm)
Mar 20	Friedrich L. Benda (Ger-cm)		Aug 2	Nathanael Gruner (Ger-cm)
Apr 25	Johann F. Beckmann (Ger-org)		Aug 18	Pierre J. Roussier (Fr-the)
May 12	Charles S. Favart (Fr-imp)		Sep 11	Nicolas Dezède (Fr-cm)
Jun	Jakob Kirckmann (Ger-pn.m)		Nov	Gaetano Guadagni (It-cas)
Jun 28	Elizabeth Ann Linley (Br-sop)		Nov 30	Ernst W. Wolf (Ger-cm)

Dec 15   Joseph M. Kranz (Ger-cm)   Dec 21   Antonio Boroni (It-cm)
Dec 19   Johann M. Schmid (Boh-cm)   Pierre de La Garde (Fr-bar)

C. Debuts:

U.S. -- Andrew Ashe (London), Joseph Gehot (New York), John Hodgkinson (New York), Mary Ann Pownall (Boston)

Other - John Field (age 9, Dublin), Józef Jawurek (Warsaw)

D. New Positions:

Conductors: Johann Georg Albrechtsberger (kapellmeister, St. Stephen's, Vienna), Pasquale Anfossi (maestro di cappella, St. John Lateran, Rome), Józef Elsner (kapellmeister, Lemberg), Johann Christian Friedrich Haeffner (kapellmeister, Stockholm), Leopold Anton Kozeluch (kapellmeister, Vienna), Cándido Ruano (maestro de capilla, Toledo Cathedral), Franz Xaver Süssmayr (Vienna National Theater), Bernhard Anselm Weber (Königstadt Theater, Berlin), Nicola Antonio Zingarelli (maestro di cappella, Milan Cathedral)

Others: Joseph Corfe (organ, Salisbury Cathedral), Louis Joseph Francoeur (manager, Paris Opera), Friedrich Ludwig Seidel (organ, Marienkirche, Berlin)

E. Prizes and Honors:

Honors: Olof Ahlström (Swedish Academy)

F. Biographical Highlights:

Felice Alessandri is dismissed from the Berlin Opera by Friedrich Wilhelm II and returns to Italy; Ludwig van Beethoven goes to Vienna where he studies a short time with Franz Joseph Haydn; Nicolas Marie Dalayrac marries actress Gilberte Sallarde; Charles Dibdin opens his own theater in London in which to produce his "entertainments"; Jan Ladislav Dussek, in London, marries singer Sofia Corri; pianist Johann Wilhelm Hässler moves permanently to Moscow; Franz Joseph Haydn, following a highly successful London adventure, returns in triumph to Vienna; James Hewitt leaves London and moves to the U.S. where he settles down in New York; E. T. A. Hoffmann enrolls in law courses at Königsberg; Antoine Lacroix, fleeing the Revolution, settles permanently in Germany; Jean Lebrun becomes prinicipal horn for the Prussian Court Orchestra; Johannes Nepomuk Maelzel settles in Vienna as a music teacher; Johann Gottlieb Naumann marries Catarina von Grodtschilling; Marcos Antonio Portugal begins an eight-year stay in Italy, composing 22 Italian operas; Joseph Boulogne Saint-Georges becomes a colonel in the French Negro Regiment; organist Raynor Taylor leaves London and emigrates to the U.S.; Isaiah Thomas moves his publishing firm to Boston; Giovanni Battista Viotti flees to London and begins conducting Italian opera; Georg "Abbe" Vogler begins a study tour that takes him to North Africa.

G. Institutional Openings:

Performing Groups: Royal Opera Co. of Berlin

Festivals: Belfast Harp Festival

Other: Johann Gerstenberg Music Store and Publishing House (Leipzig); *The Music Magazine* (U.S.); Hans Nägeli, Music Publisher (Wetzikon); Sans Souci Theater (London); Spectacle de la Rue St. Pierre (New Orleans); Teatro La Fenice (Venice)

H. Musical Literature:

Albrechtsberger, Johann, *Kurzegefasste methode, den Generalbass zu erlernen*
Forkel, Johann N., *Allgemeine literature der Musik*
Gerber, Ernst L., *Historisch-biographisches Lexicon II*
Hiller, Johann A., *Anweisung zum Violinspiel*
Holden, Oliver, *American Harmony*

Knecht, Justin H., *Gemeinnützliches elementarwerk der harmonie und des generalbasses I*
Martini, Johann P., *Mélopée moderne*
Reichardt, Johann, *Studien für Tonkünstler...*
Türk, Daniel, *Kurze Anweisung zum Klavierspielen*
Vanderhagen, Amand, *Méthode nouvelle...pour Hautbois*
Zinck, Harnack, *Kompositionen für den Gesang...II, III*

I. Musical Compositions:

Arnold, Samuel, *The Enchanted Wood* (opera)
Attwood, Thomas, *The Prisoner* (opera)
Beethoven, Ludwig van, *Piano Sonata, Opus 162*
    2 Sonatinas, Opus 163
Boccherini, Luigi, *6 String Quartets, Opus 44*
    Symphony in D Minor, Opus 45
    4 String Quartets, Opus 45
Carr, Benjamin, *Philander and Silvia* (pastorale)
Cimarosa, Domenico, *Il matrimonio segreto* (opera)
    La calamità dei cuori (opera)
Clementi, Muzio, *3 Piano Sonatas, Opus 28*
Destouches, Franz von, *Die Thomasnacht* (opera)
Dezède, Nicolas, *Paulin et Clairette* (opera)
Farinelli, Giuseppe, *Il Dottorato di Pulcinella* (opera)
Fomin, Evstigney, *Orpheus and Eurydice* (opera)
Furlanetto, Bonaventura, *Gideon* (oratorio)
Giordani, Giuseppe, *Atalanta* (opera)
Gossec, François, *Hymne à la Liberté*
Grétry, André, *Les deux couvents* (opera)
    Basile (opera)
Haydn, Franz J., *Symphonies No. 97 and 98*
    Sinfonia Concertante in B-flat Major, Opus 84
    The Storm for Chorus and Orchestra
    12 English Ballads
Haydn, Michael, *Missa Sancte Crucis*
Hewitt, James, *Overture, Expressive of a Battle (Battle of Trenton)*
Holden, Oliver, *Coronation* (hymn tune, "All Hail the Power")
Martín y Soler, Vicente, *Didon abandonée* (opera)
Méhul, Etienne, *Stratonice* (ballet)
Naumann, Johann, *Amore giustificato* (opera)
Paisiello, Giovanni, *Elfrida* (opera)
    Il ritorno d'Idomeneo (opera)
Piccinni, Niccolò, *Gionata* (oratorio)
    La serva onorata (opera)
Rossi, Giovanni, *Piramo e Tisbe* (opera)
Rouget de L'Isle, Claude, *Marseillaise* (French National Athem)
Sarti, Giuseppe, *Lo stravagante inglese* (opera)
Shield, William, *Hartford Bridge* (operetta)
Storace, Stephen, *The Pirates* (opera)
Süssmayr, Franz X., *Moses* (opera)
Tarchi, Angelo, *Le Danaidi* (opera)
Viotti, Giovanni, *Concerto No. 20 for Violin and Orchestra*
Vogler, Georg, *Gustav Adolph* (opera)
Weigl, Joseph, *Der strassensammler* (opera)
Wranitzky, Paul, *Rudolf von Felseck* (opera)
Zingarelli, Nicola, *Atalanta* (opera)
    Annibale in Torino (opera)
    Il mercato di Monfregoso (opera)

1793

World Events:
In the U.S., Congress passes the Proclamation of Neutrality in the Anglo-French warfare; a Fugitive Slave Law is passed by Congress; Eli Whitney of Mulberry Grove, Georgia, patents the Cotton Gin, but receives little compensation from business interests who steal his ideas. Internationally, the Reign of Terror begins in France under the control of Robespierre; Louis XVI and Marie Antoinette are both sent to the guillotine; Catholicism is banned in the Revolutionary Republic; the Second Partition of Poland takes place; the capitol of Upper Canada is moved from Niagara to Toronto.

Cultural Highlights:
In Paris, the Louvre Museum is opened to the public; the magazine *British Critic* begins publication; William Beechey is appointed Painter to the Queen in London; John Hoppner is appointed Portrait Painter to the Prince of Wales; Peter Francis Bourgeois is taken into the Royal Academy in London. Births in the world of art include American artist Thomas Doughty, Austrian artist Ferdinand Georg Waldmüller, British artist and critic Charles Eastlake and Irish artist Francis Danby; deaths include American artist Joseph Wright, Swedish artist Alexander Roslin, Italian artist Francesco Guardi and Flemish sculptor Pierre Antoine Verschaffelt. Births in the literary field include Swedish poet Erik Johan Stagnelius, British poet John Clare, Irish poet and author William Maginn, French novelists Paul de Kock and poet Casimir Delavigne; deaths include American novelist William H. Brown, German author Karl Philipp Moritz, Scotch historian William Robertson, Italian dramatist and librettist Carlo Goldoni and French philosopher Charles Bonnet. Other highlights include:

Art: Antonio Canova, *Cupid and Psyche*; Jacques-Louis David, *The Death of Marat*; John Flaxman, *Illustrations for Iliad and Odyssey*; Anne Girodet-Trioson, *Endymion*; Francisco de Goya, *The Madhouse*; James Hoban, *U.S. White House*; Hubert Robert, *Desecration of the Royal Tombs*; Johann G. Shadow, *Frederick the Great* (Stettin); Giovanni Battista Tiepolo, *Pulcinellos on Holiday*

Literature: Joel Barlow, *The Hasty Pudding*; Marie Chénier, *Fénelon*; Nicolas François, *Paméla*; Richard Graves, *The Reveries of Solitude*; Immanuel Kant, *Religion within the Limits of Mere Reason*; Gabriel Legouvé, *Epicharis*; Vincenzo Monti, *Bassevilliana*; Charlotte Smith, *The Old Manor House*; Elihu H. Smith, *American Poems, Selected and Original*; William Wordsworth, *Descriptive Sketches*

MUSICAL EVENTS

A. Births:

Jan 18	William Havergal (Br-cm)	Nov 19	Anna Fröhlich (Aus-sop)
Mar 6	Bernhard Klein (Ger-cm)	Nov 28	Carl J. Almquist (Swe-cm)
Apr 9	Theobald Boehm (Ger-fl)	Dec 11	Pietro A. Coppola (It-cm)
May 16	Benedetta Pisaroni (It-alto)		Giuseppe de Begnis (It-bs)
Jun 15	Julius Cornet (Aus-ten)		František Blatt (Cz-cl)
Jul 4	Franz Pechaczek, Jr. (Boh-vn)		George F. Perry (Br-cm)
Jul 25	Joseph H. Stuntz (Ger-cd)		Geltrude Righetti (It-alto)
Aug 10	August Neithardts (Ger-cd)		

B. Deaths:

Feb 9	Pascal Taskin (Bel-hps.m)	May 7	Pietro Nardini (It-vn-cm)
Feb 16	Christian G. Hubert (Ger-pn.m)	May 13	Martin Gerbert (Ger-mus)
Mar 17	Leopold Hoffmann (Aus-vn)	Aug 21	Anselmo Bellosio (It-vn.m)
		Sep 10	Marc A. Desaugiers (Fr-cm)

Sep 14 Benjamin Cooke (Br-org)
Sep 30 Andrew Adgate (Am-voc-ed)
Oct 1 Louis A. Chardiny (Fr-bar)

Oct 21 Johann E. Hartmann (Den-vn)
Dec 13 Johann J. Bode (Ger-bn)
Dec 20 Joseph Legros (Fr-ten)

C. Debuts:

U.S. -- Georgina Oldmixon (Philadelphia)

Other - Auguste Bertini (London), Johan Fredrik Berwald (Stockholm), Niccolò Paganini (age 9, Genoa)

D. New Positions:

Conductors: Domenico Cimarosa (maestro di cappella, Naples), Pietro Carlo Guglielmi, (maestro di cappella, St. Peter's, Rome), Friedrich Haack (kapellmeister, Stettin), Antonio Moreira (Teatro San Carlo, Lisbon), Joseph Preindl (kapellmeister, St. Peter's, Vienna), Vincenzo Righini (kapellmeister, Berlin), (Abbé) Johann Franz Sterkel (kapellmeister, Mainz), Johann Baptist Toeschi (kapellmeister, Munich), Nicola Antonio Zingarelli (maestro di cappella, Milan Cathedral), Johann Rudolf Zumsteeg (kapellmeister, Stuttgart)

Others: Samuel Arnold (organ, Westminster Abbey), Robert Broderip (organ, St. Michael's, Bristol), Lorenzo da Ponti (librettist, King's Theater, London), Johann Gottlieb Spazier (editor, *Musikalische Zeitung*), Raynor Taylor (organ, St. Peter's, Philadelphia)

F. Biographical Highlights:

Josef Valentin Adamberger retires from the Italian Opera in Vienna and turns to voice teaching; John Addison marries the niece of of F. C. Reinhold; Paul Alday, in London, marries harpist Adélaïde Rosalie Delatouche; Ludwig van Beethoven meets the Baron von Swieten and Prince Lichnovsky who become his friends and patrons; Benjamin Carr leaves London and moves to the U.S. where he settles in Philadelphia; Luigi Cherubini gets married and returns to Paris; Domenico Cimarosa leaves Vienna and returns to Naples; John Field's family moves to London; Franz Joseph Haydn, following his return from London, buys a home in Vienna; Friedrich Heinrich Himmel travels and studies music in Italy on a royal grant; Johann Nepomuk Hummel, back in Vienna, studies with Franz Joseph Haydn and with Antonio Salieri; Alexander Reinagle helps to set up a stock company in New York for the presentation of comic operas; Giuseppe Sarti is reinstated as director of the St. Petersburg Conservatory; Gaspare Spontini enters the Naples Conservatory; Georg "Abbe" Vogler returns to his position in the Stockholm court.

G. Institutional Openings:

Performing Groups: Newport St. Cecilia Society; New York "City Concerts"; New York Uranian Society

Educational: Groton Academy (New Hampshire--founded by Samuel Holyoke)

Other: Boston Theater; *Carr's Musical Repository* (Philadelphia); Casa de Comedias (Montevideo); Gaveaux Music Publishing Co. (Paris); Haydn Monument (Rohrau); Institute National de Musique (Paris); Moller and Capron, Music Publishers (N.Y.); *Musikalische Zeitung* (Berlin); New Theater Opera House (Philadelphia); Simrock Music Publishers (Bonn); Teatro S. Carlos (Lisbon)

H. Musical Literature:

French, Jacob, *The Psalmodist's Companion*
Gram, Hans, *Sacred Lines*
Gunn, John, *The Art of Playing the German Flute*
Hiller, Johann A., *Allgemeines Choral-Melodienbuch für Kirchen und Schulen*
Holden, Oliver, *Union Harmony*
Kimball, Jacob, *The Rural Harmony*
Koch, Heinrich, *Versuch einer anleitung zur composition III*

Langlé, Honoré, *Traité d'harmonie et de modulation*
Read, Daniel, *Columbian Harmonist I*
Reichardt, Johann, *Briefe über Frankreich*
Thomson, George, *Original Scottish Airs I*

I. Musical Compositions:

Alessandri, Felice, *Virginia* (opera)
Asioli, Bonifazio, *Cinna* (opera)
Attwood, Thomas, *The Mariners* (opera)
Beethoven, Ludwig van, *Variations on "Se vuol ballare," Opus 156*
Boccherini, Luigi, *6 String Quintets, Opus 46*
    6 String Trios, Opus 47
Boieldieu, François, *La fille coupable* (opera)
    Chant populaire pour la fête de la raison
Cherubini, Luigi, *Koukourgi* (opera)
Cimarosa, Domenico, *I traci amanti* (opera)
    Amor rende sagace (opera)
Clementi, Muzio, *3 Piano Sonatas, Opus 29*
    3 Piano Sonatas, Opus 32
Dalayrac, Nicolas, *Ambroise* (opera)
    Urgande et Merlin (opera)
Gossec, François, *Hymne à la nature*
    Hymne à l'égalité
    Hymne à la statue de la liberté
Haydn, Franz J., *Symphony No. 99 in E-flat Major*
    3 String Quartets, Opus 71
    3 String Quartets, Opus 74
    Variations in F Minor for Piano
Lesueur, Jean F., *La caverne* (opera)
Martín y Soler, Vicente, *L'Oracle* (opera)
    Amour et Psyche (ballet)
Méhul, Etienne, *Le jugement de Paris* (ballet)
    Le jeune sage et le vieux fou (opera)
    Hymne à la raison
Paër, Ferdinando, *I molinari* (opera)
Piccinni, Niccolò, *La Griselda* (opera)
Righini, Vincenzo, *Enea nel Lazio* (opera)
Rossi, Giovanni, *Pietro il grande* (opera)
    L'impresario delle Smirne (opera)
Sarti, Giuseppe, *Requiem for Ludwig XVI*
Shield, William, *The Midnight Wanderers* (operetta)
    The Relief of Williamsburg (operetta)
Steibelt, Daniel, *Roméo et Juliette* (opera)
Stich, Jan Václav, *Concertos No. 3 and 4 for Horn and Orchestra*
    12 Small Trios for 3 Horns
Süssmayr, Franz X., *L'Incanto superato* (opera)
    Piramo e Tisbe (opera)
Trento, Vittorio, *La finta ammalata* (opera)
Trial, Armand E., *Le Siège de Lille* (opera)
    La cause et les effets (opera)
Viotti, Giovanni, *Concertos No. 21-23 for Violin and Orchestra*
Weinlig, Christian, *Der Christ am Kreuze Jesu* (oratorio)
Winter, Peter, *Psyche* (opera)
Wranitzky, Paul, *Merkur, der heurat-stifter* (opera)
Zingarelli, Nicola, *La Rossana* (opera)
    La secchia rapita (opera)

1794

World Events:

In the U.S., the Battle of Fallen Timbers ends the Indian problem permanently in the Ohio Territory; the Whiskey Rebellion by the farmers of western Pennsylvania is put down by government troops; the U.S. Navy is officially formed by Congress; the Jay Treaty with Great Britain is unpopular with the general public but prevents another war with England; the University of Tennessee is founded; future Commodore Matthew Perry is born. Internationally, Robespierre himself is taken to the guillotine thus bringing to an end the Reign of Terror in France; a revolt of Polish patriots led by Thaddeus Kosciusko is crushed by the Russians; Agha Mohammed establishes the Kajar Dynasty in Persia; the École Polytechnique is founded in Paris.

Cultural Highlights:

Peter Francis Bourgeois is knighted and appointed Painter to the King in London; Jean Baptiste Huet is appointed Painter to the King of France; Thomas Lawrence is taken into the Royal Academy in London; Walter S. Landor is suspended from Oxford; Benjamin Constant begins an affair with Mme. de Staël. Births in the art world include German artists Julius Schnorr von Carolsfeld and Karl Begas and Spanish artist Francisco Bayeu. Births in the literary field include American poet William Cullen Bryant, German author and poet Wilhelm Müller and Irish author William Carleton; deaths include British historian Edward Gibbon, dramatist George Colman, Sr., author Anselm Bayly poet Susanna Blamiro, Scottish poet Alicia Cockburn, French author Sébastien Chamfort and poet André Chénier and German poet Gottfried August Bürger. Other highlights include:

Art: William Blake, *The Ancient of Days*; Asmus Carstens, *Atropos*; Jacques-Louis David, *Luxembourg Gardens*; Francisco de Goya, *Procession of the Flagellants*; Anton Graff, *Johann F. Reichardt*; Jean-Antoine Houdon, *The Negro Girl*; Philippe de Loutherbourg, *Lord Howe's Victory at Ushant*; Henry Raeburn, *Sir John Sinclair*; John Russell, *William Herschel*; John Trumbull, *The Declaration of Independence*

Literature: William Blake, *Songs of Experience*; William Dunlap, *Leicester*; Timothy Dwight, *Greenfield Hill*; William Gifford, *The Baviad*; William Godwin, *The Adventures of Caleb Williams*; Johann von Goethe, *Reinecke Fuchs*; Louis Lemercier, *Agamemnon*; Thomas Mathias, *The Pursuits of Literature*; Ann Radcliffe, *The Mysteries of Udolpho*; Jean Paul Richter, *Hesperus*; Edward Williams, *Poems, Lyric and Pastoral*

MUSICAL EVENTS

A. Births:

Jan 12	Franz Hauser (Boh-bar)	Jul 2	Samuel Graves (Am-inst.m)
Feb 11	Karl Proske (Ger-mus)	Jul 2	Antoine Prumier (Fr-hp)
Mar 21	Karl Hüttenrauch (Ger-org.m)	Jul 3	Eberhard Walcker (Ger-org.m)
Apr 7	Giovanni Rubini (It-ten)	Aug 4	Josef Proksch (Boh-pn-ed)
Apr 9	Jacques H. Farrenc (Fr-pub)	Sep 10	François Benoist (Fr-org)
Apr 13	Alexander Oulibicheff (Rus-mus)	Sep 18	Catherine Stephens (Br-sop)
Apr 17	Friedrich Berr (Fr-cl)	Oct 13	Anselm Hüttenbrenner (Aus-cm)
May 23	Ignaz Moscheles (Ger-pn-cm)	Nov 16	George Lambert (Br-org)
Jun 5	Joseph B. Hart (Br-org)	Dec 6	Luigi Lablache (It-bs)

B. Deaths:

Jan 29	Johann Breitkopf (Ger-pub)	Jun 4	Pablo Estève y Grimau (Sp-cm)
Feb 2	Marie Fel (Fr-sop)	Jun 10	Johann A. Maresch (Rus-hn)
Apr	Abraham Kirckman (Ger-pn.m)	Jul 2	Franz Pokarny (Boh-cm)
May 6	Jean J. Beauvarlet (Fr-org)	Jul 7	Pascal Boyer (Fr-cm)
May 23	Johann G. Clement (Ger-cm)	Jul 17	Jean F. Edelmann (Fr-hps)

Jul 22 Jean de la Borde (Fr-vn)	Oct 12 James Lyon (Am-cm)
Aug 11 Jakob Kleinknecht (Ger-fl)	Nov 15 Henry Mountain (Ir-vn)
Aug 25 Leopold A. Abel (Ger-vn)	Dec 16 Salvatore Bertini (It-cm)

C. Debuts:

Other - Gaetano Crivelli (Brescia), Pierre Jean Garat (Paris), Josephina Grassini (Milan), Johanna Hartig (Munich), Andrea Nozzari (Bergamo), Louise Reichardt (Berlin)

D. New Positions:

Conductors: João José Baldi (mestre de capela, Faro Cathedral), Franz Bühler (kapellmeister, Botzen), Johann Christian Friedrich Haeffner (Stockholm Opera), Franz Xaver Süssmayr (kapellmeister, National Theater, Vienna), Anton Wranitzky (kapellmeister to Prince Lobkowitz), Nicola Antonio Zingarelli (maestro di cappella, Loreto)

Others: Louis-Joseph Francoeur (director, Paris Opera), Benjamin Jacob (organ, Surrey Chapel), August Müller (organ, St. Nicholas, Leipzig), William Walond (organ, Chichester Cathedral)

F. Biographical Highlights:

Brigida Banti-Giorgi returns to London to stay and begins singing with the King's Theatre; Ludwig van Beethoven, settling in Vienna, enters into a fashionable keyboard competition with Joseph Wölfl; Antonio Bruni becomes a member of the revolutionary Commission Temporaire des Arts; Benjamin Carr moves to New York and opens a branch of his Musical Repository and also concertizes as both singer and pianist; Louise Rosalie Dugazon divorces her husband from whom she has been separated for fifteen years; Franz Joseph Haydn makes his second visit to London for Salomon's second series of concerts of his symphonies; Raphael Georg Kiesewetter settles temporarily in Vienna; Etienne Méhul is given a yearly pension from the Comédie-Italienne; Niccolò Piccinni, on returning from his Vienna trip, is unjustly put in house arrest for four years; Anton Reicha moves from Bonn to Hamburg and begins teaching piano; Franz Xaver Süssmayr is appointed a second conductor at the Vienna Court Opera; Václav Jan Tomašek begins studying math, history and philosophy at the University of Prague.

G. Institutional Openings:

Performing Groups: Philharmonische Gesellschaft (Ljubljana)

Other: Bevington and Sons Organ Co. (London); Joseph Carr Publishing House (Baltimore); Chestnut Street Theater (Philadel-phia); Drury Lane Theater II (London); Federal Street Theater (Boston); Johann D. Gerstenberg, Music Publisher (St. Petersburg); Ibach and Sons, Piano Makers (Beyenburg); Leeds Music Hall II; Motta and Ball, Piano Makers (London); Johann Traeg, Music Publisher (Vienna); George Willig, Music Publisher (Philadelphia)

H. Musical Literature:

Baumbach, Friedrich A., *Kurzgefasstes Handwörterbuch über die schönen Künste*
Belcher, Supply, *The Harmony of Maine*
Billings, William, *The Continental Harmony*
Devienne, François, *Flute Method*
Hook, James, *Guida de Musica II*
Law, Andrew, *The Art of Singing*
Read, Daniel, *Columbian Harmonist II*
Sala, Nicola, *Regole del contrappunto prattico*
Tattersall, William, *Improved Psalmody*
Vierling, Johann G., *Versuch einer Anleitung zum Präludieren*

I. Musical Compositions:

Attwood, Thomas, *The Packet Boat* (opera)
Bach, J. C. F., *Symphony No. 20 in B-flat Major*
    Septet in E-flat Major for Winds
Beethoven, Ludwig van, *Trio, Opus 87, for 2 Oboes and English Horn*
Boccherini, Luigi, *6 String Quartets, Opus 48*
    5 String Quintets, Opus 49
Cannabich, Christian, *Cortez et Thélaire* (opera)
Cherubini, Luigi, *Eliza* (opera)
Cimarosa, Domenico, *Le astuzie femminili* (opera)
    Il trionfo della fede (cantata)
Clementi, Muzio, *Piano Sonata in C Major, Opus 30*
    Piano Sonata in A Major, Opus 31
    3 Piano Sonatas, Opus 33
Dalayrac, Nicolas, *La prise de Toulon* (opera)
Gossec, François, *Symphony in C Major*
    Military Symphony in F Major
Grétry, André, *Joseph Barra* (opera)
    Denys le tyran (opera)
    La rosière républicaine (opera)
Haydn, Franz J., *Symphony No. 100, "Military"*
    Symphony No. 101, "The Clock"
    Symphony No. 102 in B-flat Major
    4 Trios for 2 Flutes and Cello
    Piano Trios No. 15-18
Haydn, Michael, *Missa tempore quadragesimae*
    Missa proquadragesimae sec cantum choralem
Hewitt, James, *Tammany* (ballad opera)
    The Patriots (ballad opera)
Isouard, Nicolo, *Artaserse* (opera)
Lesueur, Jean F., *Tyrtée* (opera)
    Paul et Virginie (opera)
Mayr, Simon, *Saffo* (opera)
Méhul, Etienne, *Timoléon* (incidental music)
    Horatius Cocles (opera)
    Mélidore et Phrosine (opera)
Naumann, Johann G., *Concerto for Piano and Orchestra*
    Davide in Terebinto (oratorio)
Paër, Ferdinando, *Una in bene e una in male* (opera)
Paisiello, Giovanni, *Elvira* (opera)
    Christus (oratorio)
Piccinni, Niccolò, *Il servo padrone* (opera)
Reichardt, Johann, *Goethes' lyrische Gedichte*
Reinagle, Alexander, *Concerto for Piano and Orchestra*
    Slaves in Algiers (incidental music)
    Preludes for Piano
Romberg, Andreas, *Der Rabe* (opera)
Sarti, Giuseppe, *Der ruhm des Nordens* (opera)
Shield, William, *Netley Abbey* (operetta)
    The Travellers in Switzerland (operetta)
Süssmayr, Franz X., *Der Spiegel von Arkadien* (opera)
    Il turco in Italia (opera)
Weigl, Joseph, *Das Petermännchen* (opera)
Wranitzky, Paul, *Das Fest der Lazzaronen* (opera)
Zingarelli, Nicola, *Gerusalemme distrutta* (oratorio)

1795

World Events:
In the U.S., the Treaty of Greenville opens the Ohio Territory to settlement by the white man; the Treaty of San Lorenzo gives the U.S. navigation rights on the Mississippi River; the Pinckney Treaty gives the U.S. the right of deposits at the mouth of the Mississippi at New Orleans; the Naturalization Act setting prerequisites for citizenship is passed by Congress; the Northwest Company founds Milwaukee; future President James Polk is born. Internationally, the French Directory is formed while Napoleon Bonaparte becomes head of the French Army in Italy; the French invade and occupy the Lowlands; the Third Partition of Poland takes place; Prussia and Spain both make peace with France; the London Missionary Society is formed; the hydralic press is invented.

Cultural Highlights:
The French Academy of Fine Arts (École Nationale Supérieure des Beaux-Arts) is founded in Paris; the Rudolph Ackermann School of Art opens in London; John Hoppner is taken into the Royal Academy in London; Jean Baptiste Regnault is taken into the French Institute; Charles Lamb, suffering from a bout of insanity, spends several months in an asylum. Births in the art field includes Dutch artist Ary Schaffer and British sculptor William Behnes; deaths include Spanish artist Francisco Bayeu y Subías. Births in the world of literature include American poets Maria Brooks and Joseph Rodman Drake, British poet John Keats, Irish poet George Darley, Scottish historian Thomas Carlyle, Russian dramatist Alexander S. Griboedov and poet Kondrati Ruleyev; deaths include Scottish author James Boswell, Swedish author Johan Henrik Kellgren and poet Karl Mikael Bellmann and Italian poet and librettist Raniero di Calzabigi. Other highlights include:

Art: William Blake, *God Judging Adam*; Asmus Carstens, *Night with her Children*; Edward Dayes, *Drury Lane Theatres*; John Flaxman, *Aeschylus*; François Gérard, *Isabey and Daughter*; Francisco de Goya, *The Duchess of Alba* (white); Charles W. Peale, *The Staircase Group*; Johann G. Schadow, *Princess Luise and Sister*; Gilbert Stuart, *George Washington* (dollar bill); Francis Wheatley, *The Cries of London*

Literature: Sebastien Chamfort, *Pensées, Maximes et Anecdotess*; André Chénier, *La Jeune Captives*; William Dunlap, *Fontainville Abbey*; Johannes Falk, *Der Menschs*; William Gifford, *The Maeviad*; Johann von Goethe, *Wilhelm Meisters Lehrjahre*; Immanuel Kant, *Zum Ewigen Frieden I*; Walter Landór, *Poems*; Charlotte Smith, *Elegiac Sonnets and Other Poems*; Johann Voss, *Luise*

MUSICAL EVENTS

A. Births:

Feb 21	Francisco da Silva (Bra-cm)	
Mar 4	Joseph Böhm (Hun-vn)	
Mar 8	Johann Bellermann (Ger-mus)	
Mar 14	Robert de Pearsall (Br-cm)	
Mar 18	Joseph Merk (Aus-cel)	
Apr 14	Pedro Albéniz (Sp-pn)	
May 27	Friedrich Belcke (Ger-tro)	

Jun 13	Anton Schindler (Aus-vn)
Aug 16	Heinrich Marschner (Ger-cm)
Sep 17	Giuseppe Mercadante (It-cm)
Nov 28	Adolf B. Marx (Ger-cm-the)
Dec 8	Jacques Gallay (Fr-hn)
	Charles Nicholson (Br-fl)

B. Deaths:

Jan 13	François J. Kraff (Fr-cd)
Jan 19	Maria Teresa Agnesi (It-hps)
Jan 26	Johann C. F. Bach (Ger-cm)
Feb 1	Giacomo Insanguine (It-cm)
Feb 5	Antoine Trial (Fr-ten)

Feb 18	Benjamin Banks (Br-vn.m)
Mar 5	Josef Reicha (Cz-cel)
May 20	Franz X. Chrismann (Aus-org.m)
May 22	Friedrich Marpurg (Ger-the)

May 28	Jeremiah Dencke (Cz-org)	Oct 25	Francesco Uttini (It-cm)
Jun 20	Pietro Florio (It-fl)	Nov 6	George A. Benda (Boh-cm)
Aug 19	Friedrich Graf (Ger-cd)	Nov 13	Christian Donati (Ger-org.m)
Aug 31	François Philidor (Fr-cm)	Nov 19	Thomas Linley, Sr.(Br-org)
Oct 3	John C. Smith (Br-org)		Hyacinthe Azaïs (Fr-cm)
Oct 11	Franz C. Neubaur (Cz-vn)		Josiah Flagg (Am-cd-cm)

C. Debuts:
Other - Angelica Catalani (Venice), Anton Dimmler (Munich), Marianne de Tribolet (Vienna), Johann Michael Vogl (Vienna)

D. New Positions:
Conductors: Domingo Arquimbau (maestro de capilla, Seville Cathedral), Friedrich Himmel (kapellmeister, Berlin), Friedrich L. Kunzen (kapellmeister, Copenhagen)

Educational: Paris Conservatory: Joseph Agus (solfège), Pierre Marie Baillot (violin), Charles-Nicolas Baudiot (cello), Henri-Montan Berton (harmony), Mathieu-Frédéric Blasius (winds), Charles Simon Catel (harmony), François Devienne (woodwinds), Heinrich Domnich (horn), Frédéric Duvernoy (horn), Pierre Gavinies (violin), André Grétry (inspector), Rodolphe Kreutzer (violin), Jean X. Lefèvre (clarinet), Jean François Lesueur (inspector), Jean-Henri Levasseur (cello), Jacques-Pierre Rode (violin), Nicolas Séjan (organ)

Others: Nicolo Isouard (organ, St. John of Jerusalem, Malta)

E. Prizes and Honors:
Honors: Joachim Albertini (life pension by Prince Poniatowski of Poland), John Goss (French Academy), François Gossec, André Grétry and Etienne Méhul (French Institute)

F. Biographical Highlights:
Ludwig van Beethoven has his first works published, his *Piano Trios, Opus 1*; Carl Czerny's family moves to Vienna in order to escape the unrest in Poland; Carl Ditters von Dittersdorf, on the death of his patron, the Prince-Bishop of Breslau, is invited by Baron von Stillfried to his estate where he spends the rest of his life; Johann C. G. Graupner leaves London and emigrates to the U.S. where he settles in Charleston, South Carolina; E. T. A. Hoffmann graduates from his law studies; Vicente Martin y Soler leaves Russia for a year in London before returning to Russia; Gaspare Spontini quits the Conservatory in Naples and, leaving for Rome, strikes out on his own in composition; Joseph Wölfl gives up his post in Warsaw and returns to Vienna as pianist and teacher.

G. Institutional Openings:
Performing Groups: Columbian Anacreontic Society of New York; Norwich Anacreontic Society

Educational: Paris Conservatory of Music (a consolidation of the Institute of Music and the École Royal de Chant)

Other: Rudolph Becker Publishing House; Thomas Boosey Book Store (London); Cramer Publishing House (Paris); *Die Hören*; Maison Pleyel (Paris Music Publisher); Duncan Phyfe Shop (New York); Schlesinger'sche Buch- und Musikalienhandlung (Berlin); Peter Urbani, Music Publisher (Edinburgh)

H. Musical Literature:
Altenburg, Johann, *Versuch einer Anleitung zur...Trompeter- und Pauker-Kunst*
Blewitt, Jonathan, *Complete Treatise on the Organ*
Chiabrano, Carlo F., *Compleat Instructions for...Guitar*
Dibdin, Charles, *History of the Stage*

Gatayes, Guillaume, *Harp Method*
Holden, Oliver, *Massachusetts Compiler*
Hüllmandel, Nicolas J., *Principles of Music, Chiefly Calculated for the Pianoforte*
Jackson, George K., *First Principles, or a Treatise on Practical Thorough Bass*
Knecht, Justin H., *Kleines..Wörterbuch...aus der musikalischen Theorie*
Mussolini, Cesare, *A New and Complete Treatise on the Theory and Practice of Music*
Vogler, Georg, *Introduction to the Theory of Harmony*

I. Musical Compositions:
André, Anton, *3 Symphonies, Opus 4-6*
Arnold, Samuel, *Elisha* (oratorio)
Beethoven, Ludwig van, *Concerto No. 2 for Piano and Orchestra*
　　Rondo in B-flat Major for Piano and Orchestra
　　12 German Dances, Opus 140, for Orchestra
　　3 Piano Trios, Opus 1
　　String Quintet in E-flat Major, Opus 4
　　3 Piano Sonatas, Opus 2
　　Adelaide, Opus 46 (song)
Boccherini, Luigi, *6 String Quintets, Opus 50*
　　2 String Quintets, Opus 51
　　4 String Quartets, Opus 52
Boieldieu, François, *Rosalie et Myrza* (opera)
　　Concerto No. 1 for Clarinet and Orchestra
　　Concerto No. 1 for Harp and Orchestra
Carr, Benjamin, *Federal Overture*
Cimarosa, Domenico, *Penelope* (opera)
Clementi, Muzio, *Keyboard Sonata in C Major, Opus 33a*
　　2 Piano Sonatas, Opus 34
　　2 Capriccios for Piano, Opus 34
Dalayrac, Nicolas, *Adèle et Dorsan* (opera)
　　La pauvre femme (opera)
Dittersdorf, Carl von, *Don Quixotte der Zweite* (opera)
　　Gott Mars und der Hauptmann von Bärenzahn (opera)
Haydn, Franz J., *Symphony No. 103, "Drum Roll"*
　　Symphony No. 104, "London"
　　Piano Trios No. 19-24
Himmel, Friedrich H., *La morte di Semiramide* (opera)
Isouard, Nicolo, *L'avviso ai maritati* (opera)
Martín y Soler, Vicente, *L'isola del piacere* (opera)
　　La scuola dei maritati (opera)
Méhul, Etienne, *Doria* (opera)
　　Scipion (opera)
　　La Caverne (opera)
Philidor, François, *Bélisaire* (opera)
Ruggi, Francesco, *L'ombra di Nino* (opera)
Salieri, Antonio, *Il mondo alla rovescia* (opera)
　　Eraclito et Democrito (opera)
Schenk, Johann, *Achmet und Almanzine* (operetta)
Shield, William, *The Irish Mimic* (operetta)
　　The Mysteries of the Castle (operetta)
Süssmayr, Franz X., *Die edle Rache* (opera)
　　Idris und Zenide (opera)
Viotti, Giovanni, *Concerto No. 24 for Violin and Orchestra*
Weigl, Joseph, *Der Raub der Helena* (ballet)
Wölfl, Joseph, *Der Höllenberg* (opera)
Wranitzky, Paul, *Die gute Mutter* (opera)
Zingarelli, Nicola, *Gli orazi e curiazi* (opera)

1796

World Events:
In the U.S., George Washington refuses to run for a third term as President; John Adams is elected President No. 2; Tennessee becomes State No. 16; Congress passes the Land Act which makes it possible sell public lands by auction; Fort Cadillac is turned over to the U.S. and Cleveland, Ohio, is founded. Internationally, Spain joins France in the war against Great Britain; Napoleon conquers all of Northern Italy and marries Josephine de Beauharnais; the Austrians push the French back to the Rhine River; Catherine II, the Great, dies in Russia and is succeeded by Paul I; Edward Jenner introduces his vaccine against smallpox.

Cultural Highlights:
The *Musenalmanach* is founded by Johann Friedrich von Schiller; the publication *Das Attische Museum* is introduced with Christoph Martin Wieland as editor; Matthew Gregory Lewis becomes a member of the British Parliament; Bertel Thorvaldsen studies art in Italy on a scholarship; William Beckford publishes his *Modern Novel Writing*. Births in the art world include American artists George Catlin, Asher B. Durand and John Neagle, French sculptor Antoine-Louis Barye and artist Jean Bapiste Camille Corot; deaths include Scotch artist David Allan, Austrian artist Franz Anton Maulbertsch and British architect William Chambers. Births in the literary field include Dutch author Florentius C. Kist, German author Karl L. Immermann, poet August Platen, Spanish novelist Fernán Caballero, poet Manuel Bretón de los Herreros and British novelist Frederick Chamier; deaths include Polish historian and poet Adam Stanislaw Naruszewicz, German poet Johann Peter Uz, Scottish historian and poet James Macpherson and poet Robert "Bobby" Burns. Other highlights include:

Art: Charles Bulfinch, *Hartford State House*: Antonio Canova, *The Penitent Magdalen*; Francisco de Goya, *Don Manuel de la Prada*; Antoine Gros, *Napoleon at Arcole Bridge*; Pierre-Paul Prud'hon, *Madame Anthony*; Hubert Robert, *View of the Grande Gallerie*; Edward Savage, *Washington Family Series*; Gilbert Stuart, *George Washington* (Athaneum and Landsdowne); Joseph Turner, *Fishermen at Sea*

Literature: Fanny Burney, *Camilla*; Samuel Taylor Coleridge, *Poems on Various Subjects*; Johannes Falk, *Men and Heroes*; Wilhelm Heinse, *Hildegard von Hohenthal*; Elizabeth Inchbald, *Nature and Art*; Matthew Lewis, *Ambrosio, or The Monk*; Thomas Paine, *The Age of Reason*; Jean Paul Richter, *Siebenkäs I*; Friedrich Schiller, *On Naïve and Sentimental Poetry*; William Wordsworth, *The Borderers*

MUSICAL EVENTS

A. Births:

Jan 24	Nicholas Moris (Br-vn-pub)	Jun 4	Melchiore Balbi (It-cm-the)
Jan 31	C. F. Martin (Ger-gui.m)	Jul 20	Edward Hodges (Br-org)
Feb 17	Giovanni Pacini (It-cm)	Jul 23	Franz Berwald (Swe-cm)
Mar 14	Anton Haizinger (Aus-ten)	Jul 28	Ignaz Bösendorfer (Aus-pn.m)
Mar 27	Louis Lambillotte (Fr-mus)	Oct 9	Carlo Conti (It-cm-the)
May 13	William Hall (Am-pn.m)	Nov 30	Carl Loewe (Ger-cm)
May 15	A. Bottée de Toulman (Fr-mus)		

B. Deaths:

Jan 9	Giuseppe Avossa (It-cm)	Feb 28	Friedrich M. Rust (Ger-vn)
Feb 16	Catterina Gabrielli (It-sop)	Sep 14	Samuel Green (Br-org.m)
Feb 17	John Jones (Br-org)	Sep 22	Georg W. Gruber (Ger-vn)
Feb 25	Giovanni Borghi (It-org)	Sep 22	Joseph Lederer (Ger-cm)

Oct 31   Thomas Haxby (Br-inst.m)   Dec 30   Jean Baptiste Lemoyne (Fr-cm)
Dec 19   Henry Delamain (Ir-org)

C. Debuts:
Other - Giovanna Guaetta Babbi (Trieste), Matthaeus Stegmayer (Vienna)

D. New Positions:
Conductors: Anton Franz Eberl (kapellmeister, St. Petersburg), Friedrich Adam Hiller (National Theater, Altona), John Christopher Moller (New York City Concerts), Christian Gottlob Neefe (Bossann Theater Co., Dessau), Luigi Piccinni (kapellmeister, Stockholm), Francisco de la Vega (maestro de capilla, Havana Cathedral), Karl S. B. Wessely (kapellmeister, Rheinsberg)

Others: Thomas Attwood (organ, St. Paul's, London), Domenico Cimarosa (organ, Naples Court), Charles Knyvett, Sr., (organ, Chapel Royal, London), Johann Reichardt (director, Halle Salt Mines)

E. Prizes and Honors:
Honors: Karl Friberth (Knight of the Golden Spur), François Giroust (French Institute), Etienne Nicolas Méhul (French Institute)

F. Biographical Highlights:
Joachim Albertini leaves Poland and begins a seven-year stay in Italy; Johann Anton André begins study of the fine arts at Jena University but his father's death puts him in charge of the family business; Ludwig van Beethoven concertizes in Prague, Dresden, Leipzig and Berlin; John Braham begins a liason with singer Nancy Storace; Domenico Cimarosa marries Gaetana Pallonte; Muzio Clementi decides to give up conducting and concentrate on performance and composition; Johann Christian Graupner gets married while in Charleston, South Carolina and soon moves to Boston; Rodolphe Kreutzer makes a triumphal concert tour of Italy, Germany and the Netherlands; Vicente Martín y Soler leaves London and returns to St. Petersburg where he remains until his death; Daniel Steibelt, in financial stress, leaves Paris for a concert tour of the Netherlands and England where he settles temporarily in London; Carl Maria von Weber receives his first formal music training when he takes piano with J. P. Heuschkel in Hildburghausen.

G. Institutional Openings:
Performing Groups: Apollo Glee Club (Liverpool); New York Harmonical Society

Other: Euroditio Musica (Amsterdam); Falter und Sohn, Music Publishers (Munich); Haymarket Theater (Boston); Lewis Lavenu (Lavenu and Mitchell in 1802), Music Publishers (London); Liceo Filarmonico (Bologna); Musical Box (patented by Antoine Favre); A. Senefelder, Fr. Gleissner and Co., Lithographers (Munich)

H. Musical Literature:
Arteaga, Esteban de, *Del ritmo sonoro e del ritmo muto nella musica degli antichi*
Blasius, Mathiew-Frédéric, *Clarinet Method*
Dussek, Jan Ladislav, *Instructions on the Art of Playing the Pianoforte or Harpsichord*
Galeazzi. Francesco, *Elementi teorico-pratici di Musica II*
Gunn, John, *School of the German Flute*
Hering, Karl G., *Praktisches handbuch zur leichten Erlernung des Klavier-Spielens*
Hook, James, *New Guida de Musica*
Kollmann, Augustus, *Essays on Practical Harmony*
Leite, António, *Estudo de Guitarra*

I. Musical Compositions:

André, Johann, *Der Bräutigam in der Klemme* (opera)
Attwood, Thomas, *The Smugglers* (opera)
Bianchi, Francesco, *Antigona* (opera)
Beethoven, Ludwig van, *2 Sonatinas, Opus 43a and 44a*
    Farewell to Vienna's Citizens, Opus 23 (song)
    6 Minuets, Opus 167, for Piano and Orchestra
    Variations on Paisiello's "Nel cour piu," Opus 180
    12 Variations on a Dance by Wranitzky, Opus 182
    "Ah, perfido," Opus 65
Boccherini, Luigi, *6 String Quartets, Opus 53*
    6 String Trios, Opus 54
Boieldieu, François, *Les deux lettres* (opera)
Carr, Benjamin, *The Mountaineers of Switzerland* (ballad opera)
Cimarosa, Domenico, *Gli Orazi ed i Curiazi* (opera)
    I nemici generosi (opera)
Dalayrac, Nicolas, *Marianne* (opera)
    La famille américaine (opera)
Dittersdorf, Carl von, *Ugolino* (opera)
    Der Durchmarsch (opera)
    Der schöne Herbsttag (opera)
Fioravanti, Valentino, *Il furbo contro il furbo* (opera)
Giordani, Tommaso, *The Cottage Festival* (opera)
Gossec, François, *La reprise de Toulon* (opera)
    Chant martial pour la fête de la victoire
Gresnick, Antoine, *Le baiser donné et rendu* (opera)
    Les faux mendians (opera)
Haydn, Franz J., *Missa Sancti Bernardi ("Heiligmesse")*
    The Seven Last Words (choral version)
    Concerto in E-flat Major for Trumpet and Orchestra
    Alfred, König der Angelsachsen (incidental music)
Haydn, Michael, *Missa hispanica*
Isouard, Nicolo, *Rinaldo d'Asti* (opera)
    Il barbiere di Siviglia (opera)
Lesueur, Jean F., *Télémaque* (opera)
Mayr, Simon, *La Lodoiska* (opera)
Méhul, Etienne, *Tancrède et Chlorinde* (opera)
Pelissier, Victor, *Edwin and Angelina* (opera)
Portugal, Marcos, *Zulima* (opera)
    La Donna di genio volubile (opera)
Pugnani, Gaetano, *Werther* (opera)
Reinagle, Alexander, *The Witches of the Rock* (pantomine)
Salieri, Antonio, *Il Moro* (opera)
Schenk, Johann, *Der Dorfbarbier* (operetta)
Shield, William, *Lock and Key* (operetta)
Spontini, Gaspare, *Li Puntigli delle donne* (opera)
Stich, Jan Václav, *3 Quartets for Horn and Strings, Opus 18*
Storace, Stephen, *The Iron Chest* (opera)
Süssmayr, Franz X., *Die freiwilligen* (opera)
    Der Retter in Gefahr (oratorio)
Titov, Alexei, *The Brewer* (opera)
Weigl, Joseph, *L'amor marinaro* (opera)
    Alonzo e Cora (ballet)
Wölfl, Joseph, *3 Piano Sonatas, Opus 2* (with violin)
Zingarelli, Nicola, *Andromeda* (opera)
    Giulietta e Romeo (opera)

1797

World Events:
In the U.S., trouble develops when France, upset with Jay's Treaty, begins the policy of interfering with U.S. shipping; the XYZ Affair when Talleyrand's agents try to extort money from the U.S. commissioner further strains relations with France; the Lancaster Pike in Pennsylvania is finished and opens to traffic; the frigate *United States* is launched, the first in the new country; Fort Adams (Memphis) is built on the banks of the Mississippi River; patents are given for the first U.S.-built clock and for the iron plow. Internationally, the Treaty of Campo Formio forces Austria out of the War of the First Coalition; Talleyrand becomes the French Foreign Minister; the British Navy defeats the Spanish fleet; Frederick William II of Austria dies and is succeeded by Frederick William III.

Cultural Highlights:
Daniel Nikolaus Chodowiecki becomes director of the Berlin Academy of Fine Arts; Sawrey Gilpin is taken into the Royal Academy in London; Manuel Maria du Bocage is imprisoned for advocating republicanism; Thomas Campbell goes to Edinburgh to study law; August Wilhelm Schlegel begins translating Shakespeare into German; William Wackenroder publishes his *Outpourings of the Heart of an Art-Loving Cloister Brother*. In the art world, French artist Hippolyte Paul Delaroche is born; deaths in the art world include British artists John Robert Cozens, William Hodges and Joseph Wright and German artist Christian Bernhard Rode. Births in the literary field include British author Mary Wollstonecraft Shelley, Scottish poet William Motherwell, Irish novelist and artist Samuel Lover, French poet Alfred Victor de Vigny and dramatist Michel Jean Sedaine, Swiss novelist Jeremias Gotthelf (Albert Bitzius) and German poet Heinrich Heine; deaths include British author, orator and statesman Edmund Burke, novelist and man of letters Horace Walpole and Irish actor and dramatist Charles Macklin. Other highlights include:

Art: William Berczy, *Joseph Brant, Mohawk Chief*; William Blake, *Night Thoughts*; John Flaxman, *Dante*; Francisco José de Goya, *The Nude Duchess* and *The Clothed Duchess*; Thomas Lawrence, *Satan Calling His Legions*; Joseph Mallord Turner, *Millbank by Moonlight* and *The Old London Bridge*; Joseph Wright, *Landscape with Rainbow, Chesterfield*

Literature: François Andrieux, *Le Meunier Sans-Souci*; Anonymous, *The Wearing of the Green*; William Beckford, *Azemia*; Isabelle Charrière, *Trois Femmes*; Samuel Taylor Coleridge, *The Rhyme of the Ancient Mariner*; Ugo Foscolo, *Fieste*; Johann von Goethe, *Hermann und Dorothea*; Friedrich Hölderlin, *Hyperion I*; Harriet Lee, *Clara Lennox*; Matthew Lewis, *The Castle Spectre*; Ann Radcliffe, *The Italian*

MUSICAL EVENTS

A. Births:

Jan 31	Franz Schubert (Aus-cm)	Aug 30	Barbara Fröhlich (Aus-alto)
Feb 13	Heinrich Steinway (Ger-pn.m)	Oct 28	Giuditta Pasta (It-sop)
Mar 28	Ernst Wiedermann (Ger-m.ed)	Nov 4	Carlo de Blasis (It-bal)
Apr 29	Ludovicus Coenen (Hol-org.m)	Nov 18	Charles F. Angelet (Bel-pn)
May 12	Johann Kufferath (Ger-vn)	Nov 20	Alexandre Vincent (Fr-the)
May 14	Charles Hart (Br-org)	Nov 29	Gaetano Donizetti (It-cm)
May 30	Johann C. Lobe (Ger-mus)	Dec 12	Lucy Anderson (Br-pn)
Jun 16	Pietro M. Crispi (It-org)	Dec 29	Aimé A. Leborne (Bel-cm)
Jul 15	Edward F. Genast (Ger-bar)		Luigia Boccabadati (It-sop)
Jul 21	Franz Schoberlechner (Aus-pn)		Edward Holmes (Br-pn)
Aug 5	Friedrich Kummer (Ger-cel)		

B. Deaths:

Jans 19	John Hill (Br-cm)		Aug 6	Stephen Clarke (Scot-org)
Jan 30	Johann A. Sixt (Ger-org)		Aug 19	Theresa Cornelys (It-sop)
Feb	Pasquale Anfossi (It-cm)		Sep 19	Johann F. Daube (Ger-the)
Feb 8	Johann F. Doles (Ger-org)		Oct 12	Pierre de Jélyotte (Fr-cm)
Feb 11	Antoine Dauvergne (Fr-cm-cd)		Nov 21	Pietro P. Sales (It-cm)
Mar 9	Vasily Pashkevich (Rus-vn)		Nov 27	Carl C. Agthe (Ger-org)
Mar 19	Philip Hayes (Br-org)		Nov 27	Johann B. Wendling (Ger-fl)
Apr 5	William Mason (Br-org-pt)		Dec 7	Giovanni M. Rutini (It-cm)
Apr 12	Josef A. Steffan (Cz-cm)		Dec 29	Anton Bachschmidt (Ger-vn)
Apr 23	Giovanni Andreoni (It-cas)			Elisabeth Böhm (Ger-sop)
May 28	Anton Raaff (Ger-ten)			Nicolas de Méreaux (Fr-org)

C. Debuts:

Other - Giovanni Polledro (Turin), Domenico Ronconi (Venice), Giuseppe Siboni (Florence)

D. New Positions:

Conductors: Bartolomeo Campagnoli (Leipzig Gewandhaus Concerts), Franz Seraph von Destouches (Erlangen), Johann Drexel (kapellmeister, Augsburg Cathedral), Marco Santucci (maestro di cappella, S. Giovanni Lateran, Rome)

Educational: Jean-Louis Adams (piano, Paris Conservatory), William Crotch (organ, St. Johns College), Bernard Sarrette (director, Paris Conservatory)

Others: Jean-Joseph Boutmy (organ, St. Baaf Cathedral, Ghent)

F. Biographical Highlights:

Ludwig van Beethoven begins teaching piano in Vienna and also receives the first recognition of his budding genius as a composer; Johannn Christian Gottlieb Graupner begins his teaching career in music in Boston; Franz Joseph Haydn begins work on his choral masterpiece, *The Creation*; Friedrich Heinrich Himmel begins a long concertizing tour through Russia and Scandinavia; Sigismund Ritter von Neukomm goes to Vienna to study first with Michael Haydn and then with Franz Joseph Haydn; Joseph Boulogne Saint-Georges resigns his position as colonel in the French colored regiment and retires from his army career, moving to Paris for the remainder of his life; Václav Jan Tomašek switches his studies to law at the University of Prague but continues his studies in music as well; Carl Maria von Weber enters the Institute for Choir Boys in Salzburg and studies composition with Michael Haydn.

G. Institutional Openings:

Other: John Gelb and Co., Organ Builders (New York); *The Pianoforte Magazine* (London); Teatro Cerri (Bergamo)

H. Musical Literature:

Aitken, John, *Scots Musical Museum*
Bunting, Edward, *General Collection of Ancient Irish Music I*
Campagnoli, Bartolomeo, *Metodo per Violino*
Daube, Johann F., *Anleitung zur Erfindung der Melodie und ihrer Fortsetzung I*
Gauzargues, Charles, *Traité de Composition*
Holden, Oliver, *The Worcester Collection*
Vogler, Georg, *Organ School*
    Method of Clavier and Thoroughbass

I. Musical Compositions:

André, Anton, *Symphony in D Major*
    Friedensfeier, Opus 7
Attwood, Thomas, *The Fairy Festival* (masque)
    Fast Asleep (opera)
Beethoven, Ludwig van, *Concerto No. 1, Opus 15, for Piano and Orchestra*
    Quintet for Piano and Woodwinds, Opus 16
    String Serenade in D Major, Opus 8
    Rondo for Piano, Opus 15
    Piano Sonata in E-flat Major, Opus 7
    Piano Sonata in D Major, Opus 6, for 4 Hands
    2 Cello Sonatas, Opus 5
    12 Variations on "See, the Conquering Hero"
Boccherini, Luigi, *6 Quintets for Flute (Oboe), Opus 55*
    6 String Quartets, Opus 56
Boieldieu, François, *La pari* (opera)
    La famille suisse (opera)
    L'heureuse nouvelle (opera)
Cherubini, Luigi, *Médée* (opera)
Cimarosa, Domenico, *L'imprudente fortunato* (opera)
    Achille all'assedio di Troja (opera)
    Artemisia (opera)
Dalayrac, Nicolas, *La leçon* (opera)
    La Maison isolée (opera)
Dittersdorf, Carl von, *Der Mädchenmarkt* (opera)
    Die lustigen Weiber von Windsor (opera)
    12 Keyboard Sonatas, Four Hands
Grétry, André, *Lisbeth* (opera)
    Le barbier du village (opera)
    Anacréon chez Polycrate (opera)
Hagen, Peter von, *Federal Overture*
Haydn, Franz J., *6 String Quartets, Opus 76*
    "Gott erhalte Franz den Kaiser" (Austrian National Anthem)
Isouard, Nicolo, *I due avari* (opera)
    L'improvisata in campagna (opera)
Lesueur, Jean F., *Artaxerse* (opera)
Méhul, Etienne, *Symphony No. 1 in G Minor*
    Le jeune Henri (opera)
    La taupe et les papillons (opera)
Paër, Ferdinando, *Tamarlane* (opera)
    Griselda (opera)
Paisiello, Giovanni, *Andromeca* (opera)
Pelissier, Victor, *Ariadne Abandoned by Theseus* (opera)
Reinagle, Alexander, *Columbus* (incidental music)
    The Savoyard (incidental music)
Salieri, Antonio, *I tre filosofi* (opera)
Schmidt, Johann, *Der Schlaftrunk* (opera)
Shield, William, *Love and Nature* (operetta)
    The Italian Villagers (operetta)
Sor, Fernando, *Telemaco nell'isola de Calipso* (opera)
Spontini, Gaspare, *Adelina Senese* (opera)
Stich, Jan Václav, *Horn Concertos No. 5 and 6*
Weigl, Joseph, *Alcina* (ballet)
    I Solitari (opera)
Wölfl, Joseph, *Das schöne Milchmadchen* (singspiel)
    3 Piano Sonatas, Opus 3
Zingarelli, Nicola, *La morte di Mitridate* (opera)

1798

World Events:
In the U.S., the Kentucky Resolutions and the Virginia Resolutions set forth the principles of State's Rights; Congress passes the Alien Act, the Alien Enemy Act and the Sedition Act; Congress authorizes all-out naval war with France over her harassment of U.S. shipping; the Naturalization Act calls for 14 years of residency before citizenship can be given; "Millions for defense, but not one cent for tribute" is coined by Representative Robert Harper. Internationally, the War of the Second Coalition begins; Napoleon Bonaparte begins his Egyptian Campaign and the Battle of the Pyramids takes place; Admiral Nelson destroys the French fleet at Abukir Bay; the Pope is taken prisoner by the French revolutionary forces; Ceylon becomes a British Crown Colony; the French experimenter in photography, Louis Jacques Daguerre, is born.

Cultural Highlights:
The publishing firm of E. Merriam and Co. is founded in Massachusetts; Francisco José de Goya is made Chief Painter to the King in Spain; Gabriel Maries Legouvé in taken into the French Academy; August Friedrich von Kotzebue becomes dramatist and librettist to the Viennese Court. The literary world sees the birth of Dutch poetss Isaäc Da Costa, German author August Heinrich Hoffmann, novelist Willibald Alexis, Italian poet Giacomo Leopardi, Irish poet John Banim, Scotch poet Robert Gilfillan and Polish poet Adam Mickiewicz; German poet Karl Wilhelm Ramler dies. In the art world, French artist Ferdinand Victor Eugène Delacroix is born and German artist Asmus Jacob Carstens dies. Other highlights include:

Art: William Beechey, *George III Reviewing the Troops*; Charles Bulfinch, *Boston State House*; Vincenzo Camuccini, *The Death of Julius Caesar*; François Gérard, *Cupid and Psyche*; Francisco de Goya, *Los Caprichos* and *The Betrayal of Christ*; Benjamin Latrobe, *Bank of Pennsylvania* (Philadelphia); Thomas Rowlandson, *The Comforts of Bath*; George Stubbs, *A Green Monkey*; Joseph Turner, *Manor House Gate*

Literature: Charles Brown, *Wieland*; Álvarez Cienfuegos, *Obras Poéticas I*; William Cowper, *The Castaways*; William Dunlap, *André*; Stéphanie Genlis, *Les Petits Émigres;* Friedrich Klinger, *Der Weltmann und der Dichter*; August Kotzebue, *The Stranger*; Walter Landor, *Gebir*; Thomas Malthus, *Essay on Population*

MUSICAL EVENTS

A. Births:

Jan 2	Désiré A. Batton (Fr-cm)	Jun 5	Alexei F. L'vov (Rus-vn-cm)
Jan 31	Karl G. Reissiger (Ger-cm)	Jun 20	Johan H. Griesbach (Br-cel)
Feb 3	Engelbert Aigner (Aus-cm)	Jun 21	Wolfgang Menzel (Ger-cri)
Apr 5	Jonas Chickering (Am-pn.m)	Sep 9	Friedrich Telle (Ger-cd)
Apr 19	Franz Glässer (Boh-cm)	Oct 7	Jean B. Vuillaume (Fr-vn.m)
Apr 25	Jean Andries (Bel-vn-mus)	Oct 28	Henri J. Bertini (Fr-pn)
May 20	Jean B. Chollet (Fr-ten)		James Bland (Br-bs)
May 28	Josef Dessauer (Boh-cm)		Henriette Lalande (Fr-sop)

B. Deaths:

Jan 4	Giuseppe Giordani (It-cm)	Aug 15	Felice Alessandri (It-cm)
Jan 20	Christian Cannabich (Ger-cm)	Sep 16	Damasus Brosmann (Cz-vn)
Jan 24	Christoph Torricella (Swi-pub)	Oct 6	Cecilia Young (Br-sop)
Jan 26	Christian Neefe (Ger-cm-cd)	Nov 15	Angelo Amorevoli (It-ten)
Feb 8	James Leach (Br-ten)	Dec 12	William Selby (Br-org)
Jun 15	Gaetano Pugnani (It-vn-cm)	Dec 16	Gaetano Brunetti (It-vn)
Jul 31	Johann Trattner (Aus-pub)		Joao de Carvalho (Por-cm)
Aug 3	Samuel Baumgarten (Ger-bn)		Aloisio Fracassini (It-vn)

C. Debuts:
    Other - Thomas Bellamy (Dublin), Friedrich Dotzauer (Kassel), Manuel García (Spain), Bianchi Jackson (Lacy) (London)

D. New Positions:
    Conductors: Bernardo Bittoni (maestro di cappella, Fabriano Cathedral), Vincenzo Fontana (maestro di cappella, S. Pietro,Bologna), José Nunes García (mestre de capela, Cathedral, Rio de Janeiro), Jeronymo Francisco de Lima (Royal Opera, Lisbon), Ignaz Schuppanzigh (Ausgarten Concerts, Vienna), Carl Stegmann (kapellmeister, Hamburg), Peter Winter (kapellmeister, Munich)

    Educational: François Boieldieu (piano, Paris Conservatory), Johann P. Martini (inspector, Paris Conservatory)

    Others: Johann Nepomuk Kalcher (organ, Munich Court), Johann F. Rochlitz (editor, *Allgemeine Musikalische Zeitung*)

E. Prizes and Honors:
    Honors: Nicolas Dalayrac (Royal Academy of Sweden)

F. Biographical Highlights:
    Giuseppe Aprile is pensioned by the Royal Chapel; Samuel Arnold suffers a bad fall and remains bedridden for several months; Ludwig van Beethoven notices the first signs of his approaching deafness; Catterino Cavos goes to Russia where he remains for the rest of his life; Louis Francois Dauprat is the first to receive first prize in horn from the Paris Conservatory; Michael Haydn visits Vienna for the very first time; James Hewitt buys out Carr's Musical Repository and begins publishing music; Frédéric Kalkbrenner enters the Conservatory of Paris; Daniil Kashin, on his return after study in Italy, is given his freedom from serfdom; Konradin Kreutzer begins the study of law at the University of Freiburg; Rodolphe Kreutzer gets to meet Beethoven while in Vienna; Vincenzo Manfredini returns to Russia at the invitation of Czar Paul I, his former pupil; Pierre Monsigny, ruined by the revolution in France, is given a pension by the Opéra-Comique; Niccolo Piccinni is released from home arrest and leaves for Paris; Gustave Vogt enters the Paris Conservatory; Carl Maria von Weber moves to Munich after the death of his mother; Joseph Wölfl marries Therese Klemm.

G. Institutional Openings:
    Performing Groups: Concentores Sodales (London Choral Group); Concerto de la Rue Cléry (Paris); United States Marine Fife and Drum Corps (beginning of the U.S. Marine Band)

    Educational: Accademia dei Costanti (Pisa)

    Other: *Allgemeine Musikalische Zeitung*; Astley's Royal Amphitheater (London); Broderip, Clementi and Co., Music Publishers (London); *Journal d'Apollon pour le Forte-Piano*; Nicolas Lupot, Violin Maker (Paris); T. Mollo and Co., Music Publishers (Vienna); Park Theater (New York); Théâtre des Jeunes-Artistes (Paris); Thomas Tomkison, Piano Maker (London); *Unpartheiische Kritik* (by C. G. Thomas)

H. Musical Literature:
    Bailleux, Antoine, *Méthode raisonnée pour apprendre à jouer du Violin*
    Cartier, Jean B., *L'Art du Violon*
    Jackson, William, *The Four Ages with Essays on Various Subjects*
    Knecht, Justin H., *Vollständige Orgelschule für Anfänger und Geübtere III*
    Langlé, Honoré, *Traité de la Basse sous le Chant*
    Relfe, John, *Guida Armonica*
    Rigler, Franz P., *Anleitung zum gesange, und dem Klaviere oder die Orgel zu spielen*
    Stich, Jan Václav, *Hornschule*
    Vogler, Georg, *Système de simplification pour les orgues*

Woldemar, Michel, *Méthode pour le violon*
Wright, M., *American Musical Miscellany*

I. Musical Compositions:

Attwood, Thomas, *A Day at Rome* (opera)
Beethoven, Ludwig van, *12 Minuets for Orchestra, Opus 139*
    Piano Sonatas No. 5-7, Opus 10
    Piano Sonata No. 8, Opus 13, "Pathétique"
    Violin Sonatas No. 1-3, Opus 12
    3 String Trios, Opus 9
    Trio, Opus 11, for Clarinet, Cello and Piano
    12 Variations on Mozart's "Ein Mädchen," Opus 66s
Boieldieu, François, *Zoraime et Zulnar* (opera)
    La dot de Suzette (opera)
Cherubini, Luigi, *L'hôtellerie portugaise* (opera)
Cimarosa, Domenico, *L'apprensivo raggirato* (opera)
Clementi, Muzio, *3 Piano Sonatas, Opus 37*
Dalayrac, Nicolas, *Gulnare* (opera)
    Alexis (opera)
    Primerose (opera)
Dittersdorf, Carl von, *Die Opera buffa* (opera)
    Don Coribaldi (opera)
    6 Keyboard Sonatas on Ovid's "Metamorphoses"
Dussek, Jan L., *The Captive of Spilberg* (opera)
Gresnick, Antoine, *La forêt de Sicile* (opera)
    La grotte des Cévennes (opera)
Haydn, Franz J., *The Creation* (oratorio)
    Missa solennis in D Minor, "Nelsonmesse"
Himmel, Friedrich H., *Alessandro* (opera)
Isouard, Nicolò, *Ginevra di Scozia* (opera)
    Il barone d'Alba chiara (opera)
Kauer, Ferdinand, *Das Donauweibchen* (opera)
Martín y Soler, Vicente, *La festa del villagio* (opera)
Mayr, Simon, *Che originale* (opera)
Naumann, Johann G., *I pellegrini al sepolcro* (oratorio)
Portugal, Marcos, *Fernando nel Messico (opera)*
Reichardt, Johann, *Die Geisterinsel* (opera)
    Lieder der Liebe und der Einsamkeit I
Reinagle, Alexander, *The Italian Monk* (incidental music)
    The Gentle Shepherd
Sarti, Giuseppe, *Andromeda* (opera)
Schmidt, Johann, *Concerto, Opus 1, for Piano and Orchestra*
Spontini, Gaspare, *L'eroismo ridiculo* (oepra)
    Il Teseo riconosciuto (opera)
Steibelt, Daniel, *Albert und Adelaide* (opera)
    Concerto No. 3, Opus 35, for Piano and Orchestra
Stich, Jan Václav, *Concerto No. 7 for Horn and Orchestra*
Süssmayr, Franz X., *Der Wildfang* (opera)
Weigl, Joseph, *Das Dorf im Gebürge* (opera)
Winter, Peter, *Der Sturm* (opera)
Wölfl, Joseph, *Der kopf ohne Mann* (opera)
    3 String Quartets, Opus 4
    3 Piano Trios, Opus 5
    3 Piano Sonatas, Opus 6
Zingarelli, Nicola, *Ines de Castro* (opera)
    Meleagro (opera)
Zumsteeg, Johann, *Die Geisterinsel* (opera)

1799

World Events:
In the U.S., Fries Rebellion, a revolt by the Pennsylvania Germans against the land tax, takes place; the government begins negotiations with France over the shipping problems; a National Quarantine Act is passed by Congress who also standardizes all weights and measures; Philadelphia receives the first public water system; Henry Lee immortalizes George Washington at his funeral with the words, "First in war, first in peace, first in the hearts of his countrymen." Internationally, Napoleon Bonaparte leaves Egypt, returns to France to overthrow the Directory and make himself First Consul; Russia withdraws from the Second Coalition; the Austrians wins several victories over the French; Alexander von Humboldt begins his explorations in South America.

Cultural Highlights:
The magazine *American Review and Literary Journal* begins publication; French troops discover the Rosetta Stone in Egypt; Henry Fuseli becomes a professor in the Royal Academy of Art in London; Walter Scott becomes the sheriff of Selkirk; Friedrich von Schiller settles in Weimar to be near Goethe; Stendhal serves with Napoleon's army in Italy; Heinrich von Kleist resigns his commission to become a civil servant; Heinrich Wilhelm Wackenroder's *Phantasien über die Kunst, für Freunde der Kunst* is published. Births in the art field include Russian artist Karl Bryulov; deaths include British sculptor John Bacon and German artists Ferdinand Kobell and Adam Friedrich Oeser. Births in the literary circles include Russian poet Alexander Pushkin, Bohemian poet Frantisek Celakovsky, Swedish poet Karl August Nicander, German novelist Ludwig Rellstab, French novelist Honoré de Balzac and British poet Thomas Hood; deaths include German author Georg C. Lichtenberg, French author Pierre Augustin Caron de Beaumarchais, author and librettist Jean François Marmontel, Portugese poet António Diniz da Cruz e Silva and Italian poet Giuseppe Parini. Other highlights include:

Art: James Barry, *Jupiter and Juno on Mt. Ida*; Jacques-Louis David, *Rape of the Sabine Women*; François Gérard, *Josephine Bonaparte*; Francisco de Goya, *Hermitage of San Isidro*; Pierre Guérin, *Return of Marcus Sextus*; Philippe de Loutherbourg, *Battle of Camperdowns*; Gilbert Stuart, *Thomas Jefferson*; George Stubbs, *Hambletonian*; Berthold Thorvaldsen, *Bacchus and Ariadne*; Joseph Turner, *Battle of the Nile*

Literature: Vittorio Alfieri, *Misogallo*; Charles Bocage, *Ormond*; Thomas Campbell, *The Pleasures of Hope*; Johann Herder, *Metakritik*; Gabriel Legouvé, *Etéocle et Polynice*; Louis Lemercier, *Pinto*; Matthew Lewis, *Tales of Terror*; Novalis, *Heinrich von Ofterdingen* (unfinished); Mungo Park, *Travels into the Interior of Africa*; Johann F. von Schiller, *Wallenstein Trilogy*; Friedrich Schlegel, *Lucinde*

MUSICAL EVENTS

A. Births:

Feb 11	Johann H. Lübeck (Hol-vn)	Jun 6	Jean Ancot, fils (Bel-pn)
Feb 24	Siegfried W. Dehn (Ger-the)	Jun 22	Aloys Fuchs (Aus-mus)
Mar 1	Alexei Vertovsky (Rus-cm)	Jul 8	Théophile Tilmant (Fr-cd)
Mar 21	Charles Mayer (Ger-pn)	Aug 28	Heinrich Enckhausen (Ger-org)
Mar 27	Jacques Halévy (Fr-cm)	Oct 20	Ferenc Bräuer (Hun-cd)
Apr 5	Vincenzo Fioravanti (It-cm)	Nov 6	Karl Böhmer (Hol-vn)
Apr 7	András Bartay (Hun-cm)	Nov 11	Giuseppe Persiani (It-cm)
May 27	George W. Doane (Am-hymn)	Dec 25	Thomas Oliphant (Br-cm)
May 28	Ernst Köhler (Ger-pn)		John A. Latrobe (Br-cm)

B. Deaths:

Feb 4   Jean Henri Naderman (Fr-hp.m)
Feb 12 František Dušek (Boh-pn-cm)
Apr 19 Pieter Hellendaal (Hol-org)
Apr 28 François Giroust (Fr-cm)
May 2   Heinrich J. Riegel (Ger-cm)
May 9   Claude Balbastre (Fr-org)
Jun 8   Joah Bates (Br-org)
Jun 10 Joseph Saint-Georges (Fr-cm)
Jun 18 Johann André (Ger-cm-pub)
Jul 28 Johann Distler (Aus-vn)

Aug 6   Joseph Friebert (Aus-ten)
Aug 16 Vincenzo Manfredini (It-cm)
Sep 20 Polly Young (Br-sop)
Oct 5   Wilhelm Cramer (Ger-vn)
Oct 16 Antoine Gresnick (Bel-cm)
Oct 24 Carl Ditters von Dittersdorf (Ger-cm)
Oct 30 Esteban de Arteaga (Sp-mus)
Dec 20 David T. Nicolai (Ger-org)
Dec 28 Gotthold Donati (Ger-org.m)
         Jan Kirkmann (Hol-org)

D. New Positions:

Conductors: Antonio Bruni (Paris Opéra-Comique), Giovanni Liverati (kapellmeister, Prague), Adamo Marcori (maestro di cappella, Pisa Cathedral), Giacomo Rampini (ii) (maestro di cappella, Udine Cathedral)

Educational: Pierre Jean Garat (voice, Paris Conservatory), Charles Hague (violin, Cambridge), Giovanni Paisiello and Giacomo Tritto (co-directors, Conservatorio della Pietà de' Turchini, Naples), Charles-Henri Plantade (voice, Paris Conservatory), Jean Baptiste Rey (harmony, Paris Conservatory)

Others: William F. Ayrton (organ, Ripon Cathedral), Matthew Camidge (organ, York Minster), John Clarke (organ, Trinity Church, Cambridge)

E. Prizes and Honors:

Honors: François-Joseph Gossec (Royal Academy of Sweden), Stanislao Mattei (Accademia Filarmonica, Bologna)

F. Biographical Highlights:

Gaetano Andreozzi separates from his wive; Domenico Cimarosa, sentenced to death for favoring the French occupation of Italy, is pardoned and banished from Naples; William Crotch receives his musical doctorate from Oxford; Jan Ladislav Dussek, on the failure of the Corri publishing firm, flees to Germany leaving his wife and family behind; Nicolo Isouard goes to Paris where he finds considerable success; Gertrud Mara leaves her husband and goes to Russia as a voice teacher; Anton Reicha goes to Paris with high hopes for performance of his operas but has little luck; Pierre Rode concertizes in Spain and meets Boccherini; Fernando Sor goes to Madrid and joins the French army; Louis Spohr's first tour is a failure but he is hired by the Duke of Brunswick; Daniel Steibelt, pardoned for army desertion, returns to Vienna and loses an improvising duel with Beethoven; Filippo Traetta escapes political prison and settles in Boston; Johann Michael Vogl begins the study of languages and philosophy at the Kremsmünster Gymnasium.

G. Institutional Openings:

Other: Lübeck Opera House; Georges-Julien Sieber, Music Publisher (Paris)

H. Musical Literature:

Abreu, Antonio, *Guitar Method*
Adam, Louis, *Méthode générale du doigté*
Albrechtsberger, Johann, *Anfangsgründe zur Klavierkunste*
Becker, Rudolph Z., *Mildheimisches Liederbuch*
Corfe, Joseph, *A Treatise on Singing*
Corri, Domenico, *The Art of Fingering*
Kollmann, Augustus, *An Essay on Practical Composition*
Sabbatini, Luigi, *La vera idea delle musicali numeriche signature*
Shield, William, *An Introduction to Harmony*

Tomeoni, Florido, *Théorie de la musique vocale*

I. Musical Compositions:
Attwood, Thomas, *The Magic Oak* (opera)
Beethoven, Ludwig van, *Symphony No. 1, Opus 21*
    Septet in E-flat Major, Opus 20
    3 Violin Sonatas, Opus 12
    10 Variations, Opus 185, on Salieri's "La Stessa, La Stessissima"
    7 Ländler, Opus 168, for Piano
Berton, Henri-Montan, *Le délire* (opera)
    Montano et Stéphanie (opera)
Bianchi, Francesco, *Merope* (opera)
Boccherini, Luigi, *6 String Quintets, Opus 57*
    6 String Quartets, Opus 58
    6 Guitar Quintets (based on earlier works)
Boieldieu, François, *Les méprises espagnoles* (opera)
    La prisonnière (opera, with Cherubini)
Cherubini, Luigi, *La punition* (opera)
Cimarosa, Domenico, *Semiramide* (opera)
    Bella Italia (cantata)
Dalayrac, Nicolas, *Arnill* (opera)
    Adolphe et Clara (opera)
Danzi, Franz, *Der Kuss* (opera)
Dittersdorf, Carl von, *25,000 Gulden* (opera)
Dussek, Jan L., *Pizarro* (incidental music)
Field, John, *Piano Concerto in E-flat Major*
Fioravanti, Valentino, *Le cantatrici villane* (opera)
Gresnick, Antoine, *Le tuteur original* (opera)
    Rencontre sur rencontre (opera)
Grétry, André, *Elisca* (opera)
Haydn, Franz J., *Missa solennis in B-flat Major, "Theresienmesse"*
    2 String Quartets, Opus 77, "Lobkowitz"
Hewitt, James, *Columbus* (ballad opera)
    The Mysterious Marriage (ballad opera)
Martín y Soler, Vicente, *Tancrède* (ballet)
Mayr, Simon, *Adelaide di Gueselino* (opera)
Méhul, Etienne, *Adrien* (opera)
    Ariodant (opera)
Paër, Ferdinando, *Camilla* (opera)
    Il morto vivo (opera)
Pelissier, Victor, *The Vintage* (opera)
    The Fourth of July (incidental music)
Reicha, Anton, *Les Français en Egypte* (opera)
Reichardt, Johann, *Lieder für die Jugend*
Righini, Vincenzo, *La Gerusalemme liberata* (opera)
Salieri, Antonio, *Falstaff* (opera)
Sarti, Giuseppe, *Enea nel Lazio* (opera)
    La famille indienne en Angleterre (opera)
Schenk, Johann, *Die Jagd* (operetta)
Spontini, Gaspare, *La finta filosofa* (opera)
Süssmayr, Franz X., *Soliman II* (singspiel)
    Der Marktschreier (operetta)
Weigl, Joseph, *Clothilde, Prinzessin von Salerno* (ballet)
Wölfl, Joseph, *Piano Concerto, Opus 43, "Grand concerto militaire"*
    6 String Quartets, Opus 10
Wranitzky, Paul, *Der Schreiner* (opera)
    Johanna von Montfaucon (opera)
Zingarelli, Nicolo, *Il ritratto* (opera)

General Musical Index

A

Abaco, Joseph dall'- 1766e
Abbey, John- 1785a
Abeille, Ludwig- 1761a, 1782f
Abel, Carl Friedrich- 1758f, 1759cei, 1760f, 1762i, 1764ef, 1767i, 1773i, 1782f, 1783i, 1787b
Abel, Leopold A.- 1766f, 1794b
Abo Musical Society- 1790g
Abos, Girolamo- 1760b
Abreu, Antonio- 1750a, 1799h
Académie de Musique de Reims- 1752g
Accademia dei Costanti- 1798g
Accademia Filarmonica (Milan)- 1758g
Accademia Filarmonica Modenese- 1771g
Ackermann Theater (Hamburg)- 1765g
Adam, Johann- 1779b
Adam, Louis- 1799h
Adamberger, Valentin- 1762c, 1793f
Adams, Harriett- 1775c
Adams, Jean-Louis- 1797d
Adams, Nathan- 1783a
Adams, Thomas- 1785a
Addison, John- 1766a
Adgate, Andrew- 1762a, 1785h, 1788h, 1789h, 1793b
Adgate Free School (Philadelphia)- 1785g
Adler, György- 1789a
Adlgasser, Anton C.- 1750d, 1752f, 1754i, 1756f, 1764f, 1767i, 1769f, 1777b
Adlung, Jakob- 1758h, 1762b, 1768h
Adolfati, Andrea- 1760bd
Adrien, Martin Joseph- 1767a, 1785c
Agincourt, François d'- 1758b
Agnesi, Maria Teresa- 1752f, 1753i, 1795b
Agrell, Johan J.- 1765b
Agricola, Benedetta E.- 1774f, 1780b
Agricola, Johann F.- 1750f, 1751ef, 1754i, 1757h, 1758i, 1759d, 1768h, 1774b
Agthe, Albrecht W.J.- 1790a
Agthe, Carl Christian- 1762a, 1782d, 1797b
Aguado y García, Dionysio- 1784a
Aguiari, Lucrezia- 1764c, 1768f, 1780f, 1783b
Ahlefeldt, Maria Theresia- 1780f
Ahlström, Olof- 1756a, 1772f, 1777d,

Aigner, Engelbert- 1798a
Aitken, John- 1787h, 1797h
Akademie-Konzerte- 1778g
Albéniz, Pedro- 1795a
Alberghi, Ignacio- 1787d
Alberghi, Paolo- 1755f, 1760d, 1785b
Albertarelli, Francesco- 1788c
Alberti, Giuseppe- 1751b
Albertini, Joachim- 1782d, 1795e
Albinoni, Tomaso- 1751b
Albrecht, Charles- 1759a, 1789g
Albrecht, Johann L.- 1761h, 1764h, 1765h, 1768bh, 1773b
Albrechtsberger, Johann G.- 1755d, 1759d, 1765f, 1768fi,1770i, 1772di, 1790h, 1791f, 1792dh, 1799h
Albuzzi-Todeschini, T.- 1760b
Alcido, José B.- 1788a
Alcock, John, Jr.- 1750d, 1755f, 1766f, 1773d, 1791b
Aldana, José M.- 1758a
Aiembert, Jean-le-Rond d'- 1752h, 1754h, 1759h, 1777h, 1783b
Alessandri, Felice- 1767f, 1777df, 1781i, 1789f, 1791i, 1793i, 1798b
Alessandri and Scattaglia, Music Publishers- 1770g
Alexander Brothers, Instrument Makers- 1782g
Alexandre, Charles- 1787b
Algarotti, Francesco- 1753f, 1755g
Allegranti, Maddalena- 1754a, 1770c, 1771f, 1772f, 1781f, 1783f
Allgemeine Deutsche Bibliothek- 1765g
Allgemeine Musikalische Zeitung- 1798g
Almeida, Francisco de- 1755b
Almeida, Inácio de- 1760a
Almquist, Carl J.- 1793a
Altenburg, Johann- 1769h
Altnikol, Johann- 1759b
Alyabyev, Alexander- 1787a
Amadé, Thaddäus- 1782a
Amalia, Anna- 1787b
Ambrosch, Joseph K.- 1759a, 1784c
American Musical Magazine- 1786g
Amicis, Anna Lucia de- 1754c, 1758f, 1762f
Amon, Johannes A.- 1763a
Amorevoli, Angelo- 1764f, 1798b

C

H

Y

Young, Cecilia- 1789b, 1798b
Young, Elizabeth- 1756c
Young, Isabella- 1751c, 1791b
Young, Polly- 1762c, 1799b

Z

Zamboni, Luigi- 1791c
Zanetti, Francesco- 1760d, 1788b
Zanotti, Giovanni- 1774d
Zelter, Carl F.- 1758a, 1791f

Zimmerman, Anton- 1781b
Zimmerman, Pierre- 1785a
Zinck, Harnack- 1791h, 1792h
Zingarelli, Niccolo Antonio- 1752a, 1768i,
    1772f, 1781i, 1785i, 1786i, 1787i,
    1789f, 1789i, 1790i, 1791i, 1792di,
    1794di, 1795i, 1796i, 1797i, 1798i,
    1799i
Zoffany, Johann- 1783f
Zumpe, Johannes, Piano and Harpsichord
    Maker- 1761g
Zumsteeg, Johann- 1760a, 1780i, 1785i,
    1787i, 1788i, 1791d, 1793d, 1798i

About the Compiler

CHARLES J. HALL is Professor of Music Theory and Composition and teacher of graduate Music History at Andrews University, Berrien Springs, Michigan. He has several music publications to his credit and is a radio personality and prize-winning composer. His compositions have been performed by the Houston Symphony Orchestra, the Fargo-Moorhead Symphony Orchestra and the Indianapolis Orchestra among others.